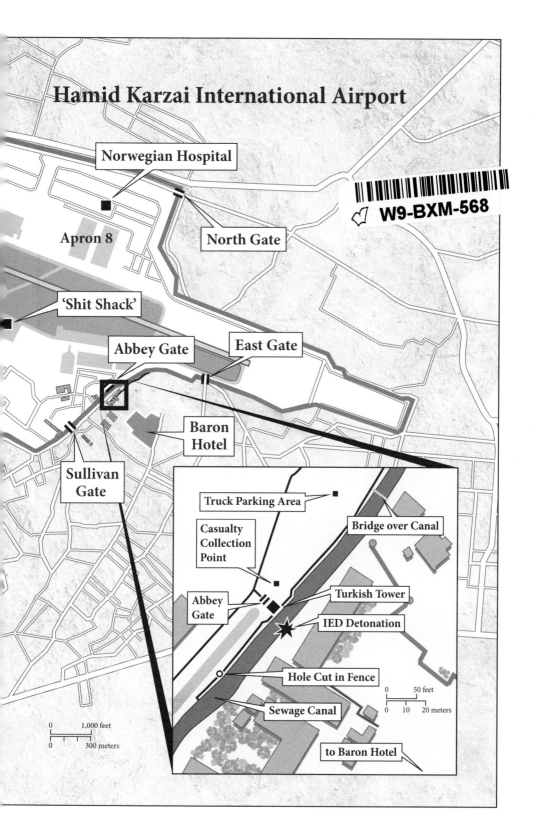

Hamid Karzai International Airport

Norwegian Hospital

Apron 8

North Gate

'Shit Shack'

Abbey Gate

East Gate

Baron Hotel

Sullivan Gate

Truck Parking Area

Bridge over Canal

Casualty Collection Point

Abbey Gate

Turkish Tower

IED Detonation

Hole Cut in Fence

0   50 feet

0   10   20 meters

Sewage Canal

to Baron Hotel

0   1,000 feet

0   300 meters

OPERATION PINEAPPLE EXPRESS

The Incredible Story of a Group of Americans
Who Undertook One Last Mission and
Honored a Promise in Afghanistan

LT. COL. SCOTT MANN (RET.)

SIMON & SCHUSTER

NEW YORK   LONDON   TORONTO   SYDNEY   NEW DELHI

Simon & Schuster
1230 Avenue of the Americas
New York, NY 10020

First Simon & Schuster hardcover edition August 2022

SIMON & SCHUSTER and colophon are
registered trademarks of Simon & Schuster, Inc.

For information about special discounts for bulk purchases,
please contact Simon & Schuster Special Sales
at 1-866-506-1949 or business@simonandschuster.com.

The Simon & Schuster Speakers Bureau can bring authors to your live event.
For more information or to book an event, contact the
Simon & Schuster Speakers Bureau at 1-866-248-3049
or visit our website at www.simonspeakers.com.

Interior design by Ruth Lee-Mui
Endpaper map by Paul J. Pugliese

Manufactured in the United States of America

1 3 5 7 9 10 8 6 4 2

Library of Congress Cataloging-in-Publication Data has been applied for.

ISBN 978-1-6680-0353-4
ISBN 978-1-6680-0365-7 (ebook)

*This book is dedicated to the
thirteen U.S. service members who
made the ultimate sacrifice
in Kabul, Afghanistan,
on August 26, 2021.*

*Your sacrifice will never be
forgotten, nor will your story.*

AFGHANISTAN TIMELINE

DEC. 24, 1979	Soviet Union invades Afghanistan
FEB. 15, 1989	Soviet Union withdraws from Afghanistan
1989 to 1992	Afghan Civil War
MAY 1, 1997	Taliban seize Kabul
SEP. 11, 2001	America attacked by Al Qaeda in New York and Washington, D.C.
OCT. 7, 2001	U.S. air campaign begins against the Taliban and Al Qaeda in Afghanistan
OCT. 19, 2001	First Special Forces detachment deployed in Afghanistan
NOV. 13, 2001	Taliban flee Kabul
DEC. 2, 2001	U.N. authorizes the International Security Assistance Force (ISAF) to help maintain security in Afghanistan
DEC. 20, 2001	Hamid Karzai selected as interim president
OCT. 9, 2004	Hamid Karzai elected president in free elections
AUG. 2010	President Barack Obama sends additional 33,000 U.S. soldiers to Afghanistan, with the total of international troops reaching 150,000
MAY 2010	Village Stability Operations begin
MAY 1, 2011	Osama bin Ladan is killed in Abbottabad, Pakistan
MAR. 1, 2013	Village Stability Winding Down
SEP. 29, 2014	Ashraf Ghani sworn in as president of Afghanistan
DEC. 28, 2014	End of U.S combat mission and transition to Afghan-led war
AUG. 21, 2017	Trump surge brings the number of American troops back to 14,000
FEB. 29, 2020	U.S. signs peace agreement with Taliban, committing the

	U.S. to a drawdown of troops and conditional full withdrawal by May 1, 2021
JAN. 15, 2021	U.S. reduces troop level to 2,500 as per the Doha Agreement
APR. 14 2021	President Joe Biden orders the complete withdrawal of U.S. troops from Afghanistan by September 11, 2021 (later revised to August 31, 2021)
JUL. 1, 2021	U.S. closes Bagram Airbase
AUG. 6, 2021	First provincial capitals fall to the Taliban
AUG. 15, 2021	Taliban recapture Kabul
AUG. 26, 2021	Suicide bomber at Hamid Karzai International Airport
AUG. 31, 2021	Last U.S. plane takes off from HKIA

At 5:36:52 p.m. on August 26, 2021, an ISIS-K suicide bomber killed eleven U.S. Marines, a U.S. Navy corpsman, and a U.S. Army special operations soldier, and approximately one hundred and seventy Afghans at Hamid Karzai International Airport in Kabul, Afghanistan. This served as a dark coda to the United States' two decades of war in Afghanistan and shut the door on the Herculean public-private efforts undertaken by a loose confederation of American, Afghan, and allied men and women to rescue as many of their Afghan partners as they could after the fall of Kabul.

This is the story of Task Force Pineapple.

CONTENTS

CHARACTER LIST

Major Characters in All Caps

AZIZYAR	Pineapple passenger. Command Sergeant Major in Afghan Special Forces. Guided by Matt.
BASHIR	Pineapple passenger. Afghan Special Forces operative who had to leave behind his wife and six children when he escaped Kabul. His sixth child was born while he was still in HKIA. Guided by James with the Hat.
BASIRA	Pineapple passenger. One of the first female NCOs in the Afghan army. Guided by Matt.
Browning, Julie	Pineapple shepherd. A former USAID senior adviser in Afghanistan, she manifested Nezam onto a charter flight.
Charles	Former Green Beret now working in U.S. inter-agency. Original member of Team Nezam.
Currie, Kelley Eckels	Ambassador-at-large for global women's issues during the Trump administration; helped shepherd Hasina Safi.
DAN	Pineapple shepherd. Dan O'Shea is a retired Navy SEAL.
DOC GUNDY	Aidan Gunderson (82nd Airborne Division, 504th Parachute Infantry Regiment, 2nd Battalion, C Company) combat medic deployed to Kabul on August 15, 2021, to assist with the embassy evacuation.
Donahue, Chris	Army major general and commander, 82nd Airborne Division during its mission to secure HKIA.

FAIZI Pineapple passenger. Afghan Special Forces operator. Guided by Zac.

Gant, Jim Retired Special Forces major. Known as "Lawrence of Afghanistan," he was one of the most visible faces of Village Stability Operations.

HAFI Pineapple passenger. Member of the Afghan NMRG, which worked closely with U.S. Special Forces. His handlebar mustache earned him the nickname "Mustache." Guided by Payton.

Hardman, Matt Commander in charge of the residual American forces securing the Green Zone and at Hamid Karzai International Airport.

HASINA SAFI Pineapple passenger. Former Afghan Minister of Women's Affairs. Guided by Kelley Currie.

Iqbal Pineapple passenger. Salaam's brother-in-law.

ISH Pineapple shepherd. Jim Gant's interpreter and closest Afghan friend.

JAMES WITH THE HAT Pineapple shepherd. Retired Special Forces officer who helped train the NMRG.

JESSE Pineapple conductor. First Sergeant Jesse Kennedy (82nd Airborne Division, 504th Parachute Infantry Regiment, 2nd Battalion, C Company) deployed to Kabul on August 15, 2021, to assist with the embassy evacuation.

JOHN Pineapple conductor, also known as "Captain Red Sunglasses." Captain John Folta, commander of the 82nd Airborne Division, 504th Parachute Infantry Regiment, 2nd Battalion, C Company, deployed to Kabul on August 15, 2021, to assist with the embassy evacuation.

JOHNNY UTAH Pineapple shepherd. Active-duty intelligence NCO. He fought with Nezam in Afghanistan.

J.P. Former Green Beret J.P. Feldmayer is a State Department political officer. He deployed to the U.S. diplomatic mission in Kabul.

JUNE Pineapple shepherd. A senior USAID official married to an active-duty Special Forces operator deployed in the Middle East. Original member of Team Nezam.

Karell, Art Pineapple shepherd. A former Marine officer.

KAZEM Former interpreter and National Directorate of Security paramilitary commander. Guided by Will.

Khalid Former Afghan interpreter for U.S. Special Forces.

Latif Pineapple passenger. Afghan Special Forces operator.

LIV Pineapple shepherd. Aide to Representative Mike Waltz (R-FL). Original member of Team Nezam.

MATT Pineapple shepherd. Retired Special Forces colonel and former Black Hawk pilot.

Meek, James Gordon ABC investigative reporter; friend to Johnny Utah and Nezam.

Miles, Kathleen Pineapple shepherd. Enabler for visa applications and former intelligence officer.

Miller, Austin An Army four-star general and Delta Force legend. He would eventually rise to become the longest-serving commander of U.S. forces in Afghanistan.

MULLAH MIKE Active-duty Special Forces battalion commander who was Nezam's commander in Afghanistan. Original member of Team Nezam.

NEZAM The Pineapple. Nezamuddin Nezami was an Afghan commando and Afghan Army Special Forces. He was the catalyst of the Pineapple Express. Guided by Scott and Team Nezam.

Nutsch, Mark The Green Beret captain who famously led the first assault on the Taliban alongside warlord Marshal Dostum after 9/11, as they swept into northern Afghanistan with Operational Detachment Alpha 595 on horseback.

PASHTOON Pineapple passenger. Command Sergeant Major in Afghan National Army. Guided by Matt

PEYTON Pineapple shepherd. Active-duty Special Forces officer who led the last team deployed to Kandahar.

QAIS Pineapple passenger. An American citizen and former foreign service national investigator at the U.S. embassy in Kabul.

Rahimi, Mohammad Pineapple passenger. A former interpreter for U.S. Special Forces in Afghanistan. Guided by Zac.

RAZAQ Pineapple passenger. A longtime Afghan interpreter for U.S. Special Forces. Guided by Steve.

Redman, Jay Pineapple shepherd. A retired Navy SEAL, he was gravely wounded in combat and became a motivational speaker and author.

SALAAM Pineapple passenger. Afghan Special Forces operator. Guided by Zac.

STEVE Pineapple shepherd. He is a former Army officer who worked on the Village Stability Operations with Scott Mann.

Tanner, Jussi Special Envoy for Finland who landed at HKIA on August 15, 2021, to arrange the evacuation of Finnish nationals.

WILL Pineapple shepherd. A former Green Beret, Will Lyles lost both of his legs in Afghanistan.

Windmueller, Kirk Pineapple shepherd. A retired Special Forces officer who had been part of Village Stability Operations.

Wookey, Ian Major in the Canadian Air Force assigned as a Chinook pilot to the 82nd Airborne Division. In charge of air operations at HKIA during the evacuation.

ZAC Pineapple shepherd. A former Green Beret, Zac Lois teaches 8th grade social studies in New York. He hatched the idea of Operation Harriet, which became the tactical backbone for the Pineapple Express.

KABUL–AUGUST 19, 2021

Nezam stacked a few bricks and squirted lighter fluid on some wood chips. He clicked open a Zippo and lit the pile. Flames jumped up in a small fire.

Morning light was just beginning to spread over the neighborhood; the power had been off all night. At one point, he had sat in his uncle's car in the dark, his powered-down iPhone plugged into the charger. The sporadic *choppa* of Kalashnikov rifles had subsided. The silence was eerie.

His phone was still off as he huddled by the fire. One at a time, he fed sheets of paper into the flames. With all the cooking fires in the neighborhood, the smoke wouldn't draw attention. The papers were colorfully adorned with commando crests, Afghan and American flags, skulls pierced with daggers, scorpions, helicopters, rifles. They praised Nezam in English or Dari. They were signed by commanders—no last names. *SF Dave. Captain Rob.* There was the Defense Language Institute English course. Commando Kandak Certificates of Achievement. Letters of recommendation from a 75th Ranger Regiment battalion commander.

It was Nezam's life that was going up in flames. It was everything the Afghan National Army recruiter in Takhar had told him he was too small to be. It was everything that made him stand tall against his corrupt uncle back home. It was what the fat mess hall sergeant had tried to lock him away from becoming.

In a way, however, maybe they'd been right. They were just looking at it the wrong way. It wasn't Nezam who couldn't do it—it was Afghanistan.

The papers burned. But they were only symbols.

He was still an elite special operator.

Besides, he had copies. He'd uploaded the documents to a cloud account belonging to several of his U.S. friends, just in case.

But then Nezam pulled out his graduation certificate from the Q Course at Fort Bragg. And the orders authorizing him to wear the blue and gold "long tab" emblazoned with SPECIAL FORCES.

I can't do it, he thought.

He folded up this and a few other original American documents, tucked them deep in his shirt, and poured water over the embers. Black smoke wafted skyward. Looking up, he noticed an old mujahideen staring at him from beyond a row of hedges twenty-five feet away. One of the neighborhood guys he played chess with. *Did he see me burning papers? Does he know who I am?*

Nezam smiled and placed his right hand over his heart, the common greeting among Afghans, waiting for a reaction. The mujahideen slowly lifted his palm to his own chest, a silent salaam, and shuffled out of sight.

The old warrior had given his blessing.

A few moments later, Nezam powered on his phone. A flood of messages popped up, ones that had been sent hours earlier.

One caught his eye.

MULLAH MIKE
Brother, it's time to go.

PART ONE

NEZAM

1

+93 78 420 9188
We know your location. We will find you and you will be dead.

Nezam's stomach clenched as he read and reread the ribbon of Dari. The text came from the same number that had called a few minutes earlier, the call he'd refused to answer. He squinted, studying the number. Country code: 93. Afghanistan. The prefix: 78. A mobile number from Etisalat, an Emirati service provider. But the sender wasn't Emirati.

He was Taliban. Nezam was certain.

Nezam sighed, scratching the knot of black hair on the top of his head. His background as one of Afghanistan's best-trained, most elite special operators gave him status. It also made him a known target of the Taliban. And now that the Taliban was resurgent, that meant something.

Nezam had been getting messages like these intermittently since 2017, when he returned from a two-year Special Forces course at Fort Bragg in North Carolina. As often as he received these threats, he never got used to them. They were one of the reasons he'd retired from the Afghan Special Forces. He had no problem fighting, or putting up with the deprivations of deployment—no issue with *action*—but he hated the messages. They were banal but terrifying and a reminder of a friend who had been assassinated by the Taliban. He never could figure out how to ignore them.

So now he worked for an American company—Five Star Global—as the security director at the Bayat power plant in Sheberghan, roughly eighty miles west of Mazar-e-Sharif and half as far as that to the Turkmenistan border to the north. It was one of the most secure corners of the country. The brand-new gas-fired plant was Afghanistan's first in over forty years, and would one day generate two hundred megawatts of power, enough for millions of Afghans. It was a jewel of new Afghanistan, and Nezam led a twelve-man team of contractors whose job was to protect it.

Sheberghan had been relatively tranquil since America's war began in the same province two decades earlier. After ten years of almost continuous combat against the Taliban, Nezam was able to finally stand down from all the killing that had given him night terrors. That was the other reason he hung up his uniform. The money from the power plant was good. There was relative peace in the area. There was an airport close by, and from there he would fly to India or Uzbekistan to run marathons. Freed of Army dictates, Nezam let his hair sprout into a bushy thatch. He grew a haphazard beard that he tugged on reflexively whenever lost in thought. He had settled into a quiet life at his outpost.

Many such outposts had proliferated across Afghanistan after U.S. and NATO forces drove the Taliban out in 2001. Hesco barriers—large chicken-wire barrels as tall as a man and filled with rubble, gravel, or soil—were stacked all around in fortifications. A fence topped with barbed wire formed a perimeter, with floodlights and a guard tower, the desolate landscape stretching off in all directions.

While life had been relatively quiet for a while, in the months before that ominous text message, the local roads had become riskier. Taliban probed the lightly armed Afghan partner police force checkpoints near the station. Nezam had even heard that soldiers in the Afghan National Army were deserting left and right. He, his men, and the power plant itself were more vulnerable because Nezam himself was now a named target.

If the man who had texted him was telling the truth, then Nezam was in danger for sure.

Each night, Nezam contacted local Afghan commanders to make sure the checkpoints were secure. He stayed awake late into the night to watch the video feeds from CCTV cameras mounted around the power plant, many of them peering outward at the barren expanse, power lines stretching into the inky night.

Nezam watched. The stillness meant nothing. The Taliban knew where he was. He was not Taliban, and he never would be. He had fought with the Americans. He was a killer of Taliban. He was their enemy, and they were his.

He turned from the larger TV screens to peer again at the smaller screen of his phone. He deleted the text message and blocked the number, as if that would do anything to safeguard him. He turned back to the images from the security cameras.

Darkness had fallen. He could still make out several of the small Afghan police checkpoints on the roads and nearby hilltops. Nezam knew that if the police would only stand and fight, they could win. He had pushed local commanders to be aggressive, but he was far from certain they would fight. There had been so much fighting, and the Americans were leaving.

He hung his head, in resignation as much as in shame. There was only one chance for him to survive.

He would have to run.

2

AFGHANISTAN

Nezamuddin Nezami, Nezam to his friends, was born into chaos.

He came into the world in 1988 in Taloqan village in Takhar province, a mountainous region north of Kabul. This ethnically Uzbek province had been a hotbed of mujahideen opposition to the Soviet invasion. The occupation was drawing to a close when Nezam was born, but that didn't stop the Soviets from ambushing a group of Afghan fighters near the Uzbek border and slaying his father.

Shortly after his mother was widowed, the roar of MiG fighter jets echoed through the valley. The villagers of Taloqan had only seconds to find shelter before the bombs rained down on their homes. Shock waves rocked the village, leveling houses and flinging debris, animals, and humans through the air.

It was only after the family reached cover that they realized no one had grabbed the baby. In the chaos, everyone assumed that someone else had snatched him from his cradle. With the jets streaking overhead, four-month-old Nezam lay alone in their dirt home.

The MiG payloads were barely empty as his mother, Hajerah, sprinted back to the ruined house and began to claw through the wreckage, screaming out Nezam's name. Other villagers came to help, pulling aside twisted metal and remnants of the roof. They heard nothing from under the rubble. They finally wrestled aside heavy wooden beams that had fallen over his crib. Then they heard a baby's giggle. Hajerah picked up Nezam, hugged him, and inspected him. There wasn't a scratch on him.

After the Soviet withdrawal, the country plunged into civil war. The Taliban battled the ethnic Hazaras, Tajiks, and Uzbeks for control. By the late 1990s, the Taliban controlled most of the country. In his village, Nezam steered clear of the Taliban, who would beat children and women in the streets with sticks and rubber hoses.

One day, the family's tiny black-and-white television showed a plane plunging into the side of an impossibly tall building in the United States. Then a second plane, into a second building. Twin towers. He'd never heard of them before. And then came a massive column of smoke and ash as the buildings collapsed.

Not long after this, U.S. and NATO military forces began flooding into his country. To young Nezam, they were conquering heroes, like Sylvester Stallone fighting the Soviets alongside Afghans in *Rambo III*—a wildly popular movie among some Afghans.

The country had new occupiers, but they were nothing like the Soviets. His countrymen learned English and took computer classes. Mass executions and public amputations ended. Girls returned to school. Music spilled from shops and car windows, and men shaved off the long beards the Taliban required.

But if things were improving for his country, they weren't for Nezam. His mother loved him, but his stepfather often beat him. He ran away. One uncle refused to let him in his house. Another tried to hang Nezam from a beam in his barn in order to steal a small parcel of farmland, part of Nezam's inheritance, but Nezam escaped. He had no home. As one of his aunts told him kindly one day, "You are a backpack man. You carry your home with you."

Nezam eventually landed on his feet in Taloqan when he came into a small inheritance bequeathed to him by the estate of his dead father. With some money in his pocket, Nezam went to school and bought clothes for his slight five-foot frame. He opened a street booth, selling cosmetics and ladies' fashion accessories—an unthinkable trade under the Taliban. A tae kwon do teacher took a liking to Nezam and gave

him a key to the dojo, where Nezam slept at night and trained during
the day. Every morning, he used a hot plate to boil an egg and warm his
milk. And then he would go for a jog, growing his endurance and speed.
Though he was small, he was fast and nimble. For the first time in his life,
he wasn't running from someone, he was just running.

When he turned seventeen, Nezam joined the Afghan National
Army (ANA). It was the family business, as two of his uncles were intelligence officers and one had even been a general. He was so short and
thin that he had to convince the skeptical recruiting officer by wearing a
pair of women's high-heeled shoes in order to add two inches and meet
the height requirement—not a particularly manly ploy, but a clever one.
It worked.

For the most part, he was bored by life in the ANA, and he became
an incorrigible prankster. The only things he enjoyed were the extra
push-ups and laps around the yard meted out as "punishment." Nezam
wanted to fight the Taliban, but the morale of his fellow soldiers was
terrible. Their combat proficiency was even worse. Inept Afghan officers and noncommissioned officers were reluctant to fight, preferring
the safety of garrison life. They'd rather have enlisted men like Nezam
perform menial tasks for them, as if they were now the warlords.

One day, the base's loudspeakers announced the arrival of a contingent of Afghan commandos and American Green Berets. It was 2008
and the U.S. was increasing its forces in Afghanistan. Nezam was on a
cleaning detail in the mess hall when he heard that the Green Berets were
looking for Afghan recruits for the commandos. Now, that! That would
not be boring.

Nezam continued mopping the floor until he heard boots crunching
on gravel. He peeked out a window. American soldiers with mirrored
sunglasses and baseball caps sauntered past in camouflage and body
armor. Nezam turned to one of his squad mates. "Man, whatever that is,
I want to go!"

"Good luck," his squad mate said. "No way the sergeant is letting you out of here." He nodded toward the fat and abusive sergeant guarding the door. "He'd sooner sit on you."

Nezam didn't care. He put down his mop and walked up to the obese sergeant. "I gotta piss."

"Fuck off. You can piss when you're done cleaning."

"No, man," Nezam said, bouncing up and down and pointing in the direction of the toilets outside. "I really need to piss."

The sergeant rolled his eyes and opened the door. "Make it quick."

Nezam leaped down the mess hall steps and took off with his high-pitched hyena giggle, sprinting toward the base classroom, where the Green Berets had assembled. The fat sergeant was angry that he'd been fooled, but he couldn't keep up.

Nezam ducked inside. Several dozen soldiers sat in rows. Afghan commandos and U.S. Green Berets stood in a line along one wall, while a U.S. officer spoke. "Most of you are here for the wrong reasons. You may think this all looks cool, but there is a good chance you will die violently. This is a dangerous mission. If you don't want to die, leave now."

The room began to empty as intimidated Afghan soldiers filed out. Nezam didn't budge. *Now's my chance*, he thought.

And he was right. Despite the odds, Nezam qualified for commando training. He never looked back. He was a born operator. His whole life had been hardship. He came ready-made for the life of an elite fighter. And he advanced quickly. He soon landed with a select group of Green Berets and Afghan special operators known as the Afghan Special Forces who, fashioned after U.S. Special Forces, would shed their uniforms and grow beards. He adopted their motto: De Oppresso Liber. Free the oppressed. Their new mission was dubbed Village Stability Operations (VSO), engineered by a handful of Green Berets including a Lieutenant Colonel named Scott Mann. Nezam and his U.S. counterparts would fan out across the country in teams to the most remote villages as vanguards working with tribes and village elders for the fledgling Afghan government.

Not long after his graduation and before his first VSO deployment, Nezam bumped into the recruiter who had allowed him to enlist while Nezam wore high heels. "Man, you're a commando!" the recruiter said in disbelief. He then wrapped Nezam in a bear hug. Like the girls in school, the music in the streets, and the businesses in the bazaars, Nezam was the future.

3

AFGHANISTAN

In May 2007, Nezam shouldered his pack and pushed into the rotor wash of a waiting Chinook with his new Afghan Special Forces detachment. They were joined by several Americans, including Lieutenant Colonel Scott Mann, a six-foot-two, mostly soft-spoken man with a light North Carolina drawl, for the short flight to Khakrez in northern Kandahar, the site of their new Village Stability Operations (VSO) platform.

Ever since Scott was the guest speaker at Nezam's Afghan Special Forces graduation, the two had been friendly. Scott had earned his Green Beret in 1996. Not that Nezam would know any different, but Scott was more of an old-school Special Forces guy. As a principal architect of the army's VSO, he was less a proponent of Green Berets as kitted-up door-kickers in Oakleys who bragged about shooting motherfuckers in the face, and more about embedding the members in Afghan villages, taking on local customs, and wearing local garb. Living alongside the tribal leaders was simply the best way to find allies in defeating the Taliban.

Scott had been in his fair share of scrapes with the enemy. But his special gift was as a problem solver: mobilizing people and assets to get his beloved Green Berets on to hard-to-reach targets and back to safety when things went to shit. At this point, he'd spent half his military career trying to determine what victory looked like in Afghanistan. The VSO were finally giving the Special Forces a glimpse of that reality. Building relationships was at the heart of it, and spending as much time visiting these outlying areas as possible. SF teams trusted Scott to get them resources they needed from headquarters. Nezam trusted him, too. In fact,

Scott had intervened back at Kandahar Airfield when he learned Nezam's team was having issues getting a helicopter transport, by assisting with the coordination and flying with them out to their new VSO site.

When the chopper landed, Nezam, Scott, and the Afghan operators tramped outside into the swirling dust. They were greeted by the site's captain, who wore cargo pants, a T-shirt, and night vision goggles. A rifle in his left hand, he clapped Scott on the back in welcome. He gathered everyone up and led the new arrivals to the hootch. Once inside, the captain went around and introduced himself to the new Afghan arrivals.

"Call me Mike."

If Nezam was born for special operations, "Mullah Mike," as he was affectionately called by teammates and local Afghans, was born for Village Stability Operations. A southern Georgia farm boy with a somnolent voice, he'd been acutely aware of prejudice. Rebelling against the conservative cultural norms around him in high school, he grew his hair long, pierced his nose, and sang in a band to overcome his paralyzing stage fright.

He also developed a near-obsession for working with people who had known oppression. In college, he spent his summers picking melons with migrant farmworkers from Central America; and though he was white, he'd joined an historically Black fraternity at the University of Georgia, where he eventually became chapter president. He learned Arabic, studied the Qu'ran, and married a Muslim woman from Tunisia.

Mike joined the Army during college, deployed to combat, and became a Green Beret officer. He found his calling in the tribal engagement program that included Green Beret legend Major Jim Gant, aka Lawrence of Afghanistan (by his boosters), aka Colonel Kurtz (by his detractors). Mike's first assignment at an isolated site in the Khakrez District was so inaccessible that food had to be air-dropped, and the men assigned to the site routinely lost twenty pounds within the first month.

As the VSO program took root throughout southern Afghanistan, Scott had taken a special interest in Khakrez. The young captain exuded the timeless Green Beret principles of working by and with indigenous people. He got the nickname "Mullah Mike" after several local farmers witnessed him publicly challenging several Taliban leaders on their distorted use of Islam to intimidate locals. More impressively, he was doing this challenging work in the most spartan of conditions, far from any kind of U.S. support. Scott was determined to help any way he could. The two had developed a close bond fueled by a persistent goal to persuade the intimidated villagers of Khakrez to stand up on their own against the Taliban.

Nezam soon learned that there were only fifteen Americans in this new VSO village, so Mike looked forward to the arrival of Pashtun-speaking Afghans to fill out their ranks. When the Chinook landed, the new operators doubled the size of the unit. Nezam—who went by "Space Monkey," on account of his agility and willingness to scamper onto rooftops to fix radios or faulty wiring—didn't disappoint. Once on the ground in Khakrez, Nezam volunteered for every patrol and combat operation in the violence-wracked province. But he had more than just combat prowess. Nezam was Special Forces through and through. He quickly built rapport with local farmers and shopkeepers, which endeared him to the villagers and infuriated local Talibs. Presence patrols to engage locals during the day were followed by surgical strike missions to root out Taliban during the night.

On one such mission, Nezam took a round through the mouth, blowing out a cheek and shattering several teeth, but not before warning the American Green Berets behind him of the waiting ambush. While he was on a stretcher waiting to be evacuated, his face covered in blood, he pleaded with Mike, "Please don't let the fucking Afghans fix my teeth." Somehow, he was still able to talk. "Can you get me a U.S. dentist? If you do I'll be right back to the fight." Mullah Mike found him an American dentist.

Upon his return, Nezam and his team transferred to the western Kandahar province, in the Maiwand District, where he met another colorful American special operations soldier, Johnny Utah. A broad and muscular Hawaiian whose forearm was inked with rows of red poppies symbolic of Afghanistan's battlegrounds, Utah was an intelligence specialist with years of combat experience. He'd initially been skeptical of Afghan special operators like Nezam, mainly due to his experience with regular ANA forces in Helmand. Those "soldiers" were constantly stoned and fled every firefight.

But Utah learned that Nezam and his unit were different. Nezam was up for every fight. In one of their first of over two hundred combat patrols together, they came under heavy enemy fire from the front. As they took fire, more shots suddenly rang out from behind. Without speaking, Nezam sprang up and disappeared.

"Why the fuck did you let him do that?" an American captain yelled at Utah.

"What the fuck are you talking about? He ran before I could even turn around," Utah snapped back. Moments later, Nezam returned, smiling, and took up his position alongside Utah. He had killed everyone behind them.

The slim Afghan commando and the bulked-up American soldier became close friends. But in time, Utah—just like Scott, just like Mike—had to say goodbye, as he was sent stateside. Nezam was reposted with no break from the action. A pattern was emerging. American special operators came and went, but Nezam stayed in the fight. Always.

About six years after Nezam joined the Afghan army, he was sent to Kunduz, in northern Afghanistan. It was 2014, and the relationship between the American and Afghan militaries was changing. Increasingly, Afghans were going into battle without American Special Forces at their side, and the rules of engagement for airstrikes had narrowed: Afghans could no longer assume that American airpower would protect them.

The enemy was also changing. ISIS-K, the Afghan branch of the Islamic State, had gained a foothold in the country. Even more brutal and ruthless than the Taliban, ISIS-K operated differently than the Taliban, and Afghan Special Forces did not always know which enemy they were fighting.

One nighttime mission in Kunduz exemplified this. Nezam, as part

4

AFGHANISTAN

Nezam got a break from the relentless bloodshed when he was selected to attend the U.S. Special Forces Qualification Course—or Q Course—at Fort Bragg. He arrived there in spring 2016. The course was rigorous, but compared to seven years of continuous combat, it was a holiday. No one was shooting at him, and he wasn't going to die on a ruck march, which he breezed through anyway since he was such a fitness nut.

While Nezam attended the Q Course, a now-retired Scott was at Fort Bragg, too, teaching aspiring Green Beret officers about the rapport-building lessons of VSO that warriors like Nezam and Mullah Mike had implemented. Over lunch, Scott and Nezam told stories and caught up on old times and friends long past. Scott marveled at Nezam's command of English now, and how he had continued to mature from the nineteen-year-old newbie SF non-commissioned officer in Khakrez. Scott also sensed an immense amount of pain and trauma just below the surface, similar to what he had seen in his American brethren returning from the war in Afghanistan. Nezam was on the edge, and Scott knew it. As they said their goodbyes in the parking lot, Scott was suddenly grateful that Nezam would have a year of training in the Q Course; while it had broken a lot of American soldiers in the past, for Nezam it was a life-saving hiatus from combat.

While he was in the United States, Johnny Utah took Nezam under his wing, taking him to the Carolina shore for surfing lessons and going on road trips to Washington, D.C., where Utah introduced Nezam to his of a team of eighty operators, was dispatched to strike an ISIS-K village compound. They began clearing buildings and destroying equipment under cover of night. Nezam knew they were in a trap. He implored his leaders to get the mission done and exfiltrate, but they procrastinated. And when the sun came up, hundreds of ISIS-K fighters materialized, surrounding the Afghan operators, firing in volleys from nearby buildings.

It was a shitshow—a blizzard of bullets and dust, the wind whipping sand off the dunes and village rooftops. The operators and the ISIS-K fighters were so close that they could hear each other's voices during lulls in the shooting. Had it not been for the deep sand Nezam and his team had burrowed into, they would never have survived.

The firefight continued as the ISIS-K fighters kept Nezam's unit pinned. At one point, sand clogged the unit's machine gun and Nezam jumped up in the middle of the fight to piss on the gun and unjam it. But as the day dragged on, there seemed to be no way out. Operators around Nezam took selfies to send to loved ones, believing their final moments had come.

Nezam wouldn't have it. He kept encouraging his team to fight, sprinting from position to position, distributing ammunition. Three times, bullets thumped into his chest armor, rocketing him to the ground, but he jumped up each time to continue. U.S. operators watched from drone cameras overhead as the hours went by, forbidden by their superiors from engaging. After twenty-four hours, Afghan helicopters finally swooped in to scoop up the men and fly them to safety. Out of eighty Afghan Special Forces, only a single man was killed.

This was Nezam's life. A boy from a broken home who was now a professional soldier. He believed in Afghanistan, but all he knew was war.

friend, the journalist James Gordon Meek, a massive man who stood six-foot-seven. He and Nezam took an instant liking to each other.

Nezam graduated from the Q Course in late 2016 and returned to Afghanistan with his coveted "long tab," the curved blue and gold shoulder patch reading SPECIAL FORCES that signified he had graduated from the rigorous training.

Nezam was now considered to be a foreign member of the U.S. Army 1st Special Forces Regiment, and while he was taciturn about this, some of his friends were less cautious. They made the mistake of congratulating him on Facebook. This earned him the attention he would eventually come to dread.

The first call came when Nezam was in Kabul in 2017. He picked up on the first ring.

"Who's this?" he asked.

"Nezam," a man said slowly. "Come home to Takhar. I know you were in the U.S. and accomplished a lot. Come back, we need you."

Nezam hung up. He texted the phone number to a friend in Afghan intelligence, and he told Nezam the number belonged to the "shadow governor" of Takhar—the region's top Taliban leader.

Nezam never returned to his birthplace. He deleted his Facebook page and stayed off social media. But the calls kept coming. One caller left a voicemail. "I am with our friend Najib," the caller said, referring to one of Nezam's childhood friends. "Najib is Taliban now. You are needed here, brother."

To Nezam, these calls amounted to death threats that showed Afghanistan's direction. The country was spiraling into instability as the U.S. forces turned security over to the ANA. The Taliban was increasingly targeting the best-trained Afghans: pilots, special operators, judges, prosecutors. Murdering Afghans with specialized experience and training, who would be impossible to replace quickly, would sow more intimidation and fear among the people. No one was untouchable. It was the ultimate mindfuck.

The constant threats, the years of combat, and the country's growing instability took a toll on Nezam. He began experiencing night terrors, waking in the darkness drenched in sweat and trembling. Like his country, he was unraveling.

Nezam's U.S. counterparts encouraged him to leave the Army and work for a private contractor. As the U.S. presence in Afghanistan dwindled, the demand for contractors grew. Security for Afghan infrastructure was falling to former Afghan Special Operations Forces (AFSOF) working for U.S. security companies. The military industrial complex was alive and well, offering Nezam an opportunity. The pay was five times the meager salary of a Special Forces Sergeant First Class like him. More important, working for a U.S. contractor made him eligible for a special visa program. An escape hatch if everything collapsed.

Unsure of what to do—fight, and likely die; go private, and likely end up fleeing—he spent hours messaging Scott. As before, Scott could sense Nezam was on the verge of losing it and he told Nezam that he needed to break away from the military, for his sanity and the sake of his life. In May 2017, Nezam decided that it was time to leave the Army. He was honorably discharged and recruited by the CIA for a top secret counterterrorism task force with SEAL Team Six. The following year, he became a security contractor for Five Star Global, a North Carolina–based security firm headed by Scott's former boss, retired Army Major General Edward Reeder Jr.

In early 2020, just before the global outbreak of COVID-19, the U.S. government suddenly announced a "peace" deal with the Taliban. In Washington, D.C., Donald Trump talked up the negotiations between his government and the Taliban: "I really believe the Taliban wants to do something to show that we're not all wasting time," he said. "If bad things happen, we'll go back." The deal, struck in Doha, Qatar, without the participation of the Afghan government or any coalition allies, set a May 1, 2021, deadline for a U.S. withdrawal. It was completely arbitrary and violated just about every rule of basic negotiation and strategic planning.

Trump had initially wanted to order all forces out by the close of 2020 but was talked out of it by his military advisers.

Nezam, like all Afghans, understood that the clock was now ticking. Once the Americans left, it would be open season on anyone who had aided them. He needed to leave immediately.

From his northern perch at the power plant, his sense of dread metastasized. With help of his other American friends, he applied for a Special Immigrant Visa (SIV)—the golden ticket that would get him out for good. Johnny Utah, Scott, and others wrote letters supporting his application. In his own letter, Nezam relayed a recent incident where he'd been pulled over and beaten at a Taliban checkpoint. Out of uniform, he hadn't been recognizable as ex–Special Forces, and the Taliban couldn't search his phone because the battery was dead. They released him, bruised but alive.

If they had ID'd him, they would have thrown a hood over him and hauled him off to torture him for days on end, beheaded him, and dumped him in a ditch, where he would return to the sand and wind.

He submitted his SIV application to the State Department on July 4, 2020.

Then he waited.

5

AFGHANISTAN

Waiting for bureaucracy—especially one halfway around the world—is never fun.

Nezam stayed alive. In September 2020, he learned that his SIV was moving through the State Department. Nezam had endeared himself to a lot of influential people who rotated through Afghanistan, and the chair of the House Foreign Affairs Committee was even in Nezam's corner, as well as a former Marine now at the National Security Council. People—important people—were fighting for him.

But in Afghanistan, the real fighting continued.

Summer passed into fall, fall into winter, winter into spring, with hardly any news. It was now early spring 2021, mere weeks from the official U.S. withdrawal date. A fact unbeknownst to many noncombatants is that war is often seasonal. Winters in Afghanistan were usually quieter. But now soldiers and insurgents were emerging from their winter strongholds and killing one another again in the mountains and valleys, over the plains and villages.

In March, the Taliban bombed a checkpoint close to the Bayat power plant, killing a police captain and wounding four of his men. Ed Reeder sent a message to Nezam offering his condolences and directing him to "recheck everyone's equipment to include their long guns. Make sure everyone is well versed on actions against the camp. Keep your eyes and ears on full alert." Things were getting hot, and Nezam and his men were on high alert. He felt terrible about wanting to abandon his country, the one he'd fought and killed for, but those days were now gone. All he wanted now was to get approval to leave.

On April 14, 2021, Nezam and countless other Afghans in similar positions caught a reprieve. There was a new American president, and on that day Joe Biden announced that the U.S. withdrawal would be pushed back four months, to the peculiarly symbolic date of September 11, 2021. Twenty years to the day after the Twin Towers fell.

This relieved some pressure on Afghanistan and also bought Nezam some time.

The power plant, once quiet, was now a hot spot of Taliban activity. Skirmishes erupted nearby, including an attack just a few miles from the station toward the end of May. Nezam dutifully reported the incidents to his American superiors at Five Star Global Security.

During this time, Nezam's comrades in the Afghan Special Forces began relaying dire messages over WhatsApp. Regular ANA units, unpaid for months, were handing over their U.S.-supplied equipment to the Taliban, who offered money for each rifle and vehicle, each box of ammunition. Fighting had intensified everywhere: in Kandahar in the south, in Herat to the west, in Kunar in the east. Village elders were approaching local commanders and imploring them to switch sides, just as they had in the days of the warlords and the mujahideen. It was the story of Afghanistan. One day you're enemies over the barrel of an AK-47, the next day you're brothers having tea.

None of this made the nightly news in Washington, D.C., which Nezam watched from afar. The Biden administration held firm to the view that the government of Ashraf Ghani would stand. As recently as April, Zalmay Khalilzad—a senior Afghan-American diplomat with silver hair wreathing a balding crown and deep bags under his eyes as if perpetually exhausted—had told the Senate Foreign Relations Committee, "I do not believe the government is going to collapse or the Taliban is going to take over." Nezam knew that he was lying. Why, he could only guess. It seemed like everyone in the U.S. and Afghan governments was in full denial.

But no one on the ground in Afghanistan was in denial. And everyone there knew that with the security umbrella folding up, they would soon have to fend for themselves.

Barring a miracle, Afghanistan would fail.

For the first time since childhood, Nezam, the cheerful and lethal warrior, was scared.

6

Nezam was reluctant to leave.

For days, Johnny Utah had been receiving reports from intel sources that Afghanistan was going to fall and soon. Utah urged Nezam to resign, get to Kabul, and fly anywhere out of the country. But Nezam didn't want to anger his boss. His supervisor sent him a text that evacuation was not in the cards. *From General Reeder: We have no plans and are giving NO guidance to the commandos to withdraw.* The next day, Reeder sent a direct message. *Nezami, I need you to be strong like a commando. I need you to lead by example. I need you to keep everyone calm.*

A country was worth dying for. But a power plant?

Nezam knew at that moment he was screwed. *I am no longer a Commando,* he thought. *I am a contractor, and I don't want to die for a power plant.*

He had to get out. He requested emergency leave in order to get his new national identification card, and that was granted. The country was falling to the Taliban and the roads weren't safe, so it would have to be by air. A helicopter to Mazar-e-Sharif was the only option, then a flight to Kabul.

Getting a jump seat on a chopper used to be relatively easy for Nezam, but no more. He messaged everyone he could think of—but there were no helicopter rides. Everyone was either fighting or fleeing or hiding, just like Nezam.

Then, a few days later, Nezam got an encouraging message from one of his friends in the Afghan Special Forces. An elite unit known as the

KKA had arrived in Sheberghan and had met with the local warlord. The upshot of their meeting: the KKA was there to push back against the enemy.

Nezam was suddenly buoyed. The KKA was among the most elite of Afghan Special Operations Forces. Their shoulder patch had a scorpion emblazoned with S.F. and the national colors of black, red, and green. Trained by Delta Force and Army Rangers, the KKA were revered as swift, effective, and lethal.

With the KKA active, maybe the roads would again be safe. Maybe Nezam could *drive* to Mazar-e-Sharif. He called Scott in what was becoming a frequent ritual. "My bag is packed and I am ready. I should be able to leave soon, sir."

"That's great news, brother. Keep me posted on the changes."

"I will, sir."

Nezam hoped that he could leave then. But a few hours later, he picked up his phone and began to scroll social media.

The KKA had disappeared.

In his heart, he knew they were dead, and a chill went down his spine. Still, he needed physical proof.

Almost immediately he found the videos and pieced together what had happened. The KKA unit, led by a handsome and dashing colonel named Sohrab Azimi, son of a famous general in Kabul, had gone to attack a Taliban position in Faryab. Azimi's convoy split into two, and about two dozen of them drove right into an ambush in broad daylight. The Taliban's elite Red Unit pinned them down. Calls for help to local ANA troops went unanswered. No one came. Azimi and his men surrendered, expecting to be treated like all other Afghan soldiers had been to that point. They would hand over their weapons and be told to go home.

Instead, the Taliban slaughtered the men on the spot.

Nezam found a video on the internet and sent it to Scott. They both watched in disgust. Less than a minute long, it panned over a dozen bloodied corpses sprawled across a dusty street lined with shuttered shop stalls. The bodies had been stripped of their kit and even their boots. Two high-cut helmets lay on the ground, helmets that were standard among Afghan special operations forces.

Nezam recognized the first bullet-riddled body in the clip—a long-bearded man with his green scarf still wrapped around his neck.

Colonel Sohrab Azimi.

As if there was any doubt, the KKA slaughter signaled there would be no quarter for the Taliban's enemies.

It didn't matter what the politicians said on TV. The Taliban knew they were within reach of winning a twenty-year war, mostly by waiting out their enemy and conducting psychological warfare like the targeted texts that the Taliban sent to Nezam daily.

7

In his office, Scott was still trying to shake off what he'd watched of the KKA slaughter. It didn't appear like the U.S. government was taking the Taliban seriously, or they were ignoring the obvious. He was receiving constant reports from his friends in intelligence and from special operators that the next couple months were going to be hell in Afghanistan; some even knew Nezam and were genuinely concerned for him.

The Taliban weren't attacking the bases because that would violate Trump's Doha Agreement, which they knew might prompt the U.S. to get back into the fight. Instead, they would take the provincial capitals, mostly by trickery and intimidation. With the exception of the Afghan special operators, the undermanned and outgunned Afghan troops wouldn't leave their bases without the dwindling air support. And so the provincial leaders would surrender in the face of any aggression, causing news of Taliban victories in the region to be spread over social media. The military would surrender without a shot fired. Scott had to hand it to them: he doubted the U.S. military could have pulled off a better smoke-and-mirrors psychological warfare trick. It was kind of genius.

And now, the Taliban were just building up momentum as large bases like Bagram Airfield and Kandahar Airfield closed.

Which would create a massive chokepoint at the Kabul airport. It was so obvious, Scott marveled shaking his head from side to side. It was like watching dominos fall and knowing how it will all end, and yet American senior officials were in denial.

And Nezam was stuck in the middle.

Scott texted Nezam. *Are you safe?*

NEZAM
Situation getting really bad but I'm safe for now.

SCOTT
Stay strong old friend.

NEZAM
Thank you, sir.

Stay strong old friend?! What a lame-ass thing to say to him. It took almost two hours for him to fall asleep, as he fought off images of the Taliban doing to Nezam what they had done to Major Azimi.

As Florida sunlight pierced the window blinds the next morning, Scott glanced at his phone and breathed a sigh of relief.

NEZAM
Good morning, brother.

At least he had survived another night.

8

Nezam felt trapped. He was having no luck finding a helo ride. He decided to make a video as a last-ditch effort to ask for help, similar to the hostage videos that had gone out on the internet. He would send it to Scott and his American friends and maybe it would get to an American official that could help. The video would explain why he was under threat, what he'd done for the Afghans and the Americans, and end by asking for extraction by the U.S. military. What did he have to lose?

Wearing a baseball cap and a khaki button-down shirt, Nezam filmed himself against the wire mesh of a Hesco barrier. He almost didn't recognize himself.

"I've been receiving many threats from Taliban for my past work with American forces as an operator." Nezam spoke haltingly into the camera of his iPhone. "I live in northern Afghanistan, where the Taliban have easily taken districts . . . towns . . . cities."

His face looked ashen, like a man facing a firing squad. His somber tone punctuated each word.

"The only way to get out from here is by helicopter and help is not coming. I know"—Nezam said in a low tone—"I know that if Taliban comes here, I will be the first one to be executed. I want American government to get me out from here. Thank you."

The video was only seventy-five seconds long, but Nezam had said everything he needed to say and he immediately shared it with Scott, Utah, and his other friends in the U.S. military.

It was Nezam's only chance at this point. He hoped it was enough.

9

On the same morning that Nezam's desperate video circulated among his U.S. friends, President Ashraf Ghani had made an urgent visit to Washington to meet with President Biden in the Oval Office. Ghani's meeting had not gone well. Publicly, Biden had promised "to stick with" the Afghans, promising to "do our best to see to it that you have the tools you need." But privately, Ghani got none of what he wanted. Primarily, training for an additional sixty-five thousand Afghan Special Operations Forces, air support for ground operations, and air-to-surface missiles for the Afghan Air Force's fleet of A-29 Super Tucanos, a light combat and reconnaissance plane. Ghani also pleaded with Biden not to evacuate Afghans, not because he wanted them to suffer, but because it would create panic, striking a mortal blow to national morale.

According to an Afghan aide, Biden's deputies derisively dismissed these urgent needs as merely a "wish list."

10

Scott Mann was up earlier than usual. He walked into the backyard and onto his dock on the Alafia River as he did every morning. The sun bounced brightly off the silty, slow-moving river as it wound its way out to Tampa Bay. It was going to be a scorcher. As he sat down in the Adirondack chair and took a slow pull from his Yeti of coffee, his thoughts drifted 7,000 miles away to Nezam trying to survive another day in the scorching heat of Afghanistan.

Usually the river helped him unwind, but not today.

Nezam was in trouble. His situation at the power plant was getting worse.

Nezam and Scott had known each other for many years, and as much as Scott didn't want to ever get involved with Afghanistan again, Nezam's plight was making things personal once more. He made a commitment to himself that if Nezam could get out of his current dilemma, Scott would kick over as many rocks as possible to help his friend get his SIV and get out of Afghanistan. His Signal app went off. It was Nezam. Scott swallowed hard and opened the chat.

> NEZAM: I made it to Mazar-e-Sharif! I am with the commando battalion
>   commander who helped me and it is a very interesting story.
> SCOTT: Did you get out on a helicopter?
> NEZAM: Yes, helicopter!
> SCOTT: Awesome man!
> NEZAM: Yes, sir! It is!

11

Nezam sent two photos. The first was of Nezam in a surgical mask, sunglasses, and a ball cap as he stood next to a camouflage Russian Mi-17 helicopter, a machine gun mounted in the door. The second photo was of Nezam and Lieutenant Colonel Zamarai Noorzai, a friend who'd graduated with Nezam from the commando training. The stocky Noorzai wore a T-shirt and camo pants as the two of them grinned, toasting Monster Energy drinks.

Noorzai had wanted to help Nezam for weeks without results, but then he had an idea. He wrote Nezam a letter on official ANA letterhead "recalling" Nezam from "leave" and ordering him to active duty at Camp Shaheen, near Mazar-e-Sharif. It was a complete ruse. There was no order, and Nezam had no such duty to report. But it didn't matter.

Nezam just needed a bird.

But it was difficult to know when an Afghan Air Force helicopter would come to Sheberghan. The sophisticated U.S.-manufactured Black Hawk UH-60s were mostly grounded since the six thousand American aviation support contractors had left the country. And Afghanistan's fleet of aging Russian Mi-17 helicopters didn't fly to the remote province regularly.

Nezam, though, had a friend at the Sheberghan airfield. He had gifted him a phone card and would periodically top it off. That morning, the tiny bribe paid off when the man called: "Helicopter inbound—come to police checkpoint! Fast!"

Nezam had grabbed his duffel, ran outside, and jumped into his

Toyota Hilux, the preferred utility vehicle of choice in Afghanistan. He gunned it, passing through the power plant's security gate just as the helo crew unloaded their last pallet of ammunition for the local police. Nezam showed his bogus orders from Noorzai to the crew chief, the man nodded, and he hopped inside.

Thirty minutes later, he was at Camp Shaheen. Noorzai then organized two trucks to escort Nezam to the airport in Mazar-e-Sharif. Flanked by fierce-looking commandos, he got there without incident and soon settled on a Kam Air flight, not quite believing that he had escaped Bayat.

The plan had worked. He had gotten out of Sheberghan. Now all he needed to do was get the hell out of the country.

12

Kabul, Nezam thought as he stepped onto the concrete apron of Hamid Karzai International Airport. *Shit.*

He'd walked down countless ramps of C-130s here, carrying his M4 carbine and rucksack through the enormous airfield on the northern side of the long runway—the military side. This was the first time he had deplaned at the civilian terminal of what everyone in the military called Aitch-Kaya, a bastardized pronunciation of HKIA. There were only a few passenger jets parked on the flight line, and the small passenger terminal was nearly empty.

Nezam strolled past giant billboards of Karzai and Ghani on the terminal walls, then hopped in a taxi and headed to his uncle's house, where he would hide until he could get on an international flight. Nezam had accepted that his application for a Special Immigrant Visa to the United States might be an exercise in futility, but he needed the relative safety of Kabul to renew his Afghan passport in the hope that Scott could somehow get the U.S. Department of State to fast-track his SIV.

Nezam's uncle Tawab lived in a seven-room house in a quiet neighborhood in the heart of Kabul. A former general in the country's intelligence services, he lived with his wife and five adult children and grandkids. Tawab offered Nezam a small room with a tiny window overlooking the garden in back. To Nezam, it seemed like the perfect safe house to lie low in while he figured out his next steps. Neighbors wouldn't think anything of one more face in a bustling household.

He kept a low profile. If he absolutely had to go out, he dressed in shabby clothes. COVID provided an excuse to wear a blue surgical mask that hid his lower face. Large sunglasses completed the disguise.

Despite the Taliban's advances in the countryside, and the occasional car bomb or kidnapping, Kabul still felt safe.

Nezam bought an iPhone 12 and a new SIM card, and Scott coached him on ways to defeat Taliban eavesdropping. Scott and Nezam would make all their calls on Signal from then on, and Nezam would make constant use of a virtual private network (VPN) to mask his location. The phone could appear as though it were anywhere in the world—even America—while Nezam prowled the streets of Kabul.

He also texted General Reeder that he was resigning but hoped to work for him in the future. *Resignation accepted*, Reeder replied curtly. He added that there would not be future employment.

Nezam also picked up some protection. "I got a Glock," Nezam told Scott one day, referring to the ubiquitous 9mm handgun, and texted a photo.

Scott couldn't believe it. It was a Glock, but not one like he'd ever seen. It had a ridiculous-looking see-through lower receiver (the part that included the grip) and an extra-long extended magazine.

Scott texted back. *You got yourself a sexy pistol there, brother.*

NEZAM: Yes, brother. It works, don't worry. I tried it.
SCOTT: Good.

Nezam also applied to renew his expiring passport, and got a new ID, the biometric Tazkira national ID card.

Mostly, though, he stayed out of sight. All he could do now was wait. Once his papers came through, he would fly.

13

It had been a year since Nezam had submitted his SIV. *A year.* Though he'd gotten to Kabul, his prospects for getting his SIV approved were dimming every day. After dozens of calls to former colleagues, help desks, and information centers, Scott had exhausted every contact he had in the government. The U.S. government had its head up its ass.

On the eve of the July Fourth weekend, President Biden held a press conference. He was practically giddy at the podium. The COVID vaccines were working, and life was returning to normal. He wanted to tout a jobs report showing that the economy had added 850,000 jobs in June. He did not want to talk about Afghanistan.

But the pool reporters did. It was practically all they asked about.

Biden snapped at one reporter, "I want to talk about happy things, man." After another Afghanistan question, he cut the reporter off, saying he wouldn't answer more questions on the subject going into Independence Day. "This is a holiday weekend. I'm going to celebrate it."

Only, the day prior, on July 1, the U.S. government had "celebrated" by officially closing Bagram Airfield. That hit Nezam and Scott in the gut. Both men had spent a lot of time traveling in and out of that base, they never thought it would close. It was the surest sign that the Americans were all but gone.

Almost the moment it was announced, Nezam was getting intel from his friends still operating on the ground. On July 3, he texted Scott, *I think the whole country is a month away to flip.*

If the administration only opened its eyes, it would see.

Little to no U.S. air support for Afghan ground troops. No mede-vac. No more U.S. contractors to manage air traffic control and aircraft repairs. No American field hospitals. Ammunition shortages and unreli-able stocks. Rampant ANA desertions. Dozens of northern districts had already fallen, a region far out of the Taliban's traditional Pashtun tribal belt, which few would have thought so vulnerable. The Taliban had also attacked Bagram, now manned by Afghans, just a few days after the last U.S. troops had left.

14

Scott was normally deep into his warmups before getting up in front of his corporate workshop clients, but not today. Just ten minutes before starting his training, he was on the phone. Again. He'd exhausted all his diplomatic options and had moved on to the military.

Scott had found the contact info for a Green Beret major who was supposedly compiling a list of "special Afghans" on behalf of the Army Special Operations.

"Yes, sir," the major said with a can-do tone. "It sounds like SFC Nezami definitely qualifies for our list since he went to the Q Course. Send me his SIV application, and I'll make sure our political advisor is working it directly."

"Roger that. Thanks," Scott said, a bit more upbeat than he'd been in a while.

After sending the visa information to the major he typed out a quick Signal message to Nezam:

SCOTT: You need to know that the highest-ranking general in Special Forces submitted your name on a shortlist of the other few Afghan Special Ops who went to our Q Course. We are working it hard.
You are in Kabul. Keep your head. You are still alive. Stay that way.

NEZAM: Thank you very much and I'll never forget.

Scott stared at Nezam's response. He'd never felt so disgusted with his own government. *What the fuck were they doing?*

15

Nezam was certain the Taliban were already in Kabul. He worked even harder to keep a low profile.

Despite the danger, he was getting by in seclusion. He spent most of his time in his tiny room monitoring news and playing chess on his phone, using an app that allowed him to compete with players across the world. It was a form of meditation, but it didn't always calm his nerves. He soon found flesh-and-blood opponents.

Behind his uncle's back garden lay a concrete yard discreetly enclosed with hedges. When Nezam peeked into the yard, he could see old men in baggy shalwar kameez sitting cross-legged on a rug laid over the pavement. As luck would have it, they were playing chess. Some were old mujahideen who had fought the Russians, wearing their iconic *pokol* rolled woolen caps. Nezam ventured through the hedge and asked if he could join them. The old muj welcomed him, and they didn't ask any questions. Nezam settled cross-legged on the rug and battled them rook-to-rook.

"You think you are young and very smart—but age and deceit will beat you!" one toothless muj needled Nezam.

Nezam's high-pitched laugh rang out across the little garden. He was a competent chess player, but against these old hands, he usually lost.

Playing chess helped pass the time while he waited for his new passport, which wouldn't be ready until later in the month. Nezam realized he needed a plan B, maybe getting a tourist visa to Uzbekistan. Tawab, his uncle, was starting to complain. He hadn't been fully aware of his nephew's work targeting Taliban and al-Qaeda leadership. Nezam was putting the family at great risk.

Nezam explored every option, no matter how tenuous or thin. It pained him to think it, but the United States could no longer be relied upon. The vague evacuation plan for SIVs like him, one that seemed to change every day, only underlined this fact.

One day, Nezam told Scott about his nervous uncle. "My uncle is pushing me to go somewhere else, but I don't know where to go."

Scott felt his heart sink. He knew Kabul was not Nezam's town.

"I understand. I'm reaching out to my network now."

"He thinks I am like Anne Frank, and there are Nazis everywhere."

"That's not far off, man."

"I need to get the fuck out of here, brother."

They talked options. Nezam asked about Mullah Mike, his former captain in Khakrez. Nezam knew that Mike had been with the CIA, and the agency had recruited Nezam at one point in 2017 for top secret work. "Maybe Mike could get me extracted from here by the CIA."

"I haven't spoken to him in a long while, Nezam. Let me see if I can locate him."

They hung up. Nezam had never felt more powerless.

All he could do was wait.

Wait, and pray.

16

For Scott, the news just kept getting worse.

His sources, some of the best experts on Afghanistan, told him that every single U.S. intelligence assessment from spring through summer concluded that the Afghan government wouldn't survive the U.S. withdrawal—estimates gave them at best until Spring 2022 and at worst early Fall 2021 before everything was under Taliban control. The Pentagon had also commissioned a secret study looking at historic examples of larger powers withdrawing from countries like Cuba or Vietnam. They found no instance of a "sponsored" government ever surviving. The one that made it the longest had lasted thirty-six months.

In mid-July, Scott also learned that American diplomats in Kabul used a rarely invoked dissent cable—a classified channel for internally protesting official State Department policy—to warn that Ghani's government was close to collapse. But nothing happened. Biden either didn't believe the drumbeat of dire predictions, or he didn't care.

Though Scott was happy Nezam had gotten to Kabul, he felt helpless to move him to the next step, get the SIV, and catch a plane to freedom.

Scott read about Operation Allies Refuge, the administration's latest attempt to evacuate at-risk Afghans. Despite the name, there was no indication that any action was imminent. Afghanistan was falling apart even faster than he thought it would. He cursed silently as he walked out toward the river to get some fresh air. Every time he thought about Afghanistan, anxiety washed over him.

It *was* shameful. After all the deployments, the work, the death, the sacrifice, and after everything America had tried to do in Afghanistan, it was crashing to an end in one final dust storm.

He suddenly felt despondent.

Scott closed his eyes and remembered losing his best friend from Ranger School, Cliff Patterson, when the towers fell. He had been at the Pentagon. When Scott deployed to Afghanistan in 2004, he was full of anger and bent on revenge. But this only got him so far. He couldn't kill his way out of being angry, and he had plenty of mistakes and empty deployments to show for that.

He eventually understood that local village engagement was the most effective counterinsurgency strategy. Bullets were still a necessity, but tea was often better ammunition.

Scott reflected on a recent interview he had sat for about Afghanistan's collapse. "A lot of guys are asking," said the reporter, "'What did my comrade die for?' You must be asking this question, watching these headlines coming out of Afghanistan. It must be a conversation you're having with guys, right?"

After a short pause, Scott had replied. "I think that what we will look back on and really regret is the way we left there. I am not good with it. A lot of us are struggling with it. I believe we are abandoning our brothers and sisters in Afghanistan. We violated a pact that we made with them. We abandoned the people with whom we made an agreement to go the long haul."

The interview had left a bad taste in his mouth.

Fuck, man, Scott thought, *I don't want to get involved in this shit.*

Shame on top of shame. It washed over him. For a split second he was transported back to that moment in 2015, when he was sitting on the floor of his bedroom closet, the door closed, room dark, a loaded .45 in his hand, tears in his eyes. Guilt gnawing his stomach lining. That was rock bottom. He had been ready. That was his time.

Only, it hadn't been.

Scott was happily married and had three sons. The only thing that stopped him that day was that one of his boys came home early from school. He had survived, and despite his trauma, he was now thriving.

The last thing Scott wanted to do was to jump back into the morass that he had pulled himself out of. The situation was grim. A little over a week earlier, a trio of bombs at a Kabul school killed dozens of young schoolgirls. He knew the Taliban had made gains in almost every part of the country, reimposing Sharia law. He knew the SIV program was stalled and failing. His Green Beret network was already swapping messages about how to get their Afghan comrades and their families out of the country.

And he knew he wanted nothing to do with any of it.

He tried to calm himself using the breathing techniques he'd learned after hitting bottom. He sat on the edge of the dock, looking at the shallow, muddy river behind his house for about ten minutes, chasing the anger from his thoughts and coaxing his pounding heart back to normal.

He walked into his garage, where he worked out for an hour until his muscles screamed and sweat poured down his neck. Finally, Scott stopped. After a shower, he headed to his office and sat behind his computer.

"Hey, Mike," he typed. "How are you, man? It's been a long time. Listen, I need your help."

PART II

THE DUST STORM

17

"What the fuck is this?" Lieutenant Colonel Kazem barked, scanning the horizon with his binoculars.

He jumped out of the bed of his Toyota Hilux and grabbed the radio handset. He needed to talk to his superiors at the National Directorate of Security (NDS), the Afghan intelligence service. "I see a line of three Humvees, Afghan police, and Army trucks fucking crossing into Iran," he said into the radio. "I need an airstrike now."

"Negative. There are no air assets available. Can you take them out?"

"With what? A fucking machine gun and some Kalashnikovs? No." The vehicles turned around a bend and disappeared. "I guess the Iranians just got some more ANA rigs from their Taliban guests."

The lieutenant colonel commanded an NDS-affiliated paramilitary unit, and he and his forty-man team had arrived to this besieged area in Nimruz six days earlier. They were there at the request of the governor, who had pleaded for help repelling Taliban attackers. Tall and lean with a cropped beard and a flip of hair across his forehead, Kazem looked too boyishly handsome to have been on the front lines. But that's where he'd been since his teens. He was quick with a grin, and gleefully salted his conversation with profanity.

Kazem had no idea how many men he had killed. His personal mission was to battle his way to a stable, multiethnic Afghanistan, and it didn't matter how many Taliban corpses lined the road to get there.

The Nimruz governor had promised Kazem a contingent of three hundred men to fight alongside his smaller force, but that didn't happen.

Just one day after the team arrived, the governor fled. To where, Kazem did not care. Once the governor was gone, morale evaporated—and so did the local security forces. They simply shed their uniforms and disappeared into the countryside.

As the security forces melted away, the Taliban called the remaining fighters' cell phones, promising a bloodless takeover if they laid down their arms. "Don't resist us. You'll be able to surrender," the Taliban promised.

But there was a caveat: "Don't get too close to the NDS elite forces. They will not be allowed to surrender. We have something special planned for them."

The vehicles crossing between Afghanistan and Iran perfectly exemplified a cardinal law of war: the enemy of my enemy is my friend. Iran's mullahs—Shiites—had no love for the Taliban—Sunnis. But these sectarian divisions could be tolerated when the United States stood in each of their ways.

The upshot was that, for now, Iran would put no pressure on the Taliban. In these barren borderlands, the Taliban had a free hand to rout the infidels—that is, the United States.

The United States, and men like Kazem.

"Fuck," he groaned. He secured the radio, climbed into his truck, and sped away through the deep sand back to NDS headquarters in Nimruz.

18

An explosion rang out across Kabul.

Gunfire followed, then more explosions. Sirens wailed. A suicide bomber had blown himself up at the home of the acting minister of defense in the high-security Sherpur neighborhood. The blast blew out windows, scattered cars, and showered the streets with debris. Four gunmen ran toward the blast site, weapons blazing. Security personnel and police closed the streets, surrounded the house, and killed the men. The minister and his family survived, but the bombing threw the capital into despair. Just as intended.

Nezam heard the explosion. The same day, his phone lit up with WhatsApp messages about the Taliban assassinating an Afghan interpreter who had worked with U.S. Special Forces. The next day, he got word that Sheberghan had fallen and that the Taliban had captured the Bayat power plant, killing one security contractor.

On August 6, the Taliban claimed control over their first provincial capital in Nimruz. Any question about whether the Taliban would target civilians was answered that same day when they assassinated an Afghan government spokesman in his car as he drove along a road in Kabul.

It wasn't just Nezam who had to get out. Everyone did.

The dust storm was here.

19

Kazem and his men holed up for four days in the largely abandoned government compound as the Taliban laid siege. The Taliban weren't killing them; his men were deserting. Kazem cursed them religiously.

Now, their dusty compound was surrounded and nearly empty of soldiers. Only Kazem's most loyal men remained—them, and two terrified NDS generals who'd barely known combat.

Kazem spent the morning wiring explosive charges inside the compound's armory, which was filled with rifles and ammunition. When he was finished, he thought, *This motherfucker is going sky high*. He exited the sweltering building and stepped into the blinding sunlight. He shaded his eyes and gazed around the walled perimeter.

Just beyond, the Taliban rode in seized coalition vehicles, prepared for a full assault. Kazem barked to his second-in-command: "Get the team to the trucks for a briefing." The Afghan operator nodded and jogged off in his heavy kit. Kazem walked to the rear of the base, where his truck was in the front of a line of idling Hilux pickups facing the perimeter. He rolled a cigarette and lit it.

The team assembled. They were haggard but resolute.

"Okay, listen up. We're going to mount up and then I'll ignite the fuse. When the ammo depot blows, the Taliban will think it's a bomb. It'll shock them for a few minutes." He took a long pull off his cigarette. "I hope."

A couple of chuckles from his bearded Pashtun operators.

"Once the depot's lit, I'm blowing that charge." He pointed to a pad of C-4 on the wall the trucks faced. "I'll haul ass out of here, and you'll follow as fast as you can. We don't stop."

He paused and looked intensely at each of his men. He held up an index finger. "We get one chance at this. One. If I get hit, you don't fucking stop." Kazem glared at the two NDS generals who cowered, pale as ghosts, in their vehicle. Disgusted, he said, "If these fucking generals get hit, you don't stop. If any of you get hit, I don't stop. If just one of us makes it out of this shit, that's a good thing. But we do it with honor—and no surrender. Understand?"

The men nodded and jumped into their respective vehicles. The trucks had NDS fighters in back with mounted PKM machine guns and RPG-7 rockets. Extra body armor vests lined the inside of the doors.

Kazem walked to the ammo depot fuse, took one last look at the compound, and pulled the igniter. The concussion wave made his teeth ache. He waited a few seconds. Then he jumped into his truck, ducked his head, and blew the second charge on the wall near the idling trucks.

"Go! Go! Go!" he yelled, and his driver gunned the truck through the massive breach in the wall. The convoy took heavy fire from Taliban vehicles in pursuit. Three U.S.-made Humvees—the very type Kazem had witnessed moving into Iran—closed in on them.

One of Kazem's gunners popped off shots with his rocket launcher and destroyed two of the vehicles. Shrapnel grazed Kazem's wrist. Two of his fighters took bullets to the legs and torso. They bounced northeast across the desert. The Taliban vehicles fell away, and Kazem's convoy sped into a cloud of thick red dust.

Kazem peered out the back window of his Hilux, not quite believing what he had just seen. He lit another cigarette. "Motherfucker."

This was no longer an insurgency. The conflict was now a "war of movement." The Taliban army was in motion across the country, with a single goal: snuffing out the Afghan government and taking unconditional control. Nimruz province was finished. The rest of Afghanistan wouldn't be far behind.

20

KABUL–AUGUST 8, 2021

Colonel Matt Hardman, the commander in charge of the residual American forces securing the Green Zone and at the Hamid Karzai International Airport, looked grim.

"Not an awesome weekend for the Afghan National Defense and Security Forces," he said at that morning's briefing in the Tactical Operations Center at HKIA. His remaining soldiers—about 650 of them—needed to hold the line against the Taliban until the State Department announced the Noncombatant Evacuation Operation (NEO), which would pull the rest of the American diplomatic staff from the country.

Colonel Hardman wasn't telling the assembled officers anything they didn't know. There were clear signs that, very soon, Kabul would be unsafe. It was not even clear that this tiny residual force could hold back the Taliban forces that were boiling over everywhere across the country and on the outskirts of the city. Colonel Hardman told them to get ready for a worst-case scenario: street-to-street fighting in Kabul.

Major Ian Wookey, a Canadian exchange officer and helicopter pilot, took notes, scribbling, *30–45 days* as the colonel talked about the timing for the NEO. An emergency evacuation was everyone's concern, but Major Wookey would have a specific role. As the aviation operations officer of Task Force Falcon for the 82nd Airborne Division, he would oversee evacuations from the U.S. embassy. He would also be piloting a CH-47 Chinook, ferrying American diplomats the short distance from the embassy to the airport.

Major Wookey had extensive experience with Chinooks, a large dual-rotor transport helicopter, but had only received his first combat aviation posting a few months earlier in May, when he deployed to Helmand province. Shortly thereafter, he was moved to Bagram. It was there that rumors began to spread: a small diplomatic security force would be tasked to the airport in Kabul, in case the embassy closed. Major Wookey scoffed when he heard this. No way that was going to happen.

But then, in June, he watched as one massive C-17 Globemaster after another taxied down the Bagram runway, carrying men and equipment out of Afghanistan. On July 1, the last U.S. forces left the base in the middle of the night, shutting off the power before taking off. The base—which included a prison holding thousands of Taliban—was now under the Afghan army's control.

Bagram would have been the ideal place for an NEO. It was defensible, and not surrounded by a city. But the U.S. no longer controlled it.

The NEO would have to be conducted from HKIA.

Major Wookey counted twelve military aircraft: four Apache gunships, four Black Hawks, and four Chinooks. This was the entire U.S. air fleet on the ground in Afghanistan. The country's vast American presence had contracted to a single square mile ringed with blast walls, chainlink fence, and razor wire.

As Colonel Hardman faced his small team in the command center, he was blunt. "Be as ready as possible for the worst day of your life. Make sure you're in the right headspace when it all goes bad."

21

Kazem lit a cigarette. He sat, slump-backed, in an abandoned clinic looking at his two wounded fighters. Their hell-for-leather escape from the base in Nimruz had been successful, but they'd taken fire.

The fighters' groans echoed off the dingy walls. They were in bad shape. Their wounds still bled, and infection was sure to set in. But the shelves of the clinic had been raided and stripped bare. There was nothing. No medicine. No morphine. Not even a bandage. The security infrastructure had crumbled overnight.

He took a long drag from his cigarette. The youngest fighter had multiple gunshot wounds to his legs. Kazem knelt beside him and placed his hand on his head. He addressed both of the wounded. "I can't take you with me, you know that. It will slow us down, and we'll all be fucking killed. So, you have two choices." He took another pull from his smoke and exhaled slowly. "I can dig two holes in the desert out back. I'll make it quick. I'll make it honorable. No more pain. Or, you can try to keep living, but you'll have to do exactly what I say."

"We want to live, Commander," the second man said.

Kazem nodded and walked out the door into the sunlight.

A few hours later, he helped both wounded men into the back seat of a taxi. The driver stood to one side, out of earshot, with two soldiers standing next to him. The engine idled. Kazem leaned into the cab and spoke to the wounded men. His voice was flat and emotionless.

"The driver will take you to Camp Bastion," he told them. "The field hospital should still be open. If not, there will still be a nurse or doctor there who can help. They'll have bandages and iodine and penicillin. It's your best chance to live. Do you understand?" Both men nodded.

Kazem handed each man a pistol. "There is one magazine in each of these. If someone stops you"—he lowered his voice—"kill the driver first. Then kill the guy stopping you. After that, the bullets will rain down as if from Allah himself. They will kill you so nicely, you won't feel a thing."

He lowered his face to the wounded men. In a raspy whisper, he said, "If you don't use the pistol to kill these men, they will figure out you are NDS. They *will* kill you, but really fucking slow. They will send out a picture of your death, or a video that lasts thirty whole minutes. That would not be good for your mom. Or Afghanistan. You fucking understand?"

The men nodded. Kazem patted each man's shoulder and stood. He paid the driver handsomely. Moments later, the cab pulled away.

Kazem chain-smoked in the abandoned clinic. When the call rang out for the evening prayer, echoing off the mud walls of the village, he signaled to his men. They went to their trucks, put them in neutral, and began to push. As the village knelt in prayer, their heads piously touching the ground, Kazem and his men silently steered the trucks out the gate and rolled them down the road. When they were several hundred yards from the village, they jumped in the trucks, fired them up, and floored it. They rumbled toward Highway 1, the Ring Road, which would lead them to safety.

It would lead them to Kabul.

22

The August sun beat down on Devils Field. Captain John Folta had been dreaming of this day for years. He was about to be placed in command of an airborne infantry company. He listened as the outgoing commanding officer gave a speech to the assembled soldiers. His wife seated nearby, John waited for his turn to deliver a speech of his own.

With his close-cropped blond hair and chiseled face, he seemed more suited to head a fraternity than command a company of the 82nd Airborne Division. But that's one thing he loved about the Army. Looks didn't mean shit. A soldier was a soldier.

Across the field, he could just make out his first sergeant, Jesse Kennedy, who had a muscular neck like a football player that made him easy to spot in a formation. Charlie Company's senior NCO stood in formation in the sweltering heat among the other paratroopers. John knew that ceremony wasn't the sergeant's cup of tea, but no matter. He was the kind of NCO a company commander hoped for.

John listened patiently to the outgoing commander, when he heard a slight buzz to his right. His brigade commander, Colonel Teddy Kleisner, pulled his phone from his pocket.

"Huh," Colonel Kleisner said. He showed his phone to John. On the home screen was a two-word notification: GREEN CORVETTE.

Those words meant one thing. His company was deploying to Afghanistan.

Immediately.

John sat stock-still, trying not to show any reaction. But his heart raced. For this one surreal moment, he and Colonel Kleisner were the only two men on the field who knew about the storm they were about to fly into.

After the speeches, as John greeted his soldiers, he exchanged a salute with Jesse. "We just got a 'Green Corvette,'" he whispered.

"Roger that, sir," the First Sergeant said with a curt nod. "Welcome to Charlie Company."

23

Master Sergeant Basira Baghrani arrived at her office in the Ministry of Defense as reports flooded in that Taliban were at the outskirts of the capital. Ministry staff swirled around her as they gathered their things before fleeing the compound.

Basira refused to run. "Where are you going? We need to fight. We can hold!" she yelled to her colleagues.

But no one listened. "You need to leave now!" an overweight officer barked at her, clutching an armful of papers as he waddled to a waiting car.

She cursed him audibly, but he paid no attention.

"Get out of here now, Master Sergeant. Save yourself. They'll be here soon," he said.

She couldn't believe it. "Stop running!" she screamed. But there was no stopping the exodus. It was like she was telling them to stay in a burning building.

"And change out of uniform before you leave," the officer yelled at her. "They'll kill you on sight in that."

Rage swelled within Basira. Diminutive and strong, a moon-shaped face framed by her green hijab, she was immensely proud of her uniform and the stature it conveyed. In 2019, she had been the first woman to graduate from the Sergeants Major Academy. Now all that meant nothing. Once the Taliban resumed their rule, she would never again be permitted to wear the uniform. Her hands began to shake. She took three deep breaths. Then she went to change her clothes.

She didn't fully comprehend it, but she was no longer a master sergeant. She was a civilian. She joined the crowd outside. She fought her way through the throng on the long walk home. When she arrived, the house was in chaos. "Where have you been?" her uncle snapped.

She ignored him. "Where's Mother?" she asked. Like many Afghan women, her mother was strong. Following the death of her husband, Basira's mother had been the rock on which the family's grief crashed and washed away.

"Out back," her uncle said with bitterness. "Doing what should have been done long ago." He never fully approved of Basira's chosen career path.

Basira slipped to the back of the house and gazed, horrified, at a fire blazing in the backyard. Her mother was feeding the last of her army uniforms into the flames.

"Mother! No!" she said. But it was too late—her mother had tossed the uniform into the fire. Basira screamed as the flames consumed evidence of her achievements, symbols of hope not only for her but for women throughout Afghanistan.

"My child," her mother said. She leveled a steely gaze on her daughter. She hadn't seen that look since childhood, just after her father had died. "It is over. We have to live. We have to survive." She touched Basira's cheek with her open palm. "I want you to get all of your military certificates and bring them out here and burn them."

As if in a trance, Basira went to her room. Her certificates hung on the wall. Next to these was a picture of her on a recruiting poster for the ANA. She was semi-famous.

The realization hit her hard. She wasn't just a target. She was a high-value target.

She pulled the certificates from the wall and stuffed them in the bottom of a bag. She piled clothes on top.

Her phone rang. It was a friend from the Ministry of Defense. "Go to the airport. The Americans are evacuating people." Basira couldn't believe it.

This could only mean one thing: the Americans really were abandoning Afghanistan.

24

Scott's phone dinged. Nezam again.

Taliban are inside Kabul, he texted Scott. *They were looking in my window earlier. They are everywhere. I'm panicking, brother.*

Scott tried to calm Nezam with a voice memo, so his friend could hear his tone.

"I know this is a scary time for you, pal, but you are one of the toughest guys I have ever met. I just need you to keep everything level, okay? You are in an unconventional war now. I need you to stay focused on lying low and preparing for the time when you need to move. Something tells me you won't have much warning, so staying sharp and focused is key. You need to stay in the shadows and just stay alive, okay, man? Just a little longer. I promise. We're going to find a way to get you out."

Scott hung up the phone and looked around his empty house. The silence was deafening. What the fuck had he just done?

This was getting far beyond helping a friend with a visa issue.

He'd just made a promise that he knew he couldn't keep.

25

The traffic had stopped. Razaq, a longtime interpreter for U.S. Special Forces, sat nervously behind the wheel of his Toyota Corolla, trapped in the gridlocked streets of downtown Kabul.

When his friend Akmal had asked him for a ride to the U.S. embassy, he'd agreed. The day before, the two former interpreters for U.S. Special Forces had gone to the passport office together and found it clogged with thousands of people. They tried to go to the bank, but all the branches were closed.

Now it was clear that he had made a mistake. Full-on panic gripped Kabul. Frightened people packed the sidewalks, running to the already closed banks for their money. Razaq chain-smoked Seven Stars cigarettes as they discussed what to do.

Razaq had only been a teenager when he first went to work for the Americans in 2004. He signed up because he wanted peace, prosperity, and development in Afghanistan. It was an opportunity for him, a kid who'd grown up with nothing. He accompanied U.S. Special Forces into firefights throughout the dangerous regions in eastern Afghanistan, all along the Pakistani border. But he'd quit in 2012 to go to school to study environmental engineering, and after that had gone to work for a waste management company.

Everything he had hoped and fought for was coming apart.

He looked to his left and saw massive lines of people at ATMs trying to get cash. Up the street, Razaq could make out abandoned Afghan police vehicles on the side of the road. The cops had stripped off their uniforms and melted into the crowds. The trucks had M240B and .50-caliber heavy machine guns sitting on their mounts. Ammunition belts hung freely from the loaded guns.

"Someone could just jump on one of those guns and kill everyone," Razaq said.

After sitting in gridlock for two hours, Akmal began freaking out. "We need to get out of here. Leave your car, man. Let's run for it."

"Dude, I'm not leaving my car," Razaq replied.

His friend grew more agitated. "Leave your car, man. We're running out of time. If you don't, I'll leave you here alone."

"Go home if you need to, man, but I'm not leaving my car." And with that, Akmal opened the passenger door and sprinted off.

Razaq leaned across the inside of the car and pulled the door shut. He locked the car, and then dialed his wife, Wajmah, who was a kindergarten teacher. Cell phone coverage was spotty, but she picked up. "Where are you?" he asked.

"I'm at work," she said.

Razaq couldn't believe it. "Why are you still at work?" he shouted. His mind raced with images of what the Taliban would do to a woman caught working at a school.

"Why are you yelling at me, Razaq?" she asked, beginning to sob.

Razaq cursed himself. She was seven months pregnant.

"I'm sorry, Waj. It's okay. I just need you to go home right now. I've got a bad feeling about all this. Lock the door. Take care of the kids. I'll be home soon."

He hung up. The situation outside was getting worse by the minute. The radio was calling out districts inside Kabul that had fallen to the Taliban. He checked that all the car's windows were up, and then lit a fresh cigarette with the butt of his old one.

Just then, his brother called. "Where are you, man?"

"I'm in my car, stuck in traffic," Razaq said.

"Are you crazy? Leave your car and get your ass home, man."

Razaq heard nearby gunfire. The Taliban had freed everyone the

Americans had held in their jails. He watched the mayhem through the window of his smoke-filled car. It was like a disaster movie, he thought to himself, and he wondered if he was dreaming. Then, with one last drag on his cigarette, Razaq opened his door and abandoned his car.

He ran through the throng of people, bumping headlong into panicked pedestrians. He went first to his cousin's house, which was closer than his own, but his cousin told him to leave because his U.S. credentials posed a danger to the family. He kept going. A hysterical woman jumped in front of him, her eyes wide with fright.

"Hey, brother, will you please help me? I'm so scared." She was a bank teller, wearing a form-fitting uniform with a European cut. She had no headcover and wore thick lipstick.

"Girl, if the Talibs see you out like this, they'll kill both of us. Where do you live?"

She pointed feverishly in the direction he was already going.

"Follow me," Razaq said. He picked his way through the crowds and blocked streets, always looking back to ensure they weren't being followed. He got the woman to her home and then ran on to his own.

As he approached his door, neighbors eyed him suspiciously. *Which one of them will rat me out?* he wondered. He slipped into his house to find his seven-month-pregnant wife staring at him wide-eyed with their three young daughters. He managed a slight smile, and then turned and locked all the bolts. He turned off the lights. He turned off his phone. Then he turned back to his family. He held them tightly in the darkness. His wife's body racked with sobs as machine-gun fire echoed in the street below.

26

The loudspeakers of the public address system within the U.S. embassy in Kabul blared, "All personnel to the pickup zone." Just a few hours earlier, the announcement had come for nonessential personnel to evacuate. Now it was everybody.

For weeks, State Department officials had believed they still had time, maybe even months. Yesterday, the Community Liaison Officer, who was responsible for organizing social events, had sent an email out notifying everyone that "today's paint and sip is canceled due to circumstance." To which someone sarcastically replied, "The terrorists have won."

No one was joking now.

Now, with only hours remaining, staff loaded boxes of classified and sensitive records onto a Gator XUV, which then lumbered down the embassy road known as "Pennsylvania Avenue" to a roaring bonfire in a huge roll-off container—a literal dumpster fire. Armfuls of documents were hastily destroyed, while the embassy's CH-46 choppers buzzed overhead, transporting their colleagues from the Green Zone to the airport two miles away.

To most, what was happening in real-time was incomprehensible. Just that morning, top embassy staff had held a meeting about the evacuation timeline for the embassy's chargé d'affaires, Ross Wilson, who was the acting U.S. ambassador. The plan was scrapped almost the moment the meeting ended as small-arms fire rang out through the streets around the embassy. Nobody had believed the situation would deteriorate in just a few hours, which was reflected in the actions of a few holdouts sitting in their office, sipping coffee, working as if they had some time left when the final alarm sounded.

Security officers rushed through the hallways, going door to door, and ordering everyone out. As the building emptied, the locks were hammered off any doors they couldn't open, just to make sure no one was left behind.

Embassy personnel donned tan body armor vests and snatched their go-bags. Overhead, helicopters crisscrossed the sky. There was a feeling of urgency as everyone knew in their hearts that soon—probably that very day—the Taliban would be inside the building. The compound believed to have been a stronghold of American power would be just another fallen monument to hubris. Everyone moved to the pickup zone.

Chinooks landed and lifted off as fast as they were filled.

Eventually, a final helicopter would carry away Ross Wilson. Surrounded by Marines, he would lower the American flag flying over the embassy, fold it, and place it into a canvas sack.

From the chopper, everyone could see the desperate gridlock in the streets. Vast tides of desperate people charged the Hamid Karzai airport, the last American foothold in the city. The three-mile trip took only a few minutes, and the helicopters descended onto the southwest end of the Kabul runway.

The CIA officers already on the airfield weren't expecting an entourage of civilian diplomats in varying states of physical fitness lugging laptops and suitcases, but the foreign service officers zeroed in on an empty building to set up their final base of operations in Afghanistan.

The room was long and contained a pool table and TVs tuned to CNN relaying news in real-time. It had been the CIA's bar not long ago. The staff set up their workstations on café tables. They plugged in radios and laptops.

Welcome to the new embassy of the United States of America in Kabul.

27

"Have you heard anything, Bashir?" asked the commander of Advanced Operations Base 750, an Afghan Special Forces company still holding out against the Taliban. "It's getting bad. We're waiting on orders to get out."

"They won't come," Master Sergeant Bashir Ahmadzai said. "Parwan and Kapisa provinces have fallen."

"What can we do?" the commander asked.

"Nothing," Bashir answered.

He stared out the window. Tall and broad with an unruly mop of wavy hair, he was a senior NCO in the Afghan Special Forces, a Q Course graduate, and one of the most trusted Afghan special operators among Green Berets.

Bashir walked to the door. He opened it and surveyed Camp Morehead. The sprawling compound about fifteen miles southwest of downtown Kabul was on the site of what had been the primary training center for the entire Afghan National Army. Commandos and Afghan Special Forces were selected and trained here. They deployed from here. It had been the heartbeat of the Afghan military, especially when things started to fall apart.

Infected by fear, politicians and Afghan National Army officers began employing commandos and other Afghan Special Operations Forces to serve their own selfish agendas: to secure and guard their property and private residences—not the country's infrastructure or strategic assets.

Bashir and all the men like him had been abandoned by the Afghan leadership.

Do they think we are made of stone? he wondered.

He was angry. No food. No ammo. No air support. No medevac. These were suicide missions—still, they fought on, plugging hole after hole in a national security dam that was bound to burst.

His home was only a few yards away from Camp Morehead. His wife and children were there. He would need to go to them soon. He had spent so little time with them as he roamed the countryside with Green Berets and other Afghans, fighting for his country. His wife never let him forget how bitter she was about this.

At 1:00 p.m., Bashir received a frantic call from a fellow Afghan special operator. "We've spotted approximately ten armed Taliban near the ammunition supply point."

The master sergeant cursed. He grabbed his M4 carbine and ordered the few remaining special operators to mount up.

He and a small band of commandos soon reached the ammo point, where they engaged and killed seven Taliban fighters. They fanned out and killed seven more—including a sniper sequestered high in a tower.

They returned to the headquarters, and Bashir watched as one Army officer after another left the compound in civilian clothes, avoiding eye contact with him and his few loyal commandos. By nightfall, they were the only ones left.

Bashir thought of his family, and of theirs. He gathered his men together. He felt as if he were speaking in slow motion as he issued his final orders at 7:30 p.m.

"Go home. Take care of your families, my brothers. We did our damnedest."

When the last soldier was gone, he took off his own uniform and shuffled down the road away from the compound one last time. He walked into his modest home and nodded to his wife. She and the kids knew to leave him alone at a moment like this.

28

The morning meeting at the palace was taking longer than expected. Hasina Safi, the acting minister for women's affairs, sat across from Afghanistan's first lady, Rula Ghani, who remained attentive and patient even as the meeting ran overtime. The two women were coordinating aid for rural women. As the Taliban advanced, more and more women were forced to assume the fundamentalists' repressive strictures. Women whose fortunes had brightened immeasurably since 2001 now needed hygiene, medicine, and other basic aid.

When the meeting ended, the two women thanked each other. Hasina did not sense that anything was amiss until she climbed into her car and her driver-bodyguard went into evasive action.

"What are you doing?" she demanded.

"Taliban everywhere," he said. "We have to get you out of here."

Hasina steeled herself. "Nonsense. Take me back to the ministry. Right now." The half-mile drive to the ministry usually took about seven minutes; that day, the trip took an hour and a half. The sound of gunfire was everywhere, and frightened people swarmed the streets, seeming to run without direction or purpose in their panic.

The driver dropped Hasina at the front of the Ministry of Women's Affairs. As she stepped into the building for what would be the last time, her heart sank. Almost all the staff had gone home. Two people defiantly remained, her deputy minister and her human relations director. *Good for them*, she thought. The deputy minister begged Hasina to go home as well, but she was determined to stay, even if the Taliban shot her, beat her, or worse.

"I must face them," she insisted. "There is no other way."

Hasina stayed throughout the afternoon, her stomach tightening as she worried about her husband and three children. As the day progressed, her two remaining staff members fed her constant reports of violence as the Taliban took control of the capital.

In the evening, the human relations director warned that the situation had grown exponentially more dangerous. Taliban were lobbing grenades at government sites, with no response from government forces. Hasina embraced her colleagues tightly and told them both to go home.

She was preparing to abandon the ministry itself when her husband called. "Hasina, do not come home. They are looking for you."

"Where should I go?" she asked. She couldn't believe she wouldn't be with her family. Would the Taliban hurt them, too, just because she loved them?

"I don't know," her husband said, his voice breaking. "But don't come here. They'll kill you."

Her bodyguard drove her to the home of a distant cousin. She would take refuge there.

Then, like so many others, she waited.

For what exactly, she wasn't sure.

29

"Mister President, it is time to leave." The blunt statement came at 3:00 p.m. from Hamdullah Mohib, the national security adviser to Ashraf Ghani. The president wanted to grab some personal items and keepsakes, but Mohib told the Afghan leader that nowhere was safe now and time was running out. He could be shot dead on sight by anyone inside the palace walls.

Ghani and Mohib gathered Ghani's wife, Rula, a Lebanese-born dual citizen of Afghanistan and the United States; the senior staff; and several armed bodyguards. Surrounding Ghani and Rula, they moved quickly to the palace helipads, where three Russian-made Mi-17s sat waiting, their rotors already spinning. Mohib led Ghani, Rula, and several others onto the first Mi-17. The rest filled the second. A mortal problem presented itself—there weren't enough seats on the third chopper.

A scuffle broke out as the bodyguards suddenly played *Lord of the Flies*. Ghani's helo took off, quickly followed by the second chopper. Mohib watched as the remaining men pushed and shoved one another, jockeying for position. Finally, the third Mi-17 tried to lift off. There were too many people. As Mohib's helo made an arcing turnover, he watched as his personal secretary and four of his bodyguards were physically pushed off the Mi-17.

They had been left behind.

Once airborne, a new problem arose. It was not entirely clear where they could go. The original plan, following what was supposed to be a peaceful transfer of power, was simply to leave with Emirati officials on a luxurious UAE government jet on Monday night. But now, and despite Mohib's many attempts to convince the Taliban leaders, there would be no peaceful transfer of power. The enemy had overrun the gates of the three-thousand-year-old city, and there was no Emirati jet at HKIA waiting to spirit away Afghanistan's elected president.

The previous day, Mohib had discussed options with Ghani, planning to fly south to the city of Khost—where Ghani had a loyal and dedicated security force—after refueling in Jalalabad.

By late Saturday afternoon, Jalalabad was gone, too.

The pilots set a course for Tajikistan before diverting to Uzbekistan, which was closer. Even after the last-minute sorting, they were still too heavy for the helicopters because the hot weather required more lift for the swishing rotors, and if they went for Tajikistan, they would run out of fuel. Ghani's protective detail was forced to jettison all their body armor, ammunition, and most of their weapons mid-flight over the Hindu Kush mountains in order for them to make it.

The Uzbeks were not expecting Ghani and his people at the international airport just across the border. When the choppers landed, Uzbek soldiers confronted Ghani's armed bodyguards before realizing that the VIP aboard was the former president of the Islamic Republic of Afghanistan—a president without an office, from a government that no longer existed.

30

First Sergeant Jesse Kennedy could see the fear on the faces of Charlie Company as their C-17 approached Kabul. And for good reason. In just a few minutes, the plane would be on the ground. Their battalion, 2nd Battalion, 504th Parachute Infantry Regiment—known as the White Devils—was part of an airborne armada descending on Kabul. They had no clue what they were flying into, or what would greet them once the ramp came down.

As far as Jesse was concerned, his new company commander, Captain John Folta, was working out just fine. He'd done a good job of getting updates while they were en route, but they were mostly from media reports, including the news that President Ghani had fled Kabul.

The tension showed on the faces of Jesse's young paratroopers, most of whom had never set foot in Afghanistan. Most assumed that they would walk off the tail ramp into a gunfight with Taliban forces occupying the capital.

Jesse had fought in Iraq and was plenty used to jumping into uncertainty, but this was also his first mission in Afghanistan. Even as the jumbo jet plunged into its lurching, nosedive descent to avoid potential antiaircraft fire, Jesse moved through the back of the plane, clapping his guys on the shoulder and cracking jokes. Jesse's whole body was tensing up, as he imagined how U.S. soldiers felt on D-Day, crouched in their amphibious landing boats just before the ramp went down and spilled the soldiers into a blizzard of bullets. Jesse kept going from soldier to soldier, asking how they were doing. He was nervous, too, but he wouldn't show it.

"Just keep your head, boys. Everything's gonna be cool."

The C-17 taxied to the south end of the runway and the paratroop door on the side of the giant plane opened. A rush of hot air flushed into the aircraft and onto their faces—but no incoming fire. The company breathed a collective sigh of relief. An even bigger relief came when the Air Force loadmaster exited the aircraft.

"See, he's not dead!" Jesse joked. "We got this!"

Charlie Company dismounted the ramp, ready for anything. "At least it doesn't smell as bad as Iraq," he said to John, who cut him a grin.

Jesse directed his platoons to establish security. John looked for other friendlies to help him get oriented. As he looked around, machine-gun fire and tracers lit up the night sky outside the perimeter.

He couldn't tell whether the Taliban were celebrating or fighting.

A few moments later, John was greeted by a distracted Marine major. "Hey, guys. Glad you're here. Anything you want, take it. Vehicles with keys, rooms with keys—take it," he said. He then spun to jog away, but stopped and shouted, "Hey, you know when we're getting the fuck out of here?"

Jesse shrugged. He had no idea.

There were radio reports that Taliban were inside the airport's wire. Jesse and John gathered their men. They scrounged vehicles, ranging from side-by-side ATVs to a bright cherry-red fire truck, and set up base in an abandoned gym. It looked like a sleepless and very violent night.

31

Fixated on the TV images of Taliban fighters celebrating in the Kabul streets, Scott was shaken out of his trance when his phone buzzed. It was his old friend Jane Horton, a Gold Star wife.

Her husband Chris had been killed while fighting in Afghanistan in 2011 when she had been only twenty-four years old. There had been a knock on her door, and her world crashed in. Since that time, Jane had battled through sadness and depression to become a voice for other Gold Star families. But equally impressive, she had become an unofficial ambassador to Afghanistan. It started with her wanting to understand the country where her beloved Chris died but quickly evolved into an impassioned mission to help other Americans understand the beauty and sincerity of the Afghan people. She made frequent trips there. She met with high-ranking leaders and everyday shopkeepers. She was a champion for Afghan women and girls.

Now after all the chaos that had happened, she called Scott. "Everything is happening so fast, Scott," she told him. "I'm trying to get a young single Afghan woman named Arianna out of the presidential palace. The Taliban will not be kind to her when they find her. She's alone and scared to death. I'm not sure what to do."

"I know, Jane," Scott replied. "I'm trying to do the same thing with my friend Nezam. It's a complete shitshow."

She sat silent on the phone, and finally spoke hoarsely. "My husband, those that died, and all of you guys . . . don't deserve to be tied to this bullshit when you were there to serve your country and give your lives if asked," she said. "I feel like my heart has been ripped out all over again."

There was so much for these old friends to say to each other at this moment. There'd be time for that later. "Jane, you've got this. Focus on Arianna. Tell her story on the news. Do whatever it takes to keep moving forward."

"You're right. If I can help this one person, it will give me something to hold onto. It's a life for a life," she sobbed. "And then I can accept that Chris gave his so I could save this one person."

As Scott hung up the phone, grief settled over him like a wet blanket. The faces of so many Gold Star family members he'd met over the years flooded in. Holly Higgins, the broken-hearted mom aching for her son, Dan, whom Scott had met performing his play. Jeff Falkel, who'd made a commemorative pen from a bullet in his son Junior's honor. Chris Piper's little boy sobbing as the bagpipes played "Ballad of the Green Berets" while Scott marched alongside him to his dad's gravesite. *My God*, he thought as he tried to keep his hands from shaking. *What were they all going through right now?* He shook off the dark thoughts. Jane's words still rang in his ears. He knew exactly what she meant. He took a breath and put his focus back on Nezam.

32

"What the hell is taking so long?" Major Ian Wookey demanded through the helmet mic to his copilot. They had been sitting in the Chinook on the Green Zone soccer field near the U.S. embassy compound with the blades turning for far too long. As the long-rumored NEO began, they were evacuating embassy staff to Hamid Karzai International Airport, and their massive twin-rotor chopper was a sitting duck on the grass. Every minute they lingered, the Taliban got closer.

After what seemed like forever, a long line of diplomats and government employees approached single-file toward his chopper in the dark. Watching through his night vision goggles, Major Wookey shook his head in disbelief. Some carried three or four massive suitcases.

"We'll never take off with all that shit," Major Wookey cursed into his mic to his loadmasters, who stood by to guide the civilians up the chopper's back ramp.

"Let me help you carry your bags," Major Wookey heard the crew chief tell a boarding passenger. Reluctantly, the man agreed, and handed him two bags. The crew chief chucked the suitcases off to the side, away from the landing zone. When they finally took off, the stack of suitcases remained.

33

Master Sergeant Bashir Ahmadzai only slept three hours the night he was forced to abandon his post. He lay in bed listening to the yelling just outside his home, adjacent to Camp Morehead's entrance. The Taliban hadn't wasted any time taking over the headquarters of the Afghan special operations forces.

He got up and walked quietly from his bedroom. His wife and children were still asleep. It felt unnatural to put on civilian clothes after so many years in uniform. He walked outside into the fresh morning sunlight. At least there weren't any gunfights underway. Nevertheless, Taliban checkpoints had been set up in every direction.

He turned his attention back to Morehead. The massive security lights that were always on at night were still on in the daylight. *Those dumbasses*, he thought. *This is who we're handing the country over to?*

He walked over to a Talib who seemed to be in charge of a checkpoint.

"As-salaam alaikum," he greeted. "Excuse me, brother."

"What do you want?" the Talib said.

"I used to be a maintenance man on Morehead," Bashir said, lying. He pointed at the lights. "Those lights must be turned on every evening and turned off in the morning. The bulbs are very expensive, and if they burn out you won't be able to get more."

The Talib looked at him suspiciously, not quite comprehending. "Thank you, brother," the wary fighter said.

Bashir walked away as calmly as he could.

34

Matt Coburn turned his Toyota pickup truck into the driveway of his family's home and shut off the engine. The former Green Beret slowly eased his huge frame out from behind the wheel. His wife, Michelle, and their two kids jumped out as he unloaded their baggage after the eleven-hour drive from South Carolina. The family vacation to Hilton Head—tranquil and full of laughter—wasn't supposed to end this way.

On the way home, his phone began lighting up with calls. One friend, who served in the Afghan Joint Special Operations Command, told Matt that President Ghani had just fled. The country was officially leaderless, and as the Afghan chain of command fell to pieces, the in-country operations were as well.

"Sir, there is no one left. What should we do?" the friend asked.

Matt had no answer. At 240 pounds, with long hair and a beard, he didn't feel like a former career Special Forces officer. The previous year had taken its toll. Hell, the last twenty years had taken their toll.

Over six deployments and twenty years, Matt had risen to the rank of full bird colonel. The first three deployments were strong. As a young Special Forces detachment commander, he had helped stand up and advise the original Afghan National Army forces. Many of those young Afghan officers and NCOs went on to become core leaders of Afghan Special Operations Forces. Throughout his deployments, he would see the same faces over and over, fighting by his side or with the Americans he commanded. He admired the Afghan fighters' persistence in the face of the Taliban, and sympathized with their many leadership challenges.

By the end of his fourth deployment, however, the war was exacting a heavy price on his body and his soul. He struggled with suicidal thoughts. Many of his friends in the 3rd Special Forces Group had been killed in action or maimed, the victims of IEDs and increasingly sophisticated attacks from the Taliban.

One particular memory haunted him. In 2009, he was accompanying a joint patrol of American and Czech armed forces when one of the Humvees hit an IED. The explosion killed two men instantly, blowing their bodies clear out of the vehicle. The Taliban had been waiting for them and immediately began firing down on the ambushed convoy.

As bullets snapped around him, Matt watched a sergeant stand up from where he'd been blown out of the truck. As he staggered toward an intact Humvee, Matt saw that flames had scorched all the hair off his friend's entire body. He later died.

Inside his burning Humvee, as if the incoming fire and danger of more IEDs weren't enough, the heat was cooking off .50-caliber shells, sending rounds in every direction.

Despite their injuries, they managed to regroup and repel the Taliban. One of his Green Berets donned flameproof mitts to remove the charred skeleton of one of his teammates from behind the wheel of his Humvee. As Matt watched, the man's legs snapped off at the knees. His remains suddenly reignited, fueled by the fresh air outside the vehicle. Matt had to use a fire extinguisher to douse the flames on what was left of his friend's body.

Compounding this searing trauma, he also began losing faith in America's military leadership. He saw bureaucracy, careerism, and risk aversion everywhere around him. During his final deployment, he was the last commander of the Combined Joint Special Operations Task Force–Afghanistan, tasked with the preparation and handoff of combat operations to the Afghan partners, working closely with top military leadership. The handoff was far from perfect, but he left feeling he had done all he could do to prepare the Afghan commandos, Special Forces, and other Afghan operators for the difficult role they would play when U.S. forces went home.

When Matt put in his paperwork for retirement, he discovered that he had not been a full colonel long enough to stay at that rank in retirement. If he chose not to stay in longer, he would retire at the lower rank of lieutenant colonel. So he did something unheard of in today's military: he hung up his boots and left the Army in the spring of 2021 as quickly as he could—in effect throwing his rank on the table.

Matt could easily have gone to work as a civilian defense contractor, but he wanted to get as far away from the military as possible. He took a massive pay cut and loss in status to take a junior-level supervisor job in an Amazon warehouse. The work was clear-cut. He liked his coworkers. There was no bullshit on the forklift or in the break room.

This did nothing to solve his post-traumatic stress or guilt. They were crushing. Decisions that he'd made had led men to die or return home maimed. His suicidal thoughts only got worse; he thought about killing himself in public to make a statement, like outside the Pentagon or in front of the White House, like the monks who set themselves on fire in Saigon during Vietnam.

Matt had worked hard in his post-Army life to put those demons behind him. Never an easy task, but one that he worked diligently on as he focused on being the best warehouse supervisor he could, and on immersing himself in his family. He was making progress. He was in a better place.

Now, as he helped Michelle unpack after their trip to the beach, all of the bullshit from this forever war came flooding back. The messages were piling up on his phone from his Afghan special operator friends, scared and alone, asking him for help.

That evening, Matt sat in his living room, staring out the window over the neat houses and close-cropped lawns of his subdivision. Seven thousand miles away a humanitarian disaster was unfolding. The Afghan special operators he'd worked with weren't even eligible for Special Immigrant Visas because they hadn't worked for the U.S. government. More bullshit. An Afghan barber at Bagram Airfield had a better chance of getting into the U.S. than the commandos who had, until recently, guaranteed that barber's freedom.

Matt didn't want to get involved. But if he didn't, his Afghan partners would be exterminated one by one.

35

Alarms began to blare in the newly created U.S. embassy. Automatic weapons fire nearby signaled it was probably a ground attack.

The previous night, hundreds of Afghans had broken through the perimeter on the airport's south side, spilling onto the airfield and interrupting the evacuation flights from the embassy. It had taken hours for U.S. and NATO forces to clear the area. The crowds outside the airport just kept growing overnight and, at daybreak, masses of people spilled back onto the runway. This time, the influx was much larger—thousands, not hundreds.

On the CCTV screens, the embassy staff could see a convoy of Hiluxes and Humvees flying white Taliban banners speeding toward the airfield. The crack of small-arms fire picked up outside the building. There was no safe room, only the bar. Panic escalated as cell calls dropped because of the overwhelmed local transmission towers. Their phones were useless. No one knew what was happening.

The situation was looking less like Saigon 1975 and more like Benghazi 2012, when Islamic militants stormed the U.S. mission and CIA annex and killed the ambassador and three other staff. They knew that the 82nd paratroopers had arrived to help with security, but that wouldn't help them if the Taliban assaulted this building. The only weapons visible were racks of cue sticks next to a dusty pool table. For any of the diplomats who chose to make a final stand, the cues and rock-hard billiard balls would have to do if it came to it.

36

On one of his last runs from the embassy, carrying security personnel, Major Wookey suddenly pulled up and hovered over the HKIA landing pad. Peering out from his cockpit, he searched for a clear spot to put down. But there wasn't one. Dozens of people swarmed below.

From his vantage point, Major Wookey had no idea who was below him. It could have been Taliban or ISIS-K with weapons trained upward, ready to shoot. He tried to get information from the tower, but there was no response. He didn't know it, but the Afghan air traffic controllers had abandoned their posts.

Major Wookey rose a hundred feet or so, banked the helicopter around, and then came back down for another approach. The hulking chopper was only about thirty feet from the ground, but much of the crowd remained. It almost seemed as though they thought they'd be able to board his chopper, as if he would ferry them to safety.

A few moments later, paratroopers from the 82nd began to appear, firing warning shots over the crowd, and lobbed tear gas canisters at them. Finally, the landing zone was cleared, and Major Wookey was able to set down.

37

Captain John Folta hadn't expected to sleep much when he arrived in Kabul with the 82nd Airborne, and he didn't. Charlie Company's first night at the airport was chaotic and uneasy, the sky flashing with tracers, gunfire echoing in the streets outside the wire. After that, he received regular reports of Afghans scaling the walls. He would dispatch a search team, but they hardly ever found anyone in the darkness.

As the sun climbed, Bravo Company requested help in its sector of the airport. Crowds had massed along an unwalled portion of the airport perimeter that had previously been home to the Afghan Air Force. When John and Charlie Company arrived, they found about fifty Afghan men hiding on the grounds, probably Afghan Air Force personnel who had shed their uniforms and hoped to board an American flight out.

They separated the men and patted them down. They were still doing this when a much bigger problem erupted.

John heard a commotion and turned to look down the airport runway. Thousands of Afghan civilians flooded across the unguarded southeastern perimeter, running straight toward Charlie Company. Warning alarms rang out immediately.

The paratroopers walked shoulder to shoulder toward the crowd, preparing to push them back from the center of the airfield. As the groups grew closer, many of the civilians put up their hands and pleaded with the uncomprehending soldiers, who couldn't understand them since they had no interpreters with them.

The soldiers struggled to push the Afghans back, sometimes shoving them, sometimes firing warning shots into the air. Tear gas canisters looped overhead, releasing clouds that wafted over the throng. In the terminal, 82nd paratroopers shot two armed Afghans. U.S. Apache helicopters thundered overhead, hovering at an angle so the rotor wash would push the crowd off the tarmac.

It was the picture of chaos.

Charlie Company spent the early morning struggling to regain order. The crowds kept coming, often milling on the airfield, blocking the runway. The most harrowing thought kept recurring to John—any number of Taliban or ISIS-K could be scattered throughout the mob.

At around 10:00 a.m., as John tried to explain to some English-speaking men there was nothing he could do to help, something caught his eye.

A huge American C-17 taxied on the runway. It had only just landed, but was now moving to take off again, without even having come to a full stop.

The plane's cargo was classified, and its call sign and tail number indicated it was *not* part of the evacuation airlift President Biden had ordered.

Unbeknownst to John, inside the plane's belly was an MH-47, a special-model Chinook used by the Night Stalkers of Task Force 160, Army aviators who ferried special-mission units to and from their most clandestine missions. The C-17's aircrew had decided they could not unload this sensitive cargo with the airport overrun. U.S. Navy Rear Admiral Peter Vasely, the top U.S. commander at HKIA, ordered the plane to turn around and take off.

Hundreds of Afghans swarmed the slow-moving C-17, some of them jogging alongside, others sitting on the landing gear hump or clinging to the fuselage. As John watched in horror, the plane gained speed, accelerating for takeoff. Its huge wheels lifted from the tarmac, and bodies fell to the ground, bouncing along the pavement like rag dolls. The plane gained altitude and roared over the city, bodies continuing to fall, tumbling first hundreds, and then thousands of feet into the city below.

John had never seen anything like it and hoped he never would again. He ordered medics to aid the Afghans who had fallen to the runway. For most of them, nothing could be done.

38

I promise, it'll work, Zac Lois had texted Mohammad Rahimi. *Go to the airport.*

A taxi dropped Mohammad and his family about a mile from HKIA. It took thirty minutes to push their way to the perimeter, Mohammad carrying one of the two-year-old twins and the other in the arms of one of Mohammad's brothers. Mohammad's wife held their three-month-old son. Their eldest boy, who was five, walked between the adults, holding the hand of Mohammad's other brother.

With all the arriving jumble of government, military, and civilian charter planes from NATO-allied countries and the Emirates, Zac was convinced this would be their way out. Mohammad agreed.

Mohammad had texted Zac in July, on the same day Bagram was vacated by U.S. forces. He needed a letter of recommendation for his SIV application. Mohammad hadn't communicated with Zac since 2017, but he knew he could count on him.

In 2012, Captain Zac Lois had led a team of Green Berets in the Village Stability Operations in Shah Wali Kot, in south-central Afghanistan. The Afghans called the team the Redbeards, since five of the U.S. soldiers were redheads, Zac included. He had excelled at the cultural connections of Village Stability work. Mohammad, who'd served as the Redbeards' interpreter, counted the man he called "Mister Zac" as not only a colleague, but a friend. He was fearless, loyal, and accompanied Zac on every mission.

Zac eventually became disillusioned with officer careerism and military politics, though, and left the Army in 2015 when his service contract was up. He and his wife settled in Syracuse, New York, where he got a master's in education, finding his new calling as an eighth-grade social studies teacher.

Syracuse, a northern city in New York close to the Adirondack and Catskills state parks, where Zac often hunted and camped, was a city of immigrants, with children from all over the world. He loved it. He amused his students by wearing Hawaiian shirts and donning period historic costumes for lessons. He hung a poster of the abolitionist Harriet Tubman in his classroom, emblazoned with the title "Original Gangsta." She'd lived in the Syracuse area after shepherding over seventy enslaved people to freedom on the Underground Railroad.

Mohammad knew none of this, but he knew he could count on Mister Zac. He was right. Zac knew he was no Harriet Tubman, but surely he could help this one old friend.

Mohammad now carried an old combat photo of him and Zac, along with his SIV application and Zac's letter of recommendation.

Mohammad and his family reached the perimeter. Afghans had dropped boards and rugs on top of the razor wire and were crossing into the airport by the hundreds. "Let's go!" Mohammad yelled.

The family shuttled the children across the wire and hurried toward the planes parked on the airfield. As they moved onto the tarmac, a huge C-17 taxied toward the runway, people chasing after it. No one stopped them. He looked everywhere for an American to show the picture to. An Apache gunship flew directly overhead, pelting them with sand and grit.

U.S. soldiers met the crowd in force. They fired their rifles in the air and pushed the crowd violently back to the perimeter. Mohammad tried to show his documents to the soldiers, but no one would listen. They just kept pushing them back, away from the runway and their lifeline to safety.

After they were pushed back outside the airport, Mohammad struggled to keep his family together. More gunfire erupted, only this time it wasn't U.S. forces firing warning shots, it was harassment fire from the

Taliban and rounds were landing right into the crowd. Mohammad's wife screamed, and the whole family dropped to the ground. A C-17 roared overhead. Mohammad's stomach turned. People were falling from the airplane.

His wife screamed again. Inches behind her was a man who had been shot in the head. Another man lay close by, his shoulder a bloody mass. Mohammad quickly counted seven other dead.

Screams everywhere. Mohammad turned to his five-year-old, lying prone in the gravel, eyes wide, unable to look away from what was left of the man's face who'd been shot in the head.

"Hey, look at me," Mohammad said, trying to break his son's stare, but it was too late. He knew trauma. It couldn't be undone.

He cursed himself. Why had he listened to Mister Zac, who was safe at home seven thousand miles away? Why had he agreed with him? Why had he brought his family here?

The shooting subsided. They slowly got up and pushed their way to Abbey Gate, which was guarded by a detachment of security forces. Mohammad begged them to listen to him, to look at his picture, but they wouldn't.

Against his better instincts, Mohammad decided to stay at Abbey Gate. The temperature had almost reached ninety degrees and there was scant shade, they had no food or water, but if they waited patiently, maybe, just maybe, they could get into the airport.

39

Rear Admiral Peter Vasely needed help. The arrival of the 82nd Airborne Division was a boon, but it wasn't enough.

When the Afghans pierced the perimeter, every soldier and Marine available had poured onto the airfield. The exodus of security personnel left the Joint Task Force headquarters all but empty. Even senior officers had rushed out to handle the chaos. Now it was just the admiral and a radio operator.

The entire NEO was on the verge of collapse. If the runway wasn't secure, no one would get out. Including his men.

One of the few remaining CIA operatives contacted Rear Admiral Vasely. This man had trained and equipped an Afghan paramilitary force known as the National Strike Unit (NSU), a poorly disciplined but brutally effective unit that had carried out the CIA's dirty work in Afghanistan for years. He was now offering their assistance as extra security around the airport's perimeter.

There were two problems with this offer. One, the NSU was not, strictly speaking, under U.S. command. They were U.S.-paid surrogate forces—mercs—and they were used to killing. Which was dangerous.

Two, if he took this deal, he had to give something in return: evacuation for the NSU and their families, creating yet one more logistical headache.

This controversial unit had already been listed for priority evacuation by the National Security Council on the August 14 evacuation guidance. And if the NSU could do what this man promised, it would take enormous pressure off the American forces and give senior leaders more latitude to deal with the NEO.

Within a couple hours, 120 vehicles brimming with paramilitary fighters in tiger-striped fatigues and AK-47s with optics showed up all along the airport perimeter. For now, order was reestablished.

40

Three miles from the airfield, Nezam heard the telltale sound of Apache helicopters swoop over the city. He leaned out of his window and caught sight of four within a few minutes. The appearance of these lithe and lethal attack helicopters flying over the city had different meanings to different people. Menacing to some, reassuring to others. But to Nezam, it primarily meant one thing: Kabul was disintegrating. The enemy was in the city.

He went to the door of his safe house and opened it. The Apaches flew low and loud just over the airfield . He didn't watch for long. The Taliban were around and looking for former Afghan soldiers. Neighbors might rat him out.

Even though the appearance of the helicopters meant the Taliban now threatened the airport—the last American outpost—Nezam was relieved to see them. For they had a secondary meaning: the Americans were still holding the airfield. There was nothing those Apaches could do for him personally, but he was reassured to know that his brothers in arms hadn't completely abandoned Afghanistan.

If Nezam felt relief, Major Ian Wookey, who sat in the airport's Tactical Operations Center, felt something different: frustration.

He swallowed hard as he listened to a pilot who had just seen a civilian execution along the airport's southwest perimeter wall.

"Enemy is in the clear," the pilot said, almost by rote. "Permission to engage."

The answer came back quickly. "Negative. Repeat, negative. Do not engage."

Apaches were some of the most advanced weapons belonging to the most powerful military in the world, and now they could not fire on insurgents who were killing innocent people.

Major Wookey understood the dire meaning of this order.

The American fight with the Taliban was over.

41

KABUL—AUGUST 16, 2021

The Americans were Basira's only hope of escape. She went from room to room, waking her mother and siblings. Leaving behind her Western-style clothes, Basira dressed conservatively in Afghanistan's traditional blue full-body burqa, shrouding her head to foot. With small bags packed, the family flagged down a taxi for the airport.

Taliban were everywhere. Basira felt her chest tighten with fear. She remembered stories of when the Taliban ruled, stoning and burning women alive who defied them. They were stopped again and again at checkpoints. They told the jihadi fighters now occupying the capital that they were going to find safety at a friend's house, and the Talibs waved them on. As they approached HKIA, the crowds swelled, people and cars mingled in the streets amid a deafening cacophony of horns. With car traffic at a stop, they got out and walked.

As they neared the perimeter, the crowds grew more and more violent, frantic voices raised in terror. Basira, barely five feet tall, was jostled as she tried to stay close to her mother and siblings. A sudden impact from behind, and Basira's glasses fell from her face under her burqa and onto the street. They shattered underfoot. Her mother fell to the ground. For a terrifying moment, Basira thought she would be trampled to death right in front of the family. But they were able to pull her back onto her feet.

Hours went by, the crowd surged like a writhing sea, and the women bobbed like tiny boats tossed in a gale. Finally, they gave up and slowly made their way back toward home.

Exhausted by the violent tempest, they were preparing dinner when they heard someone at the door. Her brother answered. A Talib stood on the stoop, holding a photo of Basira in her uniform, wearing her glasses. He peppered her brother with questions. *Does this woman live here? Does he know who she is?* Her brother said no one with glasses lived in the house.

42

Captain John Folta's Charlie Company held a thin line of security at the northwest perimeter of the airport. His soldiers grew more nervous as word spread that the Taliban would be moving into the area—not to fight the 82nd, but, in a surreal turn, to lock into the U.S. positions and provide security. Their commander, Major General Donahue, was meeting with the Taliban's Red Unit commander in the South Terminal in a parley.

First Sergeant Jesse Kennedy moved to the razor-wire strand dividing hundreds of Afghans from his nervous paratroopers. Using broken phrases and hand gestures, he tried to engage people in the crowd. He reached out to children and shook their hands. He teased them like a big brother. John watched. Jesse was showing his fellow paratroopers that the bulk of these people were desperate, not hostile.

"We've got to maintain security above all else, boys," John said, "but these people are not our enemy."

An Afghan man and his pregnant wife climbed over the fence just as Charlie Company assumed its position. The woman had broken an ankle. A medic came to the U.S. side of the wire to treat her. The Afghan man's brother brought a group of children up to the other side of the wire and called to John, just a few feet—but really a world—away.

The Afghan man on the U.S. side, the husband of the pregnant woman, looked at John and said in excellent English, "Can you let my children in? Please?"

John glanced back and forth over the wire. "I'm sorry, I can't," he said heavily. "If I do, it will be chaos. But I think we can get you and your wife back out to them. Then you all can go to Abbey Gate and get in there."

"She'll never make it. We'll lose her," the man said, weeping and shaking his head. "Can you get us to the States?"

"Yes, probably." John cocked his head. "But you don't want to leave your children, do you?"

The man was despondent. "I have to choose between losing my wife or losing my children. . . . What should I do?"

John looked him squarely in the eyes. "No, I'm not going to decide that for you," he said. "You have to decide." He paused. "If it was me, I would never leave my children."

The children called out for their parents amid the pealing crowd.

"Okay, okay," the man said, deflated. He nodded at his kids and said something to them in Dari. The soldiers helped him and the pregnant mother back over the wire. John watched them hobble back to their children.

He never saw them again.

A short while later, Charlie Company was replaced. Not by Taliban, but by an Afghan NSU paramilitary squad in their distinctive tiger-striped fatigues.

Relieved to extricate himself from the moral and ethical nightmare at the wire, John gathered his men and pulled back off the line to a secondary position within the airport.

43

At the new U.S. embassy in the old CIA bar on HKIA, the threat of immediate attack had subsided pretty quickly the day before—the airfield had been overrun by Afghans desperate to leave the country, not by the Taliban. But the gunfire continued for hours, and the reports of additional troops deploying to assist the NEO were encouraging. That morning, outside the airport, Taliban flags flew from Afghan National Army and National Police vehicles with mounted, American-made M240B machine guns in their truck beds. The Taliban's elite Red Unit could be seen strutting around in high-end, ripstop camo uniforms, brandishing Connecticut-made Colt M4 carbines. All this new gear was courtesy of Uncle Sam.

The Taliban were now providing outer-ring security at the airport. Between them and the Americans were the NSU paramilitaries—the Tiger Stripes.

The embassy staff, safe for now, turned their efforts to the massive task before them. Thousands of Afghans wanted to fly to freedom. For them, it was a matter of life or death. Would the Taliban, who was committed to the opposite of freedom, and motivated by a puritanical code of divine vengeance, agree to let them pass?

They had been told that the immediate priorities were American citizens, green card holders, and permanent residents. But what was the right thing to do? What about Kabul's countless other at-risk Afghans—NATO partners, aid workers, NGO officials, businesswomen, and their families? And how would any of them get through that massive crowd outside, growing even bigger and denser by the hour?

Their mission wasn't difficult; difficult would be a stroll in the park in comparison. For the diplomats who chose to remain behind and evacuate at the end of the NEO, their mission was more like impossible, but they would do their best. It was the only thing they could do.

TEAM
NEZAM

44

Scott couldn't tear himself from the television. Taliban fighters rolling into Kabul on U.S.-made vehicles. Talibs kitted out, helmet to boots, in U.S.-made uniforms and weapons. White flags of the Islamic Emirate of Afghanistan snapping in the wind.

Twenty years of fighting and dying—for this?

Right now, Nezam was the only person who mattered. Scott felt terrible for the other suffering Afghans, but they were oddly anonymous. Nezam was not. If Scott could find him safe passage, then Scott's service would mean *something*, however small.

And if Nezam died—Scott wouldn't be able to handle that.

He forced himself not to think about it and clicked off the television. He called Nezam on Signal.

"Hello, sir," Nezam answered glumly.

"How're you doing?"

"It is not good. Talibs were in my neighborhood today. They're walking around asking questions. It's only a matter of time. I need to leave my uncle's house or they will all die with me."

Scott sighed. "I'm going to find you another place. I know people who can help with that. Can you get to the airport?"

"It's going to be very hard, sir," Nezam said. He paused. "Taliban have taken over everything. There are checkpoints."

"Okay," Scott said. "We'll figure it out."

The line went quiet for a moment. Then Nezam spoke, almost as if he were talking to himself. "I have been in many bad situations in my life.

I faced death countless times. I have been shot in the face and wounded many different ways."

"That's for sure," Scott said.

"I am not afraid to die, sir." Another pause. "But, being here by myself—I do not want to die alone. You know?"

This was the moment he had feared from the beginning of this ordeal. It was at the heart of why he left the military.

Damn it, Scott thought.

He had to take on this mission, He had to take on this mission, but at the same time, he felt a nagging doubt that he could take responsibility for Nezam's fate. He and Nezam were half a world apart. Sure, once a Green Beret, always a Green Beret—but in reality, he wasn't a Green Beret anymore. He was a motivational speaker and a storyteller, for God's sake. Nezam wasn't exactly getting a top draft pick to lead him to safety.

Scott had been "eyes and ears" for so many of his brothers. It was, in fact, the more prominent role he'd played in his tours of duty, running the complex mission control operations to launch and recover special operators on impossible missions. But he'd had more than enough of those go badly. Not being able to get a MEDEVAC bird to his friend Pedro before he bled out in the arms of his teammates. The smile on Allen's face before he stepped off on a mission that Scott had concocted, never to return. This was the deepest reason why he had retired when a battalion command awaited him. And after retirement, these ghosts of guilt and more guilt had sent Scott into his dark closet ten years ago. Scott knew if he stepped any deeper into this situation, he might be right back there again. Losing Nezam could send him right back in.

But, if he didn't get involved at this point, if he just worked Nezam's visa issue on the edges, nothing would happen. Nezam would die alone at the hands of the Taliban. He would be beheaded or worse. Could Scott live with knowing he didn't at least try?

He steeled himself, and then spoke as if delivering an order to a unit about to plunge into a firefight. "You are *not* going to die alone, Nezam. In fact, you are not going to fucking die. We are going to get you out of there. You are going to get to the United States. And when you do, you're going to move to Tampa, Florida. You and I will be neighbors. We're going to hang out by the river, and you won't ever have to worry about being shot again. In fact, I might just train you to be a speaker. I need you to believe that. I need you to get yourself in that mindset right now. Do you understand?"

"Yes, sir. I understand," Nezam said. His voice sounded stronger.

"Good. We're going to fucking get you out of there. Are we clear, Sergeant?"

"Yes, sir. I'm clear."

"Okay. I will call you very shortly. Keep your phone charged and be ready."

"Thank you, sir. I will be."

Scott hung up. It was a quiet Monday in Florida. His youngest son, Brayden, would be leaving for college in just a few days, and then it would just be him and his wife. *Damn it*, Scott thought again. It wasn't supposed to end this way.

45

Scott's office building in Tampa was empty; everyone was working from home due to the pandemic. On the walls hung two blank whiteboards. He smiled. This was much better than his office at home cluttered with plaques and certificates. Here he could work. His employees often poked fun at him by saying that the only thing Scott needed for Christmas was more whiteboards.

He commanded Alexa to play nineties country music at volume ten. As Garth Brooks belted out "Friends in Low Places," Scott grabbed a thick black marker and wrote:

Save Nezam.

When he used to plan special operations, he would sketch out a diagram called a "scheme of maneuver." It was a tried-and-true way for military leaders to depict a combat action from start to finish. Getting Nezam out would require the same tactical precision.

First, Scott drew a square indicating Nezam's uncle's house. Underneath that he drew an alternate safe house. They would need this ASAP. On the far-left side of the whiteboard, he drew Hamid Karzai International Airport ringed with green *X*s to indicate the emerging Taliban perimeter.

He pulled up a Google Map of HKIA. What were the approaches? What were the gates? Where were the threats? Oriented west-northwest to east-southeast, the airport resembled the head of a guitar, wide in the center with a narrow neck jutting to the east. The runway bisected the airport lengthwise, with the military side to the runway's north and the civilian terminal to the south.

The main approach to HKIA was Airport Road, stretching northeast from downtown Kabul and the U.S. embassy to South Gate, the main entrance. The next gate, going counterclockwise, was Sullivan Gate. Abbey Gate was just to the northeast, close to the Baron Hotel, alongside a deep concrete sewage trench. Next was East Gate, which opened onto the guitar's "neck." Across the neck, at least four entrances lay along Russian Road, the military side. There was North Gate, aka Russian Road Gate, on the airport's northeastern corner; Northwest Gate; Glory Gate, which was also called Liberty Gate. Finally, on the airport's southern side, was West Gate, which some called "DynCorp Gate" for the contractors that used it.

Nezam's uncle's house was less than four miles from the airport—that was good. Working from memory, Scott drew a map. At each intersection along the main road, he indicated Taliban checkpoints. He didn't know exactly where they were yet, but he would find out.

In red marker, he indicated every strategic problem he could conceive of. Normally, two or three strategic challenges would be considered a serious problem. Here, Scott identified five.

The problems were:

1. How do we move Nezam through an enemy-controlled city undetected?
2. How do we get him past the Taliban perimeter around the airfield?
3. How do we guide him through a crowd of thousands?
4. How do we present him to the U.S. gate guards without them shooting him?
5. How do we get him on a flight when his SIV isn't completed?

If this had been a military exfiltration, special operators would answer these questions. They would cross the airport's wire, find Nezam, and bring him back. But that was not happening.

But while neither Scott nor a team of Green Berets could go to Nezam, he would not be completely alone.

In part due to Scott's work with Village Stability Operations, he had maintained links to the Jamaat-e-Islami network, one of Afghanistan's most established political parties. Two Afghans—close friends and former advisers who now lived in the United States—still had family in Kabul who would almost certainly help overcome Nezam's lack of support in Kabul.

Scott stepped back from the whiteboard. He had a picture of the problem. Now it was time to share that picture with others.

He went to the adjacent whiteboard and started writing names of people who would make up Team Nezam.

First was Mullah Mike. Scott needed someone who could carry out the crucial job of maneuvering Nezam through the city. Enlisting Mullah Mike wouldn't be easy, though. He was currently a Special Forces battalion commander in Europe with one of the most forward-deployed SF units in the world. He was no doubt very busy.

So Scott called him, and Mullah Mike didn't miss a beat. "Of course I'll help. That's our brother. I'll have to make some arrangements with my executive officer, but let's get him out of there."

Scott needed someone with real-time info on what the government was doing and called a Green Beret friend named Charles, who was now a special operations liaison to the intel agencies. Scott had mentored Charles through more than one deployment in Afghanistan, and it didn't hurt that Nezam had also fought alongside him in the VSO program.

Charles didn't hesitate, either, but there was a caveat. "I'll have to keep a low profile. The SIV issue is white-hot up here. If they catch me poking around on Nezam's case, they'll pull me off everything." Charles suggested that Scott call a woman he knew named June. She was a former Marine who was married to an active-duty Special Forces operator deployed in the Middle East, and was a Biden appointee working Afghan economical development issues.

"She's doing a ton with at-risk women in Afghanistan, has been for years," Charles said. "She's pissed as hell about what's happening. She should be able to swing a big stick in D.C. She's my neighbor, too. I'll talk to her tonight. Feels like we're getting the band back together, sir."

James Gordon Meek was next. Working with reporters wasn't Scott's usual MO, but James wasn't afraid to poke generals or politicians in the eye, and that was useful. He knew James was friends with Nezam and had extensive sources on both the civilian and military sides of the U.S. government, and he was ready to help any way he could.

The team was shaping up. But Scott needed another piece—someone with political clout who could cut through red tape, yell at the right people, and get things done at HKIA. Nezam's SIV would never be approved before the NEO ended and U.S. forces left forever.

He'd already contacted Congressman Mike Waltz, a Special Forces Colonel in the National Guard, to get Nezam's SIV expedited. Waltz's staff tried, but they hadn't succeeded.

Now Scott had a much bigger ask.

He thought back to 2007, when then-Captain Mike Waltz and his team were pinned down in Helmand, the Taliban closing in on all sides. Scott, who was at Bagram, served as Mike's eyes and ears on drone surveillance, and guided his team to high ground. From there, Scott orchestrated an array of drones, jets, and B-52s that hammered hundreds of Taliban fighters, opening an escape route for the beleaguered Green Berets.

Scott hammered out an email: "Mike. I've never directly asked you for anything—right? We went through a lot together in our deployment. So, I'm asking you now for help to get my friend Nezam out of a similar living hell in Kabul. You know I can get him out, Mike, but I need some added horsepower."

Waltz wrote back immediately. He was in, and he went one better. He put Scott in touch with Liv Gardner, his longtime executive assistant. She was married to an Army officer who flew Apache gunships for the 10th Mountain Division out of Fort Drum. Since childhood, she'd coped with ADHD, making her a sleep-deprived, multitasking superpower who was obsessed with Afghanistan, though she'd never set foot there.

"She's a ball of fire," Mike wrote. "And she carries my authority."

A ball of fire is precisely what we need, Scott thought. He called her.

"Sir, I'll help however I can," she said. "We're up to our eyebrows in this thing, but just let me know and I will do anything possible to help Nezam."

Scott had a team. Now they just needed to make a plan.

46

Bashir left his home near Camp Morehead the same day he'd had his run-in with the Talib at the gates. He had been told by a Special Forces contact—a former officer who was helping Afghans remotely from his home in North Carolina—to gather his family and go to HKIA. The American, who Bashir called "Commander James," had helped him apply for the special visa that would make Bashir and his family eligible to enter the U.S. on humanitarian grounds. There was every chance they could fly to safety.

Now Bashir and his family were approaching HKIA. At least, they were trying to. He pressed through the mass of people surging around the airport, his four-year-old daughter in one arm, his very pregnant wife clinging to his other arm. Their three oldest kids—ten, eight, and seven—walked hand in hand behind Bashir. His brother, carrying his own three-year-old son, brought up the rear.

The dusty road was littered with discarded shoes and clothing; crushed water bottles were everywhere. The stench of body odor—along with feces and urine—was overpowering. The people around Bashir held up anything they could to get shade. One man, though, held his infant high above his head, as if the hand of Allah would reach down and pluck the child from its misery.

Bashir's wife was growing weaker and weaker in the scorching heat. Commander James had told him to get to one of the airport's gates and he would be let in.

Commander James had been misinformed.

As the crow flies, they were seconds from North Gate, but as earth-bound humans, they were hours away. Afghan NSU paramilitaries in their tell-tale tiger-striped fatigues struggled to maintain a perimeter. Some fired their AK-47s in the air over the civilians. This only made things worse.

"Don't let go of me!" Bashir yelled to his wife. He had seen it all in his military service—only two days earlier, before disbanding his men, his team had engaged and killed over a dozen Taliban—but nothing had frightened him like this situation.

The mob was like a giant writhing organism, so dense that he could only pull his family toward the gates one inch at a time. More shots rang out, this time closer to the airport gate. Someone screamed. They kept going.

After several hours of excruciating progress, gunfire rattled his family. A few minutes later, they came to a place where the big crowd surrounded a body lying in the road. The crowd was dutifully parting around it, like a boulder in a stream. The NSU paramilitaries had shot dead a Hazara man, one of Afghanistan's most oppressed ethnic groups

Bashir looked at his panic-stricken children. His wife's eyes widened. He sighed. This was too much. As a master sergeant, he always tried to understand the limitations of those depending on him. After hours in this sea of desperation, his wife and children could barely stand. And now there was someone lying dead just a few feet away.

He spoke briefly with his brother and then set down his daughter, making sure her siblings held her hand tightly.

Then he and his brother lifted the corpse onto their shoulders, turned around, and led their family back through the crowd, which parted for them and their gruesome cargo. The dead man was passage out of the throng, but more than that, no one deserved to be left rotting in the sun.

Finally, they reached the thinner margins of the crowd. Men flocked around them, bringing water and food. Others arrived with tools and led them to a burial plot. About a dozen men took turns with shovels. Another covered the body in a tarp. It took over an hour, and by the time the last shovelful of dirt was in place, twenty-five people stood around the grave, saying the Janazah funeral prayer.

Afterward, Bashir called a taxi to return with his family to somewhere safe. They were exhausted and dehydrated, their lips chapped and their faces burned from the sun. More than anything, they were terrified.

They would try again tomorrow. Hopefully, it wouldn't be too late.

47

Jussi Tanner stepped onto the tarmac at HKIA and felt as though he'd stepped into an oven. The tan and bearded Finnish special envoy had just left Syria, where the temperatures were suffocating. But those didn't approach Kabul's oppressive heat, which soared to almost one hundred degrees that day.

In Syria, his mission had been repatriating Finnish nationals in the hellish Al-Hol refugee camp who'd lost their way and gone to fight for ISIS. He was known as an "expeditionary diplomat," someone who gladly deployed to places where diplomats did not go. The Friday before, his superior had asked him if he wanted to take some time off from his day job and go to Afghanistan. Jussi said yes.

Jussi and his security chief, accompanied by Norwegian special operators, were in Kabul to save Afghans who had worked with Finland. Almost every partner country was sending in diplomats to extract their citizens and help special interest people caught behind enemy lines. Jussi wasn't prepared for what confronted him. The airfield was awash in activity. Soldiers were everywhere. Jussi, in his 5.11 cargo pants and ripstop, button-up shirt, had the ease of a college student backpacking around the world. But the security team prowling his flanks signaled that his task was a high-stakes mission.

They made their way to the concrete blast walls at the airport's North Gate.

From this perch, he gazed down on a seething mass of people. Thousands of Afghans pressed into the outer portion of the airfield. Women held their babies aloft, trying to raise them above the burning tear gas haze that hung over the area outside the gate. The babies had been wailing for so long that their agonized shrieks made no sound.

Jussi had heard reports of Afghans being crushed to death in the crowds, and children trampled near Abbey Gate. Now he watched as an elderly Afghan man in a wheelchair toppled to the ground. A Talib had shoved him with the barrel of his AK-47. No one helped. Screams everywhere. Shotgun blasts. Flash-bangs. The guttural wails that are only made by humans who haven't had food or water in days. Jussi was in disbelief.

As if the cruelty of the situation weren't enough, rogue gunmen fired haphazardly on the crowd—killing and wounding men, women, and children. The gunfire caused violent, episodic ripples that cascaded through the sea of people. But no one dispersed. They were locked in place by each other and their own desperation.

This tableau reminded Jussi of Géricault's *The Raft of the Medusa*, the massive painting depicting the infamous aftermath of an 1816 shipwreck that hangs in the Louvre in Paris. A raft of survivors, cut loose by wealthier shipmates who had a seaworthy lifeboat, succumbed to starvation, exposure, and murder.

This was a shocking end to a NATO-led war. At least a thousand people were pressed against North Gate, and the only way through was a tall turnstile wreathed in rusty razor wire. U.S. Marines manned the checkpoint as Afghans thrust passports and documents at them. Every now and then a heavy machine gun would let off a thunderous burst over the heads of the Afghans, startling Jussi and causing brief waves of panic. The Marines were firing over one hundred rounds per minute in the air in an attempt to control the crowd.

Jussi only had a couple dozen people to exfiltrate on his first day, but a total of 414 on his list to bring inside HKIA before all NATO forces were gone. But it would be extremely difficult identifying them in this scenario. He had to let only the right people in.

Making matters worse, the security forces were exhausted. Marines, the few remaining NATO soldiers, paratroopers—their shifts hadn't allowed them much, or any, sleep. It wasn't just the physical toil; it was also the mental toll. There was no combat training for weeping mothers begging soldiers to take their babies, or fathers pleading for medical help as children died in their arms.

One thing was abundantly clear to Jussi. Getting Afghans out of this crowd was going to come down to who you knew. Generals and senior diplomats were useless. But if you had the cell number and a solid rapport with a staff sergeant manning the gate—that would be the play to get someone out.

48

Razaq was trying to make contact with the Americans at the airport. He'd never seen anything like it. Young, old, men, women, children: all pushing against each other trying to get to gates that no one could even see. He was completely exhausted and drenched in sweat.

Suddenly, Taliban fighters began yelling at him and waving their guns. Razaq looked around in fear, realizing the Taliban had divided the narrow airport gate area into male and female sides. He was on the wrong side.

He quickly retreated to the edge of the crowd.

Every man in the crowd had a beard, while his face was smooth-shaven. He'd left the house in such a hurry that he'd forgotten he was wearing a T-shirt displaying an American flag. *What are you doing Razaq?* he thought. *This is Taliban. Get it together.* He quickly took off his shirt, turning it inside out, and put it back on.

He looked again at the mass of people and turned back for home.

It had been years since he'd left his dangerous job as a combat interpreter for senior U.S. Special Forces commanders. He'd gone back to school and become an environmental engineer. All he wanted to do was work and raise his family. His wife would be delivering their third child in just a couple of months. How could it have all gone so wrong?

Razaq stopped in front of his house and took a deep breath, steeling himself for the lie he was about to tell. As he walked through the door, Wajmah rushed to him with hopeful eyes. "Did you see the Americans?"

"Yes, Wajmah. There are so many planes," he said, mustering a smile. "We will take the girls and go to the airport in the morning."

She glowed with happiness at his words, and he was glad when she turned away from him, so she couldn't see the tears rolling down his dusty face.

49

Scott set up a Signal chat room for Team Nezam, and it filled with constant chatter as they discussed how to exfiltrate Nezam.

Scott had only slept a few hours since hatching his plan. He was frustrated. It felt like they were moving backward as they tried to slice through red tape. The group cheered when former USAID foreign service officer Julie Browning managed to get Nezam on a plane manifest, but they still didn't have a way to get him across the city safely, and they hadn't found anyone to shepherd him inside the HKIA wire. They also had been unable to find him an alternate safe house.

That evening, Mullah Mike called. "Listen. Nezam needs to haul ass to the airfield—*now!*"

Scott's heart skipped a beat. "What? We've got a half-assed plan, if you can even call it a plan."

"I know. We're just going to have to build this car while it's on the road."

"But he'll burn his safe house. He'll be a sitting duck. We need a little more time, Mike."

"I know it's shitty, but time is a luxury Nezam does not have. Some of my guys working with what's left of their intel networks are telling me it's getting worse by the hour. The Taliban are locking that airfield down. If he goes now, he might be able to get out in front of any checkpoints they set up. If he waits, he's dead. Hundred percent."

Scott silently cursed. Mike was right. He was always right about shit like this, and Scott trusted Mike's instincts. But the thought of pushing Nezam out the door turned his stomach to knots.

"All right, let's do it," Scott said.

"It's the right move."

"But here's the thing," Scott said. "I want you to guide him. Just you. I don't want a bunch of people barking instructions at him. That's the quickest way to get him killed. I'm going to create a separate room in Signal for you and him. I'll put Charles and me in there also. Just in case we need to guide him in shifts. But I want you to be his primary guide."

"Roger. I'm on it."

Scott hung up. He felt like he was going to throw up.

50

U.S. Army Major General Chris Donahue arrived midday at HKIA on one of the 82nd's flights from Fort Bragg. He met briefly with Rear Admiral Peter Vasely, the top U.S. commander, and then climbed into a vehicle to see for himself the situation at the airport.

He wasn't pleased.

Taking a small protective force with him, General Donahue drove around the inside of the airfield, starting at North Gate, then East Gate, and continuing around the perimeter. Near the civilian passenger terminal, he looked up and saw two Taliban snipers in the airport tower. Antiaircraft gun trucks with Taliban behind the wheel drove up and down a section of the runway. Inside the passenger terminal, about nine Taliban fighters stood guard, and another swept broken glass from the floor.

"Get the hell out of here," General Donahue barked to the Talibs. "And get me your leader. Tell him we need to talk."

Never would he have predicted that, one day, he would be engaging his enemy in conversation instead of combat. As a Delta Force operator, he had been killing Taliban from the very first days of the war, deploying immediately after September 11 and fighting at Tora Bora, the battle in eastern Afghanistan that routed al-Qaeda but failed to capture Osama bin Laden.

In the years since, General Donahue led missions against the Taliban's elite Red Unit, a particularly ruthless branch of the Haqqani Taliban, who were responsible for numerous kidnappings of Americans. The Red Unit was the force dispersed currently around the airport. But they were no longer the enemy. They were . . . *partners*.

At around two o'clock that morning, a Taliban commander finally met General Donahue to discuss face-to-face in the south terminal. Ramrod tall with piercing gray eyes and arched eyebrows, the former Delta Force operator with the call sign "All American Six" was a study in contrasts with his bearded, robed counterpart.

General Donahue made it clear to his new partner that it wouldn't be easy, and the situation could get ugly if they allowed it to. *We need to work together, but we're prepared to do what we have to do to defend Americans and our interests,* he told the commander. *Unless we want a whole lot of killing, we need to find a way to work together and get things done.*

They hashed out some rules. The Taliban would be responsible for securing the outer perimeter of the airfield, manning checkpoints to screen those on foot crowding the gates, and to ensure that Afghans didn't overrun the airfield again. General Donahue's paratroopers, along with U.S. Marines, NATO forces, and the CIA's Afghan paramilitaries, would be responsible for guarding the gates for vetted travelers. The Red Unit's most important job would be to make sure their mutual enemy, ISIS-K, didn't get near the airport.

From then on, General Donahue would meet with the Talib commander daily around 11:00 a.m., discussing the current problems at the airport and how they could work together to fix them. Surprisingly, General Donahue found the Taliban easy to deal with.

During one meeting, the Taliban accusingly stated that he knew the Americans were pulling people surreptitiously into the airport. "We know you're putting people through without using the checkpoints," the Taliban commander said to him. "And that's not what we agreed on."

General Donahue didn't dispute it. "We have people of interest that we're going to pull through that way," he told the mullah. "I'm never going to lie to you. Yes, that is happening, and it will continue to happen."

The Talib didn't like it, but soon the airport—and all of Afghanistan—would be theirs. He let the matter go.

51

It was time for Nezam to go.

Kabul was getting worse.

They would try and get him through Sullivan Gate, near the former CIA compound on the southeastern corner of the airport. That's where Team Nezam sources said at-risk Afghans were being let in.

James had told Scott earlier that he might have contact information for a state department employee inside HKIA, a diplomat named J. P. Feldmayer. They were going to need all the help they could get for Nezam, and Scott told James to fill that guy's mailbox until he answered.

Mullah Mike was making contact with security forces inside.

It was 9:00 a.m. in Kabul.

No one had heard from Nezam for a couple of hours, but they knew he was trying to save his phone battery. Scott texted again.

SCOTT
Hey brother, contact Mullah Mike. It's time for you to go.

Minutes passed with no response. Hours. Nothing.

Scott's last conversation with Nezam haunted him. "You're going to make it." As the minutes ticked by with no word, Scott prayed he would be able to keep that promise.

52

Nezam stamped out the small fire. He'd just finished burning his documents in his uncle's backyard. Nezam powered up his phone. The night before, Mullah Mike had told him to be ready to go at any moment, but he could only charge the phone in his uncle's car because of all the electrical outages.

A flood of messages popped up.

One was from Mullah Mike. *Brother, it's time to go.*

Nezam texted back. *I will be ready in 15 mins.*

Today is the day, brother. Scott arranged a ride. He's on standby and can be to you in half an hour or less. A Pashtun taxi driver who's already driven the road today with no problems. Try the airport gates in this order: Sullivan, East, North. If you don't get in one, move to the next. If nothing works, go to Abbey Gate. Tell them Lieutenant Colonel Mike emailed their commander about you. They have an image of your passport in their email. Stay on comms if you can. Let me know when you're ready to leave. If the gates are crowded, try to work the edges. There are people being trampled in the pushes when they get too close.

Nezam grabbed his go-bag. He took his Special Forces papers that he couldn't burn from his shirt and stuffed them deep inside the bag, along with half a dozen U.S. challenge coins—medallions commemorating missions and units. He made sure that he had his passport, too, which he had gotten back two days earlier. He pulled a gray cover over the pack to conceal the military gear loops and Velcro strips. He dressed in what was practically the national uniform—a threadbare, mustard-yellow shalwar kameez, enabling him to disappear into any crowd. He took one last look at his ridiculous see-through Glock. Taking it would be too risky.

Nezam gulped down some bread and juice. He might not eat for many hours. His heart machine-gunned and his limbs shook.

He stepped outside at 10:45 a.m. A filthy, dented yellow Toyota Corolla taxi idled out front.

Nezam needed to do one more thing before leaving—record a voice memo for Scott and Johnny Utah.

"Okay, I'm moving," Nezam told them, his voice quivering. "I got the old taxi. It blends right in." He hit send. He hustled to the cab and slid into the back seat.

"Salaam," the driver said.

"Salaam," Nezam replied. He checked his phone. The battery was only at 60 percent. He set it to power-saving mode.

The taxi pulled into the street. Nezam was already thirsty as the late morning heat blasted the interior of the taxi. *I should have grabbed some water*, he thought. The taxi crept through traffic, the streets a constant din of honking horns. Every horn was like a cry for help.

The Taliban had set up checkpoints throughout the city. Now the cab pulled up to the first one. Nezam instinctively reached for the gun that wasn't there. *You're a commando*, he told himself. It was the first time he would face his enemy unarmed. *You can do this. They don't know who you are.*

The Talib wore a black turban over his sun-cracked features. A henna-dyed, rust-colored beard covered his lower face. He wore a tan shalwar kameez with high cuffs—common among devout "students" of Islam. He cradled a filched American M16A2 rifle, now the most fashionable accessory in Kabul. The Talib glanced inside the taxi for a moment as the driver greeted him in Pashto. He waved them on.

They encountered three more checkpoints as they crawled forward, but they weren't stopped again. The trip to the airport usually took twenty minutes, but this day it took forever. At about 1:30 p.m., the taxi pulled up to the curb not far from the blast walls and coiled razor wire of Sullivan Gate.

"I'll be back," Nezam told the driver. "It might be a while. Don't leave." He got out to reconnoiter, texting Mullah Mike that he'd reached the first gate.

Work the edges, Mike had instructed. Nezam scanned the crowd of hundreds of Afghans outside Sullivan Gate. Some stood, but most sat or squatted along the garbage-strewn pavement. He leaned against a tree offering some shade for about thirty minutes, watching the crowd. He couldn't see any Taliban. But the gate never opened. No one was being admitted. He walked back to the taxi, got in, and told the driver to try East Gate.

The taxi maneuvered through the industrial neighborhood on HKIA's easternmost edge. This drive normally took minutes—this time it took over half an hour. Afghan civilians clogged the roads. Traffic ground to a halt.

After not moving for what felt like an eternity, he told the driver, "I'll get out here. Thank you." The driver nodded.

Nezam grabbed his bag and stepped onto the street. He steeled himself and walked toward East Gate, texting Mike another update on his position.

Thousands of Afghans surrounded the entrance in a dense throng. Nezam hugged the edge of the crowd. U.S. Marines stood near the two-story-high concrete blast walls, and NSU paramilitaries roamed the area in their tiger-striped fatigues. The paramilitaries stood in the crowd, about fifty feet from coils of razor wire that snaked along the ground.

There were too many people. Too much shouting. Sporadic automatic-weapon fire rang out. Nezam couldn't determine who was shooting or why.

He waited patiently for his moment. The crowd suddenly got impatient and began shouting at the soldiers. Then something loud and bright popped, and the crowd recoiled.

Flash-bangs, thrown by the Marines. Smoke wafted from the far edge of the crowd, close to the steel gate, scattering hundreds of terrified civilians in every direction. Nezam remained calm and scanned the scene. A Marine fired a shotgun in the air.

Move away, or move forward?

As the crowd scattered from the flash-bangs, Nezam saw an opening.

Forward.

He bolted straight into the smoke and explosions. More flashes and booms erupted around him, sending panicked Afghans in every direction.

But they didn't frighten Nezam. Yes, it was chaos—but Nezam thrived in chaos.

Another crowd-control grenade thundered in his ears. It was close. Dozens of men and women passed him, many dragging or carrying small children. His ears rang. He elbowed his way to the coils of razor wire. He was close to East Gate now.

Then a sudden crack below the back of his neck. Stars. He dropped to the concrete, writhing in pain. He looked up. Tan tiger-striped pants stood over him in the smoky fog of the flash-bangs. An NSU thug, his AK-47's stock poised for another strike.

He didn't even say anything.

SAY "PINEAPPLE"

53

Mullah Mike emerged from a mandatory, no-phones meeting two hours after he sent Nezam to the airport. *Fucking shit timing*, he thought to himself. When he retrieved his phone, something was wrong—there wasn't a single update from Nezam.

He opened Signal. Something had glitched. He closed the app and relaunched it. Team Nezam notifications pinged through one after another, including two from Nezam himself. *Dammit*, Mike thought.

Nezam sent the first an hour earlier. *I'm at Sullivan Gate.* Then another that had just come through. *I made it to East Gate, but I don't have any name or contact to get me in.*

Mike texted back. *Nezam, sorry. My Signal app stopped pulling messages two hours ago. Sit tight. I'll holler back in a few mins.*

They were facing one of the weakest links in their plan. Getting Nezam inside the airport hinged on his ability to get in line and approach the gates in order to present himself as an Afghan Green Beret to American or NATO soldiers.

But what if there was no line for entries? What if U.S. forces were just maintaining a perimeter amid total chaos? Mike posed this question to his contacts in Kabul, and a British colonel replied almost immediately. *He will be added to our special cases list.* A Marine officer quickly promised something similar.

Exactly what these promises meant, Mike was unsure. Did it mean the men and women holding the airport perimeter had a photo of

Nezam? How would they recognize this "special case" in the heat of the moment?

Nothing is burning down in Europe today, he thought. Somehow, he had to shepherd a guy from thousands of miles away, with no drone surveillance or ground intel.

He dialed the number for the 1st Battalion, 8th Marines Tactical Operations Center at HKIA who were positioned near East Gate. A female Marine corporal answered. Mike explained that he was a Special Forces battalion commander following up on the case of an Afghan Green Beret who was, at that moment, outside East Gate. He was a prime target of the Taliban, and his life was at risk.

The corporal asked Mike to email Nezam's contact information and passport, and she would send it to the watch commanders at East Gate. Mike thanked her and hung up.

54

Thankfully, the NSU soldier didn't strike Nezam again. After standing over him for a few seconds, he moved on to harass other people in the crowd.

Nezam sat and massaged his neck. It throbbed. A lump was already rising at the point of impact. He slipped the straps of his rucksack off his shoulders.

The acrid, hazy smoke was clearing. Nezam's throat stung. He was desperate for some water. If the goal of the flash-bangs and the NSU shock troops had been to thin the crowd temporarily, it had worked. But it was already reassembling.

Nezam stood. Were people being allowed to pass through East Gate? He still couldn't tell.

Now what? he wondered. There was no obvious way to present himself to the Americans guarding the gate. The Marines and a few 10th Mountain Division soldiers were sixty feet away, too far to talk to. He checked his phone. Fifty percent. No messages in the two hours it had taken him to reach this spot. He typed a short note to Mullah Mike. *I made it to East Gate, but I don't have any name or contact to get me in.*

Nezam glanced up from his phone. The Tiger Stripe who'd struck him was back, this time with another, more muscular paramilitary wearing a full beard, black sunglasses, and a ball cap. This one wore green tiger-striped fatigues and had a radio. He looked almost American. Nezam raised his iPhone and snapped a photo of the soldiers near the gate so his friends could assess the scene.

Green Stripes spotted him. "Hey! Hey!" he barked in Dari. "No photos!" He dropped to within inches of Nezam's face and grabbed his phone.

"It's okay, it's okay," Nezam said, smiling at the man. Nezam's phone—his only remaining lifeline—was in this man's left hand. The man's right hand held the grip of his M4 rifle.

Nezam placed his hand over his heart. Green Stripes was already scrolling Nezam's photos. "Brother, I am Special Forces, it's okay," Nezam said. "I'm SF. Please give my phone back."

The man looked him up and down and handed him his phone. "No more photos," he growled, and walked away.

Nezam exhaled and looked at his phone.

> **MULLAH MIKE**
> Nezam, sorry. My Signal app stopped pulling messages two hours ago. I'll holler back in a few mins.

Nezam waited.

The crowd swelled again, as if the flash-bangs from a few moments ago were a distant memory. People pushed forward, trying to get the attention of anyone who would listen. The shifting tide of bodies slowly pushed Nezam against the sharp cables of wire forming East Gate's outer barrier. Then the rumble of the crowd was interrupted by a loudspeaker at the gate.

"Nezamuddin Nezami," a voice said in Pashto. "Please come forward and identify yourself." Nezam wasn't sure he'd heard correctly. He looked around as if there might be another Nezamuddin Nezami.

"Nezamuddin Nezami, please come forward," the loudspeaker repeated. He had no idea how the Marines had gotten his name, or that Mullah Mike had passed his name to the Marine TOC. But it didn't matter—he was on his way in.

Green Stripes was only a few feet away. Nezam took two steps and tugged his sleeve. "Hey, brother, that's me!" Nezam couldn't see Green Stripes's eyes behind his glasses, but his lips curled. "They're calling me on the speakers!" Nezam explained. "They just called me! Can you bring me forward?"

Green Stripes shrugged, then nodded. Nezam slung his backpack over his right shoulder and the paramilitary took Nezam's left hand. Other tiger stripes pushed people aside as Nezam was pulled forward to a break in the razor wire.

Just then, Nezam felt a hard tug on his bag. His pack slipped away. He spun. Someone had grabbed it! Nezam just caught sight of him as he turned and disappeared into the crowd. Green Stripes pulled him in the opposite direction, but Nezam let go of his hand and stopped.

All of his Q Course documents and most important mementos were in that backpack—and now they were gone.

He looked in every direction as the crowd reformed around him. Green Stripes had given up and moved away.

55

Scott was worried and couldn't think about sleeping, a man's life was at stake and he felt the responsibility weighing him down. Nezam had gone dark after leaving his uncle's house. For two hours, they heard nothing, and Team Nezam's chat room was ominously quiet.

Around 4:00 a.m., sporadic updates filtered in. Nezam was still alive and on the move. He was at one airport gate, and then another.

> **MULLAH MIKE**
> He is at East Gate. I'm speaking to the Marine TOC there and they are calling the commander at the gate to hopefully let him in.

Scott grumbled at the update. Nezam was out in the open for the first time after almost two months in hiding, and neither Scott nor the rest of the team knew what he was facing on the ground.

It was 4:43 a.m. *Thirty-two minutes since the last Nezam note. Twenty-four minutes since the last Team Nezam message*, Scott thought. Brutal math in the dead of night.

Toward daybreak, activity on the Signal chat room picked up. Mullah Mike relayed his conversation with the corporal at Marine TOC.

> **MULLAH MIKE**
> I've pleaded with generals and former ambassadors, but at the end of the day a Marine corporal is getting shit done because she picked up the phone and gave a fuck. Crazy world.

Scott continued to monitor his phone, praying for more good news. A short while later, Mike messaged the team that Nezam was within feet of the American troops. Mike insisted that Nezam stay at East Gate. If he just stayed put, he would eventually get in.

Scott texted Nezam to stay calm and he would get inside.

Nezam didn't answer.

There was radio silence for a full hour.

At 7:38 a.m., Nezam finally sent a text that sent a chill through Scott.

Two people died next to me. I'm just one foot away.

56

Nezam was surrounded by more than a thousand people standing shoulder to shoulder. The crowd surged unexpectedly, knocking two men violently to the ground. Their heads smashed on the concrete. One of the men had fallen within two feet of Nezam. He lay on his back in a pile of crushed water bottles, plastic bags, and a pair of pink plastic sandals. His half-open eyes had glazed over. Dark blood oozed from his nose and mouth, staining the top of his mustard-yellow shirt. Nezam leaned over. The man still breathed.

"Hey! Marines! Sirs!" Nezam shouted. He waved to get the attention of the Marines, just fifty feet away, but they only stood, expressionless. He and several other men picked up the man's limp body, yelling at the Marines for help.

"He's dying! He's dying!" Nezam cried.

The Marine riflemen stayed at their posts. Nezam and the other Afghans carefully settled the man in the bed of rubbish. A different man, twenty-ish, called out to the dying man. "Uncle!" he said. He kneeled and tried to comfort him. Nezam watched as the man's breathing came to a stop.

Just then, four Marines crossed through the break in the wire. They picked up the dead man and carried him past the wire.

Do I have to die to get inside the airport? Nezam wondered.

Nezam was close to giving up. His throat crackled with thirst. His bag was gone. His military documents were gone. His challenge coins and patches were gone. And his phone was now at 30 percent. No phone, no chance.

Take a selfie and send it to me so we can send it to the Marines for near-recognition, Scott suggested.

Nezam snapped a picture of himself, gazing at it for a moment. He looked ashen. He hit send.

Received, Scott wrote. *We'll get it to somebody and get you in.*

MIKE
Got it. I forwarded it to the corporal and said she sent his selfie over to the gate and they will pull him in. I just have to keep pushing the Marines.

57

J. P. was able to look for opportunities to help Afghans escape now that the new embassy wasn't under direct threat of being overrun. Major General Chris Donahue was holding regular meetings with the Taliban's Red Unit about keeping the airfield from being breached again by civilians, or—and this was the nightmare scenario—being bombed by ISIS-K, which appeared in fifty to sixty threat reports each day.

J. P. checked his email. He had more than five hundred unread messages. Most were marked urgent. One of these was yet another from the persistent journalist James Gordon Meek. It had arrived nearly four hours earlier. J. P. opened it.

"J. P., Nezam was told to go to the East Gate by SF guys and he's there now but needs someone to pull him in ASAP. He is manifested on a charter flight. Can you help? The Marine TOC has been notified he's there."

Another from James included a selfie of Nezam in the gate area. It had landed in his inbox much more recently. "I'm sending this on the chance that you receive this in time—Nezam is at the East Gate. He's still outside. The Marine TOC has his information—I don't know why they haven't sent anybody to grab him."

The top priority was to evacuate American citizens, green card holders, and lawful permanent residents, not random Afghan commandos. J. P. replied, "We aren't grabbing people. To do that we would need to open the gate, which would lead to people rushing the runway, chaos inside, U.S. forces needing to engage, etc. This is a horrific scene and we are trying to sort it out."

James's response was lightning-quick. "OK so you're saying there's absolutely no way to get Nezam inside?"

"Hold on."

J. P. remembered that name from another email, an email from one of his best friends, another Green Beret. He searched for the name Nezam and read it again. "J. P.—in a roundabout way, I received Sgt. Nezamuddin Nezami's case from Lieutenant Colonel Scott Mann and Lieutenant Colonel Mike, both SF brethren. See attached email and pictures."

The attached photo showed a different picture of the exact same man.

J. P. dashed off another email to James. "Working on this now."

58

Nezam was close to physical collapse from hunger and dehydration. He looked at his watch. More than seven hours since he'd left Uncle Tawab's. Nezam was so near to the wire that he could just get the attention of the American Marines. He opened his mouth and pantomimed drinking. A sympathetic Marine saw him and tossed him a bottle of water.

Nezam smiled gratefully and twisted off the cap. But as he raised the bottle to his lips, a hand swooped in and snatched it. He whipped around prepared to fight. It was an older woman in a black hijab who he'd seen off and on for hours. She poured the water over her baby, who was the color of a bright red steak and coated in perspiration. She took a long swig for herself and handed the bottle back.

"Thank you, thank you," she said.

"No problem," Nezam muttered. Those last few ounces were the best he'd ever tasted.

Nezam heard an especially loud commotion approaching from behind. He turned. A family of five were elbowing their way to the tiger stripes. The family members were brandishing blue U.S. passports. The tiger stripes indicated they'd be allowed to enter the gate.

Nezam got an idea. He pressed in close to the family, so close he could smell their sweat. He followed them through the fencing as they held their blue passports high, past a dozen Marines, and through the steel main gate.

He was in.

A Marine momentarily put his hand on Nezam, but he smiled and shouted, "It's okay, I'm with them!" They all walked to a holding area across the wire. Another cluster of Afghan civilians waited there while passports and visas were checked. After a pat-down, Nezam stepped away from the family to stand beside a tall concrete blast wall. Next to him, pouches of Meals Ready-to-Eat were stacked on a wood pallet for anyone who needed one. Near that stood a nervous-looking Afghan man. Nezam blinked. The man was wearing a very familiar-looking backpack.

His pack.

Nezam walked up behind the man and surreptitiously checked the carry handle—it had a London Bridge Trading tag. It *was* his. He tapped the man's shoulder.

"Thank you so much for carrying my bag inside," Nezam said.

"This is my bag," the man answered in Dari.

Nezam gave the thief a hard look and lowered his voice. "I am Special Forces. That is mine. All my documents are inside. Thank you for bringing my bag here." He pulled the bag off the man's shoulders. The man stood there, dumbfounded. If he created a scene now, they were both screwed.

Nezam stepped back to the MRE pallet, shaking his head at his incredible luck. He grabbed an MRE and tore it open, pulling apart the seal on a bag of cold spaghetti. It tasted like a gourmet delicacy.

He then sent a short text to Mullah Mike: *I passed through the first checkpoint. There is another where I get the bus.*

Mike texted back. *Awesome! Can't wait to see you in the States, brother!* As Nezam chewed the first food he'd had since leaving his uncle's house, he watched the line carefully. The Marines were turning many of the Afghans around and sending them back out of the gate because they didn't have a U.S. visa or an American passport. His heart sank.

Nezam had neither.

59

Scott's phone pinged.

MIKE: *He's in.*

The chat room erupted in celebration.

JAMES: *Holy shit! Great work! I'm doing a happy dance right now.*
SCOTT: *Yes! This fucking team right here!!*
LIV: *Holy hell you guys are incredible.*
MIKE: *I'm a little misty-eyed. His picture in line is killing me. So happy this worked. Thanks to everyone who helped.*

Scott was in shock. They'd done it. The chat room was already talking about other Afghan friends and colleagues they could help.

Scott asked Mike to stay in the chat until they knew Nezam was rolling toward the terminal. *If something goes south, he'll still need you*, he wrote.

Minutes later, Nezam texted with unexpected bad news, *I'm at the second checkpoint. I need to show a U.S. visa to get through and I don't have one.*

Fuck, Scott thought, then texted James to contact J.P. to see if there was anything he could do.

SCOTT
Liv, we need help right now.

She promised to keep working the phones.

SCOTT
James, I know you emailed, but can you call J.P.? Somebody needs to put a call into the checkpoint and tell them not to turn Nezam away.

JAMES
Roger that.

60

J. P.'s phone rang and he answered on the first ring. "Hello?"

"Man, I'm sorry to bother you so much," James sputtered. "I know you're in a burning shithouse right now—but Nezam is in real danger of being ejected by the Marines at East Gate."

"It's all right," J. P. said calmly. "What's happening?"

"Nezam is no ordinary Afghan who helped the Americans. He's a graduate of Q Course at Bragg. He's an Afghan Green Beret. He has a pending SIV that we tried to fast-track, but it's stalled." James paused. "If he's sent back out—one biometric scan and he's done. On the spot. He's as high-value as they come. He'll be swinging from a tree on Airport Road by sundown."

J. P. cleared his throat. "Well, you know what? I was a Green Beret, too. I just ran into my interpreter from my first deployment here seventeen years ago. We had a pretty emotional reunion by the cafeteria. And we Q Course grads gotta stick together," J. P. said. "I'll find your buddy, man."

They hung up and J. P. started making calls to his contacts at the gates, verifying that if Nezam didn't have any paperwork, then he would be thrown out. The only option would be if they gave him a special code-word and told the gate guards to let anyone in who used it.

J. P. immediately called James back, hoping it wasn't too late.

"Hey, man, you gotta get hold of your buddy right now. Tell him to say 'Pineapple' as loud as he can to every American within earshot. Do you understand? 'Pineapple!' 'Pineapple!' That's the codeword that will get him into HKIA."

"*Pineapple?*" James asked. "You're fucking with me."

"I'm not fucking with you. Just tell him to say, 'Pineapple.' Right now. Text him on WhatsApp, Signal—call him before he gets kicked out."

"Thank you; I'll get him on the line now."

61

Nezam was still in the holding pen for what felt like forever. His phone was only at 10%. Had he come so far only to get thrown out? Suddenly, his phone rang

"Bro," said James, "say, 'Pineapple' as loud as you can to everybody around you. To all the Marines—right now."

"'Pineapple?' Okay, sir, okay. I got it. Pineapple." Because of Nezam's Afghan manner and preference for not making a scene, he didn't feel comfortable just yelling out the word. He spotted a bearded American in a ball cap by the Marines' guard booth. He was clearly a special operator in civilian clothes, an M4 slung over his chest, and a push-to-talk earpiece. Nezam walked past the line of civilians and approached him. This was it.

"Hi, sir," he greeted the bearded American with a warm smile. The American just nodded.

"I am . . . Uh, I am the *Pineapple*," he told him loudly.

The American's eyebrows lifted. "*You're* the Pineapple?"

"Yes, sir. I am the Pineapple," Nezam said proudly, with a smile.

"Okay, head down the walkway to the next checkpoint for bag check. You're good to go," he said, gesturing toward more Marines.

"Thank you, sir."

62

The Signal chat group erupted with adrenaline-fueled relief. This time there was no doubt. Mullah Mike got on the phone with the Marine TOC and sang the corporal's praises directly into her ear. She and her commanding officer assured Mike that Nezam would not be thrown out now.

Scott was in his driveway when he got the news. He literally fell to his knees on the pavement and began sobbing. His wife—fearing the worst had just happened—ran over to comfort him.

He looked up at her. He was smiling. "He made it, baby."

Scott thumbed a message into Signal. *Where the fuck did you come up with Pineapple?!*

> LIV: *Is this real life?*
>
> MIKE: *I can't fucking believe it.*
>
> JAMES: *J.P. told me that was Nezam's code word. I shit you not, when he told me that, I nearly spit out my coffee.*

Scott posted a GIF with PINEAPPLES! spelled out in big block letters. He was utterly exhausted, but he felt exhilarated. The U.S. government might not be able, or willing, to help at-risk Afghans, but he and this team *could*.

> SCOTT: *We can do this again. We can get more people out.*
>
> LIV: *Agreed.*

Someone changed the Signal group's name from TEAM NEZAM to TASK FORCE PINEAPPLE.

Nezam had made it. But their work had only just begun.

PART III

TASK FORCE PINEAPPLE

63

This time, Master Sergeant Bashir Ahmadzai went alone to HKIA's North Gate.

After his first attempt a few days earlier—when his pregnant wife had nearly passed out and they buried a dead man—he and his family had tried two more times. Neither attempt got them any closer to North Gate. The second attempt ended due to exhaustion; the third ended with Bashir and his brother getting beaten by several Taliban.

The beating had partially been Bashir's fault. Stubbornly, he'd refused to part ways with his ANA uniform, his Q Course certificate, and a folded Afghan flag, all of which were in the bottom of his rucksack. When a very young Talib fighter demanded to inspect the bag, Bashir refused. He lied, telling the teenage fighter that it contained "woman things," hoping that would offend his twisted piety and send him away. Instead, it sent Bashir—and his brother—to the ground under a flurry of blows from the young Talib and others who had joined in for the sport of it. They'd only escaped because of an intervention by a more wizened Talib, who admonished the young men.

Bashir was prepared to give up and stay in Afghanistan for now—it was too difficult and his wife was in too delicate a condition. She was only days from delivery. But Commander James had convinced him otherwise.

Bashir didn't really know Commander James. He didn't know that he was a man who'd been spiritually wrecked by his Army service and his long experience in America's forever wars. He didn't know that James hardly slept, or that he blamed himself for the deaths of other men. He didn't know that he'd been hit by an IED while deployed, or that he suffered from crippling arthritis due to his injuries, or that he had regular seizures due to brain trauma from the blast. He didn't know that after leaving the Army, James became a premier counter-IED expert who did numerous rotations training members of the Afghan National Mine Removal Group. He didn't know that James became an NMRG adviser because he was racked with guilt over losing one of his men to a roadside bomb. He didn't know that James saw—as early as 2008—that the U.S.-led war was lost. He didn't know that James drank too much. He didn't know the depths of James's guilt, his rage, his bitterness, his feelings of helplessness.

What Bashir *did* know was that he needed help. He was truly desperate, and he listened to Commander James when he encouraged him to do something he never would have considered on his own.

"Bashir," James had said on the night of their third failed attempt, "you need to go alone."

Bashir protested. How could he leave his family? How could he leave his wife in her state? He couldn't. It was impossible.

Despite Commander James's many afflictions, he was clear-eyed in his assessment. "You have to go alone. Hear me out. I can protect your family in Afghanistan, but I can't protect *you* in Afghanistan. You have to leave now. I'll take care of your family, Bashir. I'll get them to you. I promise."

For better or worse, Bashir had agreed.

Now he was back along the edge of the throng. This time, he left his military mementos behind.

Without the presence of his family, he was able to be both immersed and above the situation. He could observe like the operator he was. Before descending into the crowd he stood near it, watching for patterns.

There was no rhyme or reason to the gate access process. It would open now and then for about a minute for no consistent reason. Sometimes American soldiers would spot an exfil from above and dash out to drag the person in. Sometimes a mad rush of desperate Afghans would surge through the gate, eighty or ninety people getting through. The opening and closing created an accordion effect—a rush of forward momentum followed by a sudden stop, mashing people against the fence. Frail and strong alike were trampled underfoot. The mob neither chose nor discriminated. Bashir watched as children, adults, and elderly were alternately crushed to death before his eyes.

Still, people *were* getting in. Especially people who were alone.

He took a deep breath and entered the crowd. He pushed his big frame forward, being mindful not to crush anyone. When he got within sight of the gate, the crowd closed tightly around him. He shouldered past one human being after another as they snapped at him, cursing him or begging for water.

Commander James had been right. There was no way he could have gotten his family through this crucible. But he was still unsure as to whether he could trust the American stranger who had promised to take care of his wife and children.

After eight hours, Bashir was within striking distance of the gate. Even though he knew better, primal instincts had compelled his tongue to wet his chapped lips. He'd run out of water hours earlier, and had no money to pay the exorbitant cost of one dollar per bottle—five times the normal cost.

He could now almost touch the gate. He could hardly breathe or call out, as the air was squeezed from his lungs by the pressure.

Just then, North Gate opened for some unknown reason. Without thinking, Bashir surged forward, like he'd done hundreds of times when moving down a corridor in a gunfight, heading for his target, eyes fixed.

Moments later, he was inside. He'd made it. He grabbed two bottles of water from a pallet, downing one and pouring the other over his head. He got out his phone and texted Commander James.

I'm in.

64

Task Force Pineapple. Scott chuckled just thinking about the new name, but it worked. Pineapple emojis and memes flew throughout the chat room.

Nezam was inside the airport, but Kabul was in free fall. In addition to the crush of people trying to flee the country, there was an emergent push and pull between the Taliban and U.S.-led forces over security around the airport. Liv and June discussed accessibility at the various airport entrance gates for other people they might try to get past the wire. An interactive map of Kabul was quickly posted, enabling the team to drop GPS pins showing locations of Taliban checkpoints as they learned of them in real time from Afghans on the ground.

In just a matter of hours, Pineapple evolved into a virtual war room for intelligence gathering and analysis. It was similar in some respects to the joint operations centers Scott and the other special operators on the team had known in their past lives. Except the purpose of this one was to save lives instead of fighting the enemy.

As original members like June, James Meek, and Charles receded back into their day jobs, Pineapple continued to evolve at a breakneck pace. New people were folded in. There was Julie Browning, a former USAID senior adviser in Afghanistan, the woman who'd manifested Nezam onto his charter flight and was working to put other Afghans on similar flights. There was Kathleen Miles, a former intelligence officer who had volunteered to file SIV and humanitarian parole applications with the State Department for hundreds of Afghans who needed to get manifested on military airlift out of Kabul. There was Mick Mulroy, a career CIA paramilitary officer who was involved with a different group of veteran volunteers dubbing themselves Task Force Dunkirk, after the infamous evacuation from France in 1940. Another was retired lieutenant colonel Kirk Windmueller, a former Green Beret who had been part of the Village Stability Operations program with Scott.

And there was another James, a West Pointer and former Special Forces major, whose Afghan friends called him "Commander James." He had just helped another Afghan Green Beret—Master Sergeant Bashir Ahmadzai—get inside HKIA, and he knew Nezam, who had put him in touch with Scott.

When this Commander James popped up on Signal for the first time, everyone saw his avatar—a photo of him wearing a ball cap pulled low on his brow, casting his face in shadow. To avoid confusion with James Gordon Meek, Liv immediately dubbed him as "James with the Hat," or "James WTH," or, sometimes, just "Hat."

As soon as James WTH was brought in, he texted Scott directly. *Is Pineapple for Nezam specifically, or more dudes as well?*

Scott immediately answered. *We are keeping it open for more.*

Cool, James WTH replied. *And what about Nezam's family?*

You mean his uncle? I think they're staying, Scott answered.

No, man, James WTH texted. *When I hired him onto a team in 2018, he had a wife and three kids.*

Seriously? Scott wrote. *He never said a word to us about having a family.*

Scott thanked James WTH and put in a call with Nezam, who was still at HKIA. "Bro, what the hell?" he bellowed. "You have a *wife and children*?"

65

Lieutenant Colonel Kazem scanned the horizon with his binoculars from the back of his truck's bed. The orange disk of the setting sun had just touched the horizon. After dark, they'd be able to move again. He pulled out his satellite phone and dialed NDS headquarters. No answer. He'd tried the phone number at least a hundred times since the fall of Nimruz. Nothing.

"Fuckers took all the money and ran," Kazem said to his driver, who was beside the truck, pulling security.

"Sure did, boss," came the reply.

Kazem shifted his body and looked to his right. In the gloom of dusk, he could just make out that his men had nearly finished covering the cache site. They'd carefully bagged their weapons, tactical gear, and satellite phones and placed them in the hole. He marked the location with his wristband GPS unit and committed the geographic features to memory. *Motherfuckers will never find this spot*, he thought.

When the time was right, he would return with some pipe hitters, the special operators who did some of the war's hardest and dirtiest work. They would dig up these guns and ammo. Then they would turn the tables on the Taliban. He smiled at the thought. He would come back to this place. He would return to the fight. "There will be a lot of dead motherfuckers," Kazem said to the desert. He never called the Taliban anything but "motherfuckers."

"Sure will, boss," said his driver, who'd apparently been eavesdropping.

Kazem entered one more number into his phone. He had one last option. He called up one of the NDS senior leaders in Kabul. Remarkably, the man picked up.

"Hello?" the voice answered.

"Sir, it's Kazem."

"Where are you?" the chief asked.

"In the desert, boss. Nimruz is gone. I won't surrender. I want to make a stand."

"Come to Kabul quickly, then," the chief said. "We'll figure something out. Be careful, the city is in their hands now."

Motherfuckers.

"Yes, sir. We'll be there soon."

It took half the night to reach the outskirts of Taliban-occupied Kabul. He then sent his men, two by two, into the capital carrying counterfeit bus tickets. If they were stopped, the tickets had stamps showing they had traveled across the country from Helmand over the past month.

Kazem went last. On his way into Kabul, he spied an abandoned NDS vehicle sitting on the side of the road, a .50-caliber machine gun mounted in the back. Small kids scampered over the vehicle, playing soldier and pretending to fire the massive gun. Kazem paused to watch them. *How could they just abandon their vehicles and weapons? How could they disgrace Afghanistan like this?*

Tears welled in his eyes. He mashed them with his palm. Everything he had fought for was gone. In that moment, he realized he and his men also had to leave their country. Not to abandon it, but to live—so that they could return.

Kazem banged numbers in his phone's list of contacts. No one picked up. Finally, someone answered at the HKIA ops center for the National Strike Unit, the CIA-sponsored black ops groups. Kazem identified himself and asked to speak with the commander.

"My commander is out of Afghanistan," the man replied.

"Look, I'm fucking elite forces of NDS—can I bring my guys in for exfil?" Kazem pleaded firmly.

"It's not our call. It's up to the Americans."

Americans? He knew Americans.

He thought of Will Lyles, a Green Beret he'd translated for in the Village Stability Operations program before Kazem became special operations himself. In 2010, Kazem had helped pull Will to safety after an IED blew off Will's legs. Will had been telling Kazem for months to put in an SIV application, but Kazem always scoffed at the implication. He would stay and fight, he assured Will.

But no more. He picked up his phone and dialed Will.

"Hey, boss," Kazem said. "Can you get me the fuck out of this place?"

66

Peyton was furious. Four days had passed since Kabul had fallen, and as far as he could tell, U.S. Special Forces hadn't lifted a single fucking finger to help their Afghan comrades. "Why isn't anyone doing anything? We're fucking Green Berets. They were our partner force for twenty years," he angrily pounded in an email to his entire chain of command.

A mass email like this was risky, but who cared. *Fuck it*, he thought, and hit send.

The reply-all response he received moments later was an order to report to his company commander's office, which he did.

"That's a pretty passionate letter, Peyton," the major said. "Maybe a little out of line to send it to the battalion and group commander? I know you're upset about this. We all are. But we've got to focus on our own theater of operations. Not a lot we can do in Afghanistan."

Peyton marched out, fuming inside. His detachment had been the last Special Forces team sent to Kandahar and had turned the lights out at the airfield in May. A base that had once housed over forty thousand troops had been reduced to a dystopian industrial landscape. They even bulldozed the Tim Hortons and TGI Fridays.

His team had spent days exploring the airfield and taking stock of the millions of dollars' worth of abandoned equipment in warehouses and hangars. On one sweep, he opened a padlocked door to discover several tons of toilet paper. They also destroyed equipment. Peyton sent a video to a friend showing bearded American operators laughing as they tossed grenades into generator shacks.

He made an Afghan friend on that deployment—Hafizullah, aka "Hafi," who sported a magnificent handlebar mustache. Some of the Americans called him "Cheech," but that was too arcane for the Afghans. His call sign, unsurprisingly, was "Mustache."

Hafi told Peyton that up until 2010 he'd been a maintenance contractor, but that year he put down his wrench to join an Afghan unit called the National Mine Removal Group, which regularly worked with American Special Forces. The NMRG were experts at spotting and removing every manner of IED. They were also the guardian angels of U.S. special operators against insider attacks.

The NMRG were also fighters. Hafi himself had been on over three hundred missions. He and his fellow Afghan fighters attached to the NMRG trained and ate together, and when they weren't conducting operations, they would walk around in flip-flops and T-shirts sporting U.S. flags, dipping Copenhagen and dropping f-bombs. Peyton regarded them as practically American in appearance and manner.

When Peyton departed Kandahar and returned to the States, he couldn't believe they were just leaving Hafi and his fellow Afghans to fend for themselves. Why wasn't more being done for Afghans like Hafi? It was as if everyone had become resigned to the idea that Afghanistan was a lost cause.

It was shameful.

The only person Peyton had recently met who seemed to give a shit was a congressional staffer he'd been introduced to by a Gold Star widow: Liv Gardner.

67

Nezam had a family. Who knew? thought Scott.

Nezam had been sheepish when confronted with the fact, stating it was a very complicated situation.

Nezam's corrupt uncle had forced him to marry his wife, Uldoz, in order to lay claim to his army salary. The uncle had kept the family near him in Takhar in order to ensure control of payment. Nezam had never lived with his wife for more than a few months. They had a girl and two boys, all under eleven years old.

When pressed about his plan for them, he'd said, "I put them on my SIV application, but it was never approved. When Kabul fell, I would be no good to them dead, and the Taliban did not know about them. My plan was to just leave Afghanistan and bring them later."

Scott put the case before J.P. as quickly as possible.

"Not the first time I've heard this story," J.P. said. "Anyways, I think I can get her and the kids inside since Nezam is already here. I'll bring them in a back door, a secret entrance called Liberty Gate. I should be able to pull them in there."

Nezam called Uldoz in Takhar, and a male cousin agreed to bring the family to Kabul and deliver them to Liberty Gate, as a woman traveling alone in Afghanistan—with or without the Taliban in power—was taboo. With luck, they would be at HKIA within nine hours.

68

A few hours after Nezam made it into HKIA, Scott boarded a plane to Kentucky to spend a few days visiting his parents, Rex and Anita. Rex had recently suffered a severe stroke and was in rehabilitation. Scott's mother was exhausted caring for him.

Scott settled into his room and thought about the last week.

Nezam wasn't the only one to be left behind. It appeared as if the whole Afghan special operations community was being abandoned. Messages were flooding in from active duty military needing help moving their counterparts: the KKA, the specially trained strike forces who worked shoulder-to-shoulder with Rangers and Delta Operators. The Commandos who had fought alongside Green Berets since 2008 and who had conducted unilateral missions even as provinces fell all around them. The Afghan Special Forces teams who had worked alongside U.S. Special Forces to secure rural villages. The Afghan Special Mission Units who had flown the high-risk aviation missions to insert Afghan SOF and provide air cover to the sensitive missions. The NMRG who did everything from interdicting IEDs to preventing insider threats against Green Berets and other units.

Surely there was a plan; it would be ludicrous to squander all of those organizational relationships, combat capabilities, and intelligence assets.

Scott reached out to his peers still serving in the U.S. special operations; they informed him that there was zero will among senior leaders to intervene on behalf of partner forces. Some active duty friends asked if Scott and the other volunteer group could fill the gap until the SOF community decided to get involved, they believed that the leaders could be convinced to act.

Scott breathed deeply, some tension leaving his body. He could do that. He could fill the gap for his SOF brothers, if that is what they needed. For a short while, anyway.

Scott's phone rang. It was Liv.

"Scott, I need you on a Zoom call with me and an active duty SF officer," she said. "I think this is an emergency."

SCOTT
James with the Hat, I need you in a call with Liv and a new guy. Can you join?

Soon there was a *Hollywood Squares* of video faces streaming from Colorado, Florida, North Carolina, and D.C.

Liv kicked off the call. "Hey, guys," she said. "I want to introduce you to an active-duty Green Beret, Peyton, who's trying to figure out how to exfil his guys from the NMRG force who used to operate out of Kandahar."

They all said hello and introduced themselves, and Peyton got right to it. "The NMRG are like brothers to me, and I need to get them out for that reason—but there's another one, too."

"What's that?" Scott asked.

"The Taliban know all of their real names, meaning they're in trouble. But the NMRG dudes know all of *our* names—hundreds of SF guys who've cycled through Kandahar over the last ten years. They know our phone numbers. They know our tactics, techniques, and procedures. It would be an intelligence jackpot for China or Russia. If any of them are captured and interrogated, think of what they could share."

James with the Hat chimed in. "I'm also working a hundred and eighty NMRG from the east. I agree. If these guys get rolled up, it's a serious national security threat."

Silence fell on the line. Then Scott sighed. "Okay, I got it. Peyton, Hat—send us names and numbers. No promises, but we'll bring our resources to bear and get your guys the support they need."

"Thank you, sir," Peyton said. "This restores a little faith in the SF Regiment."

"Give it time, I'm sure we'll bring that expectation crashing down," Scott said. "Liv, bring Peyton into the group. Let's get moving."

Scott was worried. This was a new, dangerous development. He knew from experience how badly, say, Russian military intelligence would like to get their hands on men like those in the NMRG. What puzzled him though was how mitigation of such an obvious national security risk could fall to a young captain—one who was working in a seemingly unofficial capacity.

69

After the exhilarating outcome for Nezam, Scott wondered what was next. It had been one thing to help Nezam, but what Peyton and James WTH were presenting was far more complex. When all the flocks were accounted for—including some 75 from Peyton, another 180 or so from James with the Hat—it added up to more than 250 Afghans. It was a huge number of desperate people with significant national security implications. This was a mission for *active* special operators, not retirees. It made no damn sense.

His phone was now blowing up with Pineapple messages. Extraction by committee was cumbersome, to say the least. Julie Browning, the former USAID senior adviser, relayed intel that Haqqani fighters from the Taliban's Red Unit were now providing "security" around HKIA, posing a clear threat to anyone trying to get out. June said there was no indication that Delta Force teams were being permitted to conduct surgical extractions, and Steve Rulli, who had worked with Scott in VSO, confirmed that. Kathleen Miles relayed the most ominous piece of intelligence: there was a credible threat of an ISIS-K suicide bombing in the dense crowds around HKIA.

Scott walked outside to watch the sunset. The cattle grazing on the surrounding, lush green hillsides were a stark contrast to the storm raging in his head. *We are not supposed to be doing this,* he thought. *This is an Uncle Sam–size problem. The State Department and the Department of Defense should be getting these guys out.*

His phone buzzed. It was James WTH.

"Dude, Pineapple is too chaotic," he said. "You need to take charge."

"What am I supposed to do? I got my guy out. Special operators—guys who are there, on the ground, with weapons and support—should be doing this. The fucking U.S. government should be doing it."

"Yeah, well, they're not," James WTH said. He paused. "Scott, the cavalry is not coming. And we need a leader, or it won't work."

Scott hung up. He had no choice.

When he was alone a short while later, Scott picked up his phone and recorded a voice memo for Task Force Pineapple. "Everybody's doing amazing work," he said. "Let's use this forum to collaborate and, when necessary, conduct tasks that the U.S. government can't. Remember, when it comes to our Afghan partners, we know who they are, we know where they are, and they trust us to help them move to friendly lines. Love this group. Keep going."

70

Scott did media hits from his parents' den in addition to juggling the exponential growth of Task Force Pineapple. He was impatient to get the word out about the trapped Afghans in Kabul, especially Afghan soldiers, and the U.S. government's total abdication of its duty to extract them. Scott mainly stuck to Fox and CNN, appearing on about half a dozen shows.

Media was not his thing anymore. He'd done some TV hits after his retirement in 2013—mainly to discuss the plight of damaged war veterans, flawed Afghan strategy, and ISIS—but he found them repetitive and, for the most part, ineffectual. He'd given them up years ago, hoping he'd never need to appear on TV again.

This situation, however, called for awareness by telling the truth about what was happening on the ground. The need was so urgent, the timeline so constrained, and the absence of U.S. leadership so profound. This time, maybe his words would have a meaningful effect. If nothing else, maybe some nongovernmental organizations would step up and get involved in Task Force Pineapple.

The private sector response was overwhelming. Veterans and citizens across the country were pissed at the government's abandonment of Afghanistan. The messages poured in on Facebook Messenger and Instagram by the hundreds, offering help and encouragement.

Following one news hit that weekend, his phone rang with a number he hadn't seen in a long time—one belonging to a former Green Beret named Mark.

Scott answered. Mark had just seen Scott on Fox. "Seems like a big project. Need any help?"

"One thousand percent we need help, man. In the past three or four days Pineapple's become unwieldy. Not only can we not meet demand, I'm worried this thing is going to get out of hand."

"I have an idea," Mark said.

He told Scott that before calling, he'd spoken to three other former special operators, who all worked in senior law enforcement or intelligence positions. Mark asked them if they would be willing to take a couple days off to help Scott, an old Green Beret buddy of his. All three were in.

"We're offering to come down to Tampa so you can off-load some staff planning shit on us. We'll expand the operation that got Nezam out so it can move hundreds of people, not just a few. We'll identify threats and obstacles. Plan for contingencies. Basically, we're ready to lay out everything you need for a scaled up mission. How's that sound?"

Scott was speechless.

"Good—I thought you'd like it," Mark said. "We'll meet you in Tampa."

"I'll be back on Monday. Can you come then?"

"We'll be there."

"Mark, I—"

"Don't mention it. We have one request, though. It has to be completely off the books. We all get fired if this gets out. No names, no identification, no trace, no records."

"I've already forgotten."

"Good. See you Monday."

Scott hung up. He let out a big sigh. This was exactly what they needed. If Pineapple was going to help anyone, they had to get better organized. They needed to figure out how to work at *scale*. But damn. The vicious churning in Scott's stomach could only mean one thing. He was getting sucked back in. Scott had left the military world nearly a decade ago. Pineapple was now something more than helping an Afghan buddy get to freedom. This was a government problem of epic proportions. Who the hell was he to be getting involved in something of this scale?

From the corner of the room, Scott's father cleared his throat. Scott didn't realize Rex had been sitting there all along. He turned and looked at the man he'd considered his hero since he could walk. Scott felt like a little kid again, trying to figure out a world that was way bigger than he was. Battle damaged from two bouts with cancer and a recent stroke, Rex's old weathered face bore the pain, but his eyes still danced the way they always had. Especially when duty called. He'd spent almost forty-three years fighting big wildland fires, running toward the smoke, while everyone else ran away. "You guys are doing the right thing, Scotty," he said. "You don't want to be on the wrong side of this. You'd never get over it."

71

Finnish special envoy Jussi Tanner walked with purpose toward the Abbey Gate. There were 450 Finnish citizens and Afghans of importance to his government still in Kabul, and his mission was to bring as many of them inside the airport as he could before the U.S. and NATO forces were gone. Today, he and his security chief, Pat, were planning to pull in a pair of young Afghan women highly at risk for Taliban retribution.

But as Jussi walked past the Turkish Tower, now manned by a Marine Corps sniper, he saw that Abbey Gate was no longer in business. The two-lane vehicle entry control point had been blocked off due to the growing fear of IED attacks. What had once been the gate area was a pile of concrete rubble and the smashed remains of a fence. He could still see the rusty sign with the words TURN OFF LIGHTS, SHOW YOUR ID in English and Dari. The rubble blocked the incoming and outgoing lanes of the airport road there.

The two young women he was assisting were pushing their way through a crowd of perhaps a thousand Afghans wedged between the high walls of the Baron Hotel compound and the sewage canal that ran along the airport perimeter. He texted them to say the gate was out of action.

They texted that they were along the sewage canal, down from the guard tower, and the diplomat soon spotted their light blue headscarves—the far-recognition signal they had been instructed to wear.

More than a dozen British soldiers milled around, and Jussi asked a sergeant if there was any way to bring people in from the canal. The

Brit said he'd be happy to cut a hole in the chain-link fence; that was the only way. He ordered one of his men to grab a set of bolt cutters from the breaching kit in their truck and was soon at work clipping a half moon-shape just big enough for a person to duck through. Jussi signaled the two women to cross the sewage canal, and British soldiers pulled them up over the retention wall and helped them through the fence.

Two more in, Jussi thought.

The Finn had no idea that hundreds of Afghans would ultimately make their way to freedom thanks to the hole he'd just punched in the airport's perimeter.

72

Liv had barely slept in four days. Since joining Pineapple, she had worked twenty-hour days cross-legged on her apartment's white sofa. Comms was two cell phones and a laptop. Her apartment had a view of Capitol Hill, where she had a real office in the Cannon House Office Building. These days, she almost never went there because of COVID. She couldn't remember the last time she'd showered or done her hair—her camera was always off for Zoom meetings. Thor, a black service dog she was minding for a friend, lay next to her while her cat, Otto, stalked the room.

She had been reluctant when her boss, Representative Mike Waltz, connected her to his old Special Forces friend Scott Mann. She was eager to help however she could. "Sir, I'm going to have to do some real weird shit, probably breach a lot of doors," she had told the congressman. "What are my limitations?"

"Do whatever it takes, Liv," he said. "Just get as many people out as you can."

The task was overwhelming; so many Afghans needed help. Her husband, an Apache attack helicopter pilot, was completely behind her. His unit had been slated for deployment to Afghanistan until President Trump struck a deal with the Taliban for the U.S. to withdraw.

The day after Nezam got into HKIA, she had texted a "gate pass" graphic to a constituent's interpreter named Khalid. The "gate pass" was provided by the State Department to be used by Afghans they had cleared for travel to the U.S. Khalid was now already inside HKIA, along with his wife, Marzia, eight months pregnant, and their two-year-old daughter. Khalid had assumed that once they were in the airport, they'd just sip on water and wait for their flight. But HKIA had gone from an international airport to a decrepit slum. It was overflowing with more than fifteen thousand people. There was no food, no water, no place to go to the bathroom, and there was practically no shelter from the sun.

Liv posted a plea for help on Pineapple, fearing that Marzia might lose the baby. They had to get on a flight ASAP. She dropped photos into the chat and dropped GPS pins for their location inside HKIA. Scott flagged Liv's message and put out a call to some contacts in the 82nd, including to Steve Rulli and his wife, Kim, who was an Army helicopter pilot at Fort Bragg.

"Don't give up, Khalid," Liv told him. "I'm working it. Leaders in the 82nd Airborne Division have been alerted, and someone will come for you."

73

Zac Lois had been trying to help his former interpreter, Mohammad Rahimi, for over a month, but nothing was working. And Mohammad wasn't the only one. There were two other Afghan Special Forces guys he wanted to bring in as well. He'd called the State Department, but folks who sounded like interns kept directing him to websites he had already scoured or asked for documents he had already submitted. His congressman wouldn't do a thing. *There must be a better way to get guys out of Kabul*, he thought.

Sitting on the couch in his summer cabin, he opened his LinkedIn account and typed:

This is a Hail Mary post, please help if you can:

I have Afghan Special Forces friends that I served with who are in Kabul and trying to get inside the airport. I have been working with them for weeks to get them, their wives, and their children out of Afghanistan. They finally have all the paperwork they need. However, the Taliban are blocking the roads leading to the airport and have beaten my friends. They can't show their ID to the Taliban since the Taliban have a list and are executing former Afghan Special Forces members. Does anyone have any contacts at all on the ground in Kabul that can meet them at the gate? This apparently is working for others. Obviously, this is a one in a million chance but we have exhausted all options and the situation is dire. Thank you!

He then hit *post*, closed his laptop, and went to bed.

The next morning, he checked the post on his phone while he was canoeing on a nearby lake with his father and two boys. Someone named Kirk Windmueller had messaged him. *DM me*, he wrote. Lois couldn't remember ever meeting anyone by that name, but Windmueller's LinkedIn profile identified him as another former Green Beret officer.

Within the hour, the two were on the phone. Apparently, Kirk was part of some kind of volunteer group called Task Force Pineapple. Later that day, Kirk ushered Zac into the Signal chat group.

> Team, give a warm welcome to Zac Lois. He is a former Green Beret and schoolteacher in Syracuse, NY. He has 3 Afghan SF plus their families seeking passage to HKIA and a way out. He has direct comms with them.

Zac was quickly brought into the fold. As he fielded "Welcome!" messages from Scott and other new teammates, he scrolled through the list of twenty or so people in the group. He recognized Mark Nutsch, a Green Beret legend; his unit had galloped on horseback into Afghanistan just weeks after 9/11. There was Jay Redman, a Navy SEAL whose face was disfigured by combat wounds, who had become an author and inspiring motivational speaker. And there was Jim Gant, aka Lawrence of Afghanistan, one of Zac's personal heroes. Zac felt like he'd been seated in a VIP lounge by mistake.

During the sons' naptime, Zac wandered out into his backyard garden, his place of peace and reflection. He checked on his summer tomatoes, squash, and asparagus as he pondered what lay ahead. *This is all as Sun Tzu wrote 2,500 years ago*, the history major thought. *"It is better to be a warrior in a garden than to be a gardener in a war."*

74

After dashing into HKIA, Bashir had avoided getting escorted out mainly because he had a pending SIV application, thanks to Commander James. His English skills helped as well. Over the twenty-four-odd hours he'd been in HKIA—sleeping under a large generator and trying to find food, which had run out at the airport—he'd grown friendly with some of the American Marines and soldiers. When he told them he had been a master sergeant in the Afghan army, no one questioned him or asked for his papers, and when he could, he happily helped them as a translator. They left him alone.

But Bashir was in limbo. He wanted to get on a flight, but his family was outside HKIA. He reminded himself that Commander James had been right—it was the correct call to keep his pregnant wife and five little ones in hiding while he came to HKIA alone. She never would have made it.

Besides, if they *had* made it and then been forced to live at HKIA like he had, it could have been even worse than pushing through the crowd. The conditions were far beyond what he'd experienced as a young refugee in Pakistan after the Soviet invasion. He had barely eaten since gaining entry to the airport yesterday afternoon, and water was becoming scarce, with thousands of hungry and thirsty people inside the perimeter. He occasionally got water from troops he engaged, but mostly he made do with sips of water left in discarded bottles. He was a special operator and he knew how to survive, but he wondered how any of these families with small children were going to make it. He'd seen so many of them lose their little ones over the last few days. It pained him to see this level of suffering in his own people.

On this, his second day at HKIA, Bashir finally found a half-eaten MRE in a dumpster. When he was finished with it, he did what he always did when he couldn't decide what to do: he called his dad, though he had generally been staying off cellular for personal security up till that moment.

His father had news for him—Bashir's wife had just given birth to their sixth child, a baby girl. "Congratulations, my son. She is here. Zainab is here. She is healthy and beautiful," his father said.

Bashir was elated and devastated all at once. His precious daughter had been born—but without him to witness it or to be there for his wife. He was silent for a moment.

"What is it, son?" his father asked.

"Dad, I should be there, not here. I should leave," he said.

"What? No! They would kill you on sight if you came back. There is no hope for that," his father said. "Put it from your mind."

"But, Dad, at least I could be there. Commander James has told me I'm going to fly out of here tomorrow no matter what," Bashir said.

"Good! Then you go," his father said sternly, chiding him as only a father could.

"What? How can you say that?"

"My son," he said, "the Taliban came to your home yesterday." Bashir's breath stopped. His father went on. "Your brother was there. They came asking for you. They searched your home and they saw all of the patches and certificates from your American friends. They joked with each other and asked if you were a tailor, knowing full well what you are."

"What happened?" Bashir asked.

"Your brother told them that you were in the Army but no one special and that you left the country. They then said it was good that you had fled. Then they took all of your uniforms, papers, and patches out into the street and burned them for all of us to see."

Bashir tried to hold back tears as hundreds of people milled all around him.

"Get on the plane, my son. We will find our way to you."

"Yes, Father," Bashir said, barely audible. He hung up the phone.

75

Hafi's phone vibrated. It was SF Peyton.

"Hafi, where are you?"

"We're in Jalalabad, boss. We're safe, but we cannot move."

Peyton took a deep breath. "You're going to have to move. To the airport in Kabul. You're going to have to move right now."

On a good day, Kabul was a three-hour drive due west from Jalalabad. Needless to say, none of these days were very good. Hafi was in his living room, where his four children—two daughters, seven and three, and two sons, six and two—were playing quietly. "It will be extremely dangerous, boss. Think about my kids."

"I am. You're NMRG. They'll hunt you *all* down."

Hafi knew Peyton was right. "Okay."

"Good. Do you have good comms with the other NMRG guys?"

"Yes, yes, of course."

"Then get on the horn and tell them the same thing. Load up and get to Kabul. We have people working on getting you out. All of you. All information will flow from me and to them through you. Got it?"

"Got it, boss."

"Good. Keep that phone charged. And be careful, brother."

"Yes, boss."

Early the next morning, the family loaded into Hafi's brother's car for the long trip. Hafi sat in the passenger seat, stroking his mustache, watching his house vanish in the side-view mirror.

He wondered if his children would ever have a home again.

76

Scott had just got off the phone with an old contact from USSOCOM, a war-tested retired Marine named Art with contacts in the CIA. Those contacts were requesting that Task Force Pineapple assist an American citizen named Qais and his fourteen family members get to the airport.

An American citizen? Really?

Once again Scott was amazed why the American government wasn't more involved. And they were the freaking CIA for god's sake! Had the world gone crazy?

The story was that Qais came to the United States in 2014 on an SIV and had since become a U.S. citizen. His wife, Rania, as well as two of their children were U.S. citizens, but their younger two children didn't hold U.S. passports. The eight others were Qais's Afghan relatives. The family had returned to Kabul for his sister's wedding in July, also hoping to find a way to get his family out. Instead, they all got trapped by the sudden fall of Kabul and had been hiding out in a cousin's house ever since. They were still expecting to get out through the State Department, but Qais was leaving no stone unturned and reached out to his employers, the U.S. government. He was a counter-terrorism expert. His name had ended up on the CIA short list.

As Scott reflected on this difficult case, he decided to enlist the help of Dan O'Shea. Dan, who had recently been added to the Pineapple Signal chat room, was a retired SEAL with significant inter-agency experience that would prove necessary for this complex task. Additionally, his work in dealing with horrific terrorist kidnappings in Iraq suited him for this highly emotional and sensitive situation.

An American citizen. Scott shook his head in disbelief. *What a clusterfuck. This is getting out of control.*

77

Charlie Company, of the 504th Infantry Regiment (the White Devils) of the 82nd Airborne Division shared responsibility with the U.S. Marines for security in an area of HKIA that went from the southern passenger terminal to Abbey Gate, a gnarly half mile of razor wire, jersey barriers, high blast walls, a rickety chain-link fence, and a putrid sewage canal alongside a waist-high concrete retaining wall. Marines guarded Abbey Gate, and Captain John Folta's paratroopers assumed a defensive line behind the primary perimeter. Afghan civilians lined the "shit trench," swarming and crushing each other. Few dared to descend into the knee-deep filth.

First Sergeant Jesse Kennedy could barely believe the situation they'd been thrust into. The airfield had a *Road Warrior* vibe, with soldiers cruising in beat-up Toyota pickups spray-painted with the name of their country—Turkey, Finland, New Zealand, Norway, Germany. Afghans who had slipped into the perimeter wandered everywhere.

John had received a message that a former interpreter for one of his paratroopers would be coming to Abbey Gate and needed to be pulled into safety. They were going to check to see if he'd arrived. Jesse drove the captain to Abbey Gate, while the company's medic, Specialist Aiden "Doc Gundy" Gunderson, followed in another Toyota Hilux. Just crossing the runway was tricky, as there was no way of knowing when a plane was about to take off or land. Jesse looked both ways, floored it across the tarmac, and hoped for the best.

He had little confidence they could find a lone Afghan in the huge crowd jostling outside Abbey Gate. They had just parked on the air-port's edge, when an Afghan man already inside the gate approached them.

"Hey, 82nd Airborne! You're here to help me," the man said, stopping Jesse with a pleading hand and pointing to his shoulder patch with the AA, All American, of the storied division.

"I don't think so," Jesse replied, puzzled.

"No, you're here to help me." He dialed a number on his phone. "They told me to look for you. My wife is pregnant. She's in really bad shape." He gestured to a woman stretched out in the dust with a little girl. "Liv is trying to talk to you, from Congressman Mike's office. Here, you can talk to her." He held out his phone.

Jesse stopped. "What's your name?"

"Khalid."

Jesse checker his roster. "Look, we're not here for you," Jesse said.

The Afghan man stepped back awkwardly. He waved his hands in acknowledgment and obvious disappointment. "No problem, sir, no problem. I am sorry."

I am sorry, thought Jesse. That was odd. Afghan civilians who'd made it this far usually wouldn't take no for an answer.

The three paratroopers continued on foot to Abbey Gate. As they strode through the heat, Jesse couldn't shake the feeling that they should have helped the man and his family. After checking in with the Marines on the threat posture, they spent five minutes surveying the sewage canal. As expected, there was no sign of the man they had come for, only a sea of desperate, pleading faces.

As they walked back to their Hilux, Jesse couldn't stop thinking about the Afghan man and his pregnant wife. He had a compassionate streak that refused to let him pass by someone in duress. Growing up dirt-poor in southern Georgia, he had learned from his dad, before he had passed away, that no matter how bad his life might seem, there was always someone who was worse off. When the two of them went fishing, his father would always give away the fish on the way home. "Dad, we don't have hardly enough to eat at home," Jesse would protest. "Someone needs it more than us, Jesse," his dad would remind him.

"Hey, sir, let's stop by and check on the pregnant woman," he said to John. The captain nodded.

The Afghan was overjoyed when they returned. Doc Gundy checked on the man's wife. She was suffering from exposure and severe dehydration.

"We need to get her to the Norwegian field hospital now," Doc Gundy said. "They'll give her an IV and try to keep her from going into labor."

The family piled into the bed of the Hilux. Neither John nor his first sergeant knew the exact location of the Norwegian medical clinic where they were taking the couple. Jesse drove toward Apron 8, the general location of the medical clinic, craning his neck to look for clues to its location while keeping an eye skyward for incoming C-17s. The First Sergeant, who had been hoarding some Twizzlers they had scavenged from a convenience store in the terminal, passed the candy through the cab window for the little girl. As they searched for the hospital, Khalid pushed his phone through the window into the Hilux cab. Jesse took the phone. The line was open and on speakerphone. An American woman was on the other end. "This is Liv Gardner from Congressman Mike Waltz's office," she said. "Who am I speaking with?"

"This is First Sergeant Jesse Kennedy, Charlie Company, 2-504, 82nd Airborne." Anxious about the suffering woman in the back, he tried to keep the truck moving slowly, but he was having a hard time driving while speaking on the phone and watching for aircraft all at the same time.

"Hi, First Sergeant, thanks so much for helping Khalid and his family. He's very important to us. I've been trying for hours to find help for them. There is someone else here who wants to talk to you," she said.

Jesse scanned the buildings alongside the airfield aprons as a male voice spoke over the speaker on the dodgy cell connection.

"This is Congressman Mike Waltz—who is this?"

Jesse introduced himself as he shifted into third. The little girl was starting to cry, and he finally spotted the Norwegian clinic. Jesse gave up on polite conversation with Waltz. "Can't talk, sir—here," he said abruptly, and handed the phone to John, who curtly thanked Waltz and hung up on the congressman as they pulled in next to the clinic. The first sergeant grinned at his commander.

"I'm pretty sure we both just got fired, sir."

John laughed. "Fuck it."

To everyone's relief, the baby was fine. They called Liv back to let her know that Marzia and her baby were healthy, she had been given an IV, and that they were arranging to get them on an evac flight. The day before, Charlie Company had escorted sixty-one Afghans to the flight line and learned how U.S. consular officers were processing and manifesting them on military airlift flights out. They'd get Khalid's family out.

"First Sergeant, is it okay if I reach out to you again as we work through some other high-profile cases?" Liv asked. "I promise they'll be highly vetted—only at-risk people who really need special focus to get into HKIA."

John, who could hear their conversation, nodded.

"Sure," Jesse replied. "We'll do what we can."

78

Scott tried to focus on his parents—his dad needed help with physical therapy, and little jobs around their family farm had been neglected for weeks. But it was no use. Pineapple and the situation in Afghanistan were all-consuming.

What Scott and Pineapple's growing membership knew was that time was running out. The 82nd was gearing up for its own departure—what the military calls a "retrograde." They would be the last boots on the ground. Once they left, HKIA would be under Taliban control.

Despite all their efforts, sleepless nights, and good will, TF Pineapple still had no reliable way to get their people into HKIA. Nezam had been a lucky break. They'd had a few successes since, but this "system" of theirs could not serve the hundreds of people that needed help *right now*.

With the addition of Zac Lois and several others, Pineapple now had thirty-plus members. Conversations were darkening, turning to worst-case scenarios. What would they do if ISIS-K—the common enemy of both American forces and the Taliban—sent suicide bombers into the crowd around HKIA, as intelligence reports were warning? What if cell phone service suddenly went down in Kabul? What if the many HKIA gates shut once and for all? What if the Taliban stopped cooperating?

Scott had his own dark concerns. He messaged, "What happens if our only options are long-term overland movements? We'll need dozens—hundreds!—of safe houses spread over hundreds of miles. We should start efforts to answer these questions while we continue to get people to the airport."

Their inside guy, J.P., had been trying to receive roughly thirty Afghans—men who were part of SF Peyton's NMRG contingent—into the airport. They were waiting in nearby safe houses and could get to the airport in under thirty minutes, but no one in TF Pineapple had come up with any feasible way to present them.

J.P. wanted to help Pineapple, but he had his hands full processing all the people already inside HKIA. Despite the dereliction of duty toward interpreters and Afghan special operations forces, the U.S. government was still managing to spirit away about ten thousand people a day—Afghans, Americans, coalition partners, you name it. And J.P. was also dealing with the chaos that was HKIA. And the harsh reality was that there were many thousands of Afghans who still needed evac, including all of the embassy's three thousand local Afghan staff members. These were J.P.'s responsibility. He'd made it clear to Scott that they had to take priority over anything Pineapple was throwing at him.

Scott was running out of ideas, and it looked like, despite reassurances from members of the U.S. special operations, the cavalry was not coming. Whoever was going to get out of that airfield would be doing it with the help of the Pineapple Express and other volunteer groups.

That evening, Scott convened a call to try to crack the code. Liv joined, along with the new guy, Zac Lois. "We have a growing list of Afghan special operations forces and interpreters and their families to push inside," Scott said. "But time is not on our side. I'm hearing from a lot of my friends on the inside that the 82nd's retrograde is about to begin. Maybe only a couple days at most. We aren't moving the numbers we need to see move. I'm out of ideas. Anyone got anything?"

There was a pause. Then Zac asked, "Does anyone have someone on the inside of HKIA? Like a brigadier general or a janitor? Anyone? Doesn't matter who—we just need them to be on the inside."

"Wait," Liv said excitedly. "I might have a connection."

She told the group about Captain John Folta and Jesse Kennedy, and how they'd helped Khalid and his family. "I mean, First Sergeant Kennedy said it was okay if we reached out to them if we have other special-interest Afghans who needed help," she said.

"Let's find out," Scott said. "What choice do we have?"

OPERATION
HARRIET

79

A wall of heat hit Nezam and his family as they stepped from the ramp of their U.S. Air Force C-17 cargo plane onto Al Udeid Air Base.

All around them, hundreds of Afghans formed a long line for check-in with U.S. consular officials, agents from the Department of Homeland Security, and uniformed military, after which the Afghans were led to a giant tent lined with hundreds of cots. This would be their temporary home; their first rest stop on their long journey to America. All around him, he recognized fellow commandos, KKA members, and other Afghan Special Forces—soldiers he'd fought with, translators who'd been at his side, and even Mahdi, his close friend from the Commandos. Smiling from ear to ear, he clapped his friends on the back and took selfies. They were joyful scenes but undercut with the knowledge that more friends were still trapped back in Kabul.

As soon as Nezam had a free moment, he texted Scott.

> Dear brother, I hope you are well I am in Doha! It's very hot here but much better than Afghanistan. The team here is working on my case and they told me they will do anything to get me clear and get me out of here.

The reply was practically instant.

> Dude! I'm so happy you are there, I can't even tell you. Tell them to call me if they need to. Please send a photo of your family so I can show it to TF Pineapple. Need to motivate everyone!

Nezam brought his family outside. Before heading to another tent to get some food, he flagged an American airman and asked if he'd snap a photo of all of them. The airman happily obliged.

Nezam put the photo in a text message and hit send.

Soon, the photo was circulating in the Task Force Pineapple Signal chat room with the caption: "Nezami, Mr. Nezami. Party of seven. Your table is ready."

The photo showed Nezam in sunglasses, his wife, Uldoz, his two sons, and their daughter—as well as a young woman in a black hijab and a teenage boy, whom Nezam had identified as his cousins. All of them were beaming.

80

The U.S. State Department instructed Qais and his family to go to a rally point on the southwest side of HKIA at 4:00 p.m. This area was under Taliban control, but he was told someone from the State Department would be there to load them onto buses and bring them inside.

As soon as they arrived, a Taliban commander greeted them, instead of the emissaries from the State Department that they expected. "Where are you and your family going?" he demanded.

Qais calmly presented his U.S. passport. "We're going to the airport," he explained.

The Talib, who struck Qais as very well-educated, only gave the papers a cursory glance before looking angrily at him. "Why would you leave Afghanistan? We need people like you to stay and help us rebuild our country after the occupiers leave."

"I have a business in America. I own a restaurant," Qais lied. "I have to get my kids back to school. I love this country and want to help rebuild. But at this moment, I need to leave."

The commander's face darkened.

"I have to get in," Qais pleaded. "My entire family has U.S. passports," he lied again.

Qais's words only angered the Talib.

"Listen to me—I will shoot you in your head." The Talib took one step back and raised his AK-47, leveling the barrel on Qais's forehead. "I don't care if you're George fucking Bush, you're not going through that gate."

Qais protested. The Talib liked that even less. He pointed his rifle just above Qais's head and fired three quick bursts. His terrified children and wife were shrieking and crying.

"Okay, okay," Qais said, backing away.

All fourteen of them pushed their way back down Airport Road and began the two-and-a-half-mile trek back to his cousin's house. He tried to calm his wife and kids, but it was no use. Qais fumed with anger. *These idiots almost got us all killed.*

Once they were safe at his cousin's house, Qais received a call from Dan O'Shea. After introducing himself, he said, "I was asked to help get you out."

Qais immediately began to vent, relaying what had happened to his family. "No one was there from the State Department," he complained. "The Taliban refused to let us pass, even with our passports. The guard came this close to killing me in front of my entire family. And he would have killed them, too, if he looked carefully at my documents. We cannot stay here. My agency can provide documents showing my family is on a hit list. We need to get out of here now."

"Wait, wait—do you think I work for the government?"

"Do you not?" Qais asked, audibly perturbed.

"No, brother, I don't. Some CIA contacts asked my organization to help on your case. Task Force Pineapple isn't official. It's mainly veterans and other current and former government employees. We're volunteers, man."

"Volunteers for whom?" Qais asked.

"Volunteers for you," Dan replied.

"I can't believe this," Qais said.

"Neither can we. . . . I'm curious, though—why's your family on a hit list?"

Qais explained that he'd been a foreign service national investigator at the U.S. embassy in Kabul, and then, after moving to the States in 2014, a contractor for federal law enforcement. "I have top secret clearance," Qais said. "I've investigated the Haqqani network for ten years.

They know who I am. They nailed a night letter threatening to kill me to my dad's front door. We had to leave there. My whole family is targeted."

"Have you heard from your office in D.C.?" Dan asked.

Qais exhaled with a weary sigh. "No, not really," he said. "I can't get anyone on the phone."

"All right. Sit tight. We'll try to help you," Dan said.

They hung up. For many hours that night, Qais puzzled over this peculiar call. *A volunteer group was asked by the CIA to get me out? What kind of D.C. bullshit is this?* He was a U.S. citizen creeping through the streets of Kabul with his family like they were common criminals.

Later, he finally got through on a State Department hotline. "If you don't feel safe, I want you to just go back home," the woman on the other end told him.

Home? he thought. *With Haqqani after me? Yet another fool bureaucrat.*

81

Master Sergeant Basira Mohammadi stood alert and vigilant just as she had been trained. She was grateful not to be inside that horrible Abbey Gate crowd anymore. The chaos, stench, and death would always haunt her dreams.

The American military advisers she had worked so closely with hadn't answered her calls or texts. But her mentor, Command Sergeant Major Pashtoon Peer Mohammad at the Kabul Training Center, had, as had Command Sergeant Major Azizullah Azizyar at Special Operations Command, who saw her as a little sister. They were working their contacts to get themselves out, and they weren't going to leave Basira behind.

At five o'clock that morning, CSM Pashtoon called her. "Basira, can you get here by taxi?" Her phone pinged with a text message—a GPS pin from CSM Pashtoon. "Colonel Matt Coburn is speaking with Azizyar. We have a safe house and a possible way out of Kabul. You will have to pose as my wife when we travel."

She hurried to say goodbye to her mother, gathered up her documents, donned her blue full-body burqa, and found a taxi with her two sisters accompanying her. The taxi delivered her to the safe house, where she met Command Sergeant Major Pashtoon and Command Sergeant Major Azizyar.

The next morning, after a long and restless night, they took a taxi to the Panjshir pumping station—a closed gas station—on the north side of HKIA. The station was near a gate rumored to be sealed shut but was in fact open for rare, CIA-approved exfiltrations. There was a bus at the station. When Basira, Pashtoon, and Azizyar filed on, dozens of faces turned toward them—a large group of Afghan commandos and NMRG, along with their families, were already there. Everyone was waiting to be let into HKIA through the secret gate. Peering through the mesh of the burqa, Basira found a seat and waited.

82

Zac Lois's house was quiet. His wife, Amanda, and their two boys were asleep. Zac was thinking about the past—but not his past in Afghanistan. Harriet Tubman, the Underground Railroad conductor whose likeness hung on the wall of his eighth-grade social studies classroom, had inspired him to look at the problem of trapped Afghans in a new way. Tubman had helped ferry enslaved people to freedom in the nineteenth century, so why couldn't a bunch of former special operators do the same for Afghans today? He had a name for the idea that was taking shape in his mind: Operation Harriet. She had gotten her passengers to safety by telling them to travel at night on certain days such as Sundays, when their absence wouldn't be noticed immediately, and using the North Star to find waypoints. There was no reason that the shepherds of Pineapple couldn't adopt the same kinds of tactics. They just lacked what Harriet had—"conductors" to physically bring the passengers into HKIA.

Zac paused for a moment to consider the phone call he was about to make. Liv had passed him Captain John Folta's number, and Scott had tasked him with making the call. Hopefully the paratroop officer would agree to be a conductor. He *had* to—it was the missing link. It all depended on his agreeing to do it.

Zac dialed. John answered on the first ring.

"Hi, Captain Folta, I got your number from Liv Gardner with Congressman Waltz's office. Do you have a minute?"

"I'm pretty busy—"

Zac risked cutting him off. "My name is Captain Zac Lois, I'm a 7th

Group guy. I know you're busy, but I wanted to see if I could coordinate with you on some exfils we are working on?"

There was a pause. "Go on," John said.

"I'm with a volunteer group called Task Force Pineapple. We've been moving small numbers of highly vetted Afghan SOF brothers into HKIA, but we need to move larger numbers, including families, in the next couple of days," Zac told him.

"I might be able to help a little bit," John offered. "Security is our first priority, but we do have a mechanism in the vicinity of Abbey Gate to pull people from the crowd. We haven't really used it yet."

"Great," said Zac. "How do we connect to it?"

"We position ourselves offset from the main Abbey Gate guard tower, along the sewage canal that runs parallel to the Abbey Gate perimeter. Your exfils will have to come during the night and wade across the concrete sewage canal," the captain continued, "allowing them to bypass the massive in-process line. From there, we can move them through a hole in the fence and right to processing at the State Department facility across the airfield. We have the trucks, contacts, and everything to do that. Reaching the trench and crossing it is the tricky part, and that's on your people. I can relay exact coordinates for where they need to go into the trench. Then we can meet them at the right place and the right time on the other side, exchange far and near-recognition signals, and pull them in."

Zac furiously scribbled notes.

"Great. Who's at Abbey Gate?"

"Marines. We're working closely with them. If they're cool about us moving through their line and pulling people in, we can do it. But if the security posture is high, it won't work. And like I said, we have security tasks that are the priority. If we're free and available, I'll contact you, and we can go to work when windows present themselves."

Zac could barely contain himself. "Can I just talk hypothetical logistics with you if you have another minute?"

"Sure."

Zac described his underground railroad plan. "You and your guys would be the 'conductors' of the railroad," he told John. Zac would be the "engineer," personally providing the paratroopers with information about vetted individuals—interpreters, commandos, ANA Special Forces, Afghan officials, along with their families. He would text names, photos, and the number of people in each exfil group directly to John on single-page "baseball cards." Zac could also suggest time windows for those families to present themselves to John and his people. "What do you think? Did I miss anything?"

Another pause as John processed and did some on-the-spot planning. "Tell your people this has to happen after dark. That's when things calm down a little. Tell the Afghans that when they get to the canal near Abbey Gate, they should look for a green glow stick—one of our guys will wear one at the linkup point, which will be the bridge over the canal. When they get to the far side of the shit trench, they will hold up some kind of unique graphic on their smartphone. My 'conductors,' as you're calling them, will then call out the Afghan's name. The conductor will check this and the number in their party. If it all matches what you send me in advance, he'll tell them to enter the trench and approach on the other side. Our guys will count them through, search them, load them into our trucks, and move them to processing and departure."

"Can we run it tonight?" Zac asked, almost giddy.

"Why not?" John agreed. "Let's give it a try."

83

Zac pored over Task Force Pineapple's HKIA maps. Toy bulldozers and race car tracks littered the living room floor between the counter and a widescreen TV tuned to CNN reporting frequent updates on the mayhem in Kabul. His laptop displayed a fast-moving stream of messages while Signal notifications pinged over and over on his phone. Pineapple was humming. A small whiteboard, the headline *OP HARRIET* scrawled on top, listed Afghans who headed each flock, the number of family members in each group, and black check marks under columns headlined *Plan*, *Pics*, and *Abbey*.

One of these names belonged to his former translator, Mohammad Rahimi. There also was a group of three Special Forces guys Zac had never met: Salaam, Faizi, and Latif. He'd gotten these names from another Afghan operator, and Nezam had vouched for them. Salaam would travel to Abbey Gate with his brother-in-law, Iqbal, and his family. Zac's loyal partner, Taqi, who had been at his side in combat, was also on the list.

So many lives were in Zac's hands. He was pretty sure that Operation Harriet was a viable system—an "underground railroad"—for bringing Afghans into HKIA, but it hadn't been tested.

He went over the plan one more time in his head. The map and GPS pin Zac had dropped into TF Pineapple showed a spot along the airport's southeastern yard's perimeter, in the vicinity of Abbey Gate guard tower known as the Turkish Tower (before this sector was handed to the Marines and 82nd Airborne, Turkish forces controlled it). It was no longer a gate exactly, but a chain-link fence about fifty yards long, running southwest from the guard tower along a concrete-walled canal—the "shit trench," as John had dubbed it. About forty meters from the Turkish Tower was the spot in the chain-lilnk fence where British soldiers had snipped the hole for Jussi to pull through Finnish nationals, tying near it a bright orange cloth panel about two feet long and one foot wide.

Outside the fence was a foot path that ran along the top of the canal. About 450 feet to the northeast of the hole lay a wide footbridge that spanned the canal. A barrier of coiled concertina wire blocked the footbridge from pedestrian traffic that would ordinarily have been able to cross to the airport side. The bridge was the lookout point where the conductors like John would be stationed, scanning the crowds on the opposite side and down in the muck itself. From the walkway, the paratroopers could pull people up from the trench and onto the footpath. It was then just an easy walk to the gap in the fence, and into HKIA. He picked up his phone and called Scott.

84

After Scott's flight from Kentucky touched down in Tampa, he went to his office to meet his former Green Beret friend Mark and the three men accompanying him. They clasped hands, laughing, greeting one another as if no time had passed. Together, they drove to a larger office covered in whiteboards that one of Scott's clients had given them unlimited access to. They settled in. Scott briefed them for an hour, and then spent another two hours answering questions.

Then Mark said, "We got this. Go home." He led Scott to the door. "We'll call you when we're finished."

Scott's phone rang soon afterward. It was the new guy, Zac Lois.

"I've been on the phone with Liv's 82nd Airborne contact, Captain Folta. We made a plan. It's pretty aggressive. I call it Operation Harriet."

"Operation *what*?" Scott asked.

"Operation Harriet—as in Tubman. See, I'm an eighth-grade social studies teacher—she was the former slave who helped run the Underground Railroad before the Civil War. She had really good tradecraft. I think we will, too. At least, if it works."

"I know who she is, man. I'm just intrigued by the plan. Go on," Scott said.

Zac explained everything he and John had discussed. "Instead of an oil lamp in a conductor's hand guiding enslaved people through the darkness, it'll be a paratrooper on the wall with a green chem light looking for an iPhone screen with a bright yellow graphic, like all the penalty cards I used to get in rugby," Zac said. "It worked in 1857. I think it'll work in 2021, too."

There was only one choice. "You've got the lead on this," Scott said. "I'm here for whatever you need. Work your plan."

Operation Harriet. It was an audacious idea, an underground railroad to ferry Afghans to safety. Scott had to hand it to Zac—he had come up with a brilliant tactical framework that seemed like it would work, if all the pieces came together on the ground. A big if. But they still needed a big-picture strategy, the operational framework to make the gritty work on the ground in Kabul manageable within the Task Force Pineapple chat room.

Mark found the answer to that. When Scott was called back to see his friends' work, they'd covered every inch of the whiteboards. The men had planned out the operation in the same way Special Forces staff would plan a tricky mission for a commander.

Mark walked him through their work. He started with the mission essential capability that DoD didn't seem to have right now. "Pineapple shepherds—guys like you and Zac here in the States—know the location and the status of their flocks—Afghans in need. Each shepherd knows who's at risk and where their people are in Kabul, and these flocks trust you—and only you—to help move them. This is what Task Force Pineapple can do that none of the government agencies can—not DoD, not State. No one." He went from board to board, tapping on each one. "These are your five focal points to accomplish your goal. Operational focus. Vetting. External communications. Situational awareness. Managing crises and moving fast to pivot as the operation changes." He explained each one in detail and how to adapt them to the limited focus of a Signal chat room. Mark turned to face Scott. "What do you think?"

Scott was stunned, barely able to breathe. These men had created an architecture for a type of digital task force that could adapt to rapid growth and continue to move people en masse out of Kabul. No way he would have been able to structure this on his own. He had been too consumed with the tactical tempo. "I don't know how to thank you guys," he finally said.

"Hey, you were the one who taught me this stuff back in the day," Mark said with a grin. He grew more serious. "But, listen, you need to treat this like a military operation," Mark said, holding up his hand. "That's the only way it will work. Set right and left limits for the members. Use discipline in your communication to people inside HKIA. Limit calls to those guys in HKIA to a few key communicators in Pineapple. There's risk here, a lot of risk, for everyone involved, because this is unprecedented governmental inaction. The scale of the private effort is massive. Focus on the humanitarian side of this. Don't get sidetracked by other efforts like a resistance. No politics either. That will sink you guys in a heartbeat. Your job is to responsibly put as many of the right people as you can into the hands of the right people—people at HKIA who are willing to pull them in. There's no time for anything else."

Scott thanked his ghost staff. They shook hands, and then they disappeared, back to the airport and back to their lives serving the nation.

85

Salaam's fate rested in the hands of the man he had never met in person: a former Green Beret he knew only as Captain Zac. One of Salaam's Afghan SF brothers had vouched for Captain Zac, and that was all he needed. Now his family's life was in Captain Zac's hands.

Salaam had been instructed to go to a GPS pin and wait for the go-ahead to move toward Abbey Gate with his family. Salaam's brother-in-law, who had sheltered them all in Kabul, was with him. He also had his family. In addition to these flesh-and-blood relations were two of Salaam's brothers in arms—Faizi and Latif. They had their families, too. In all, this flock of Zac's numbered sixteen people.

Salaam was twenty-eight years old and had been in the Afghan Special Forces for eleven years. His entire adult life had been spent waging counterterrorism ops with the Americans. He was a short and skinny operator who had risen to become a team sergeant. In mid-July—just a month earlier—he had received a battlefield commission. He'd led his men into combat in Daykundi province right up to August 15, the day that President Ghani fled Afghanistan.

That evening, Salaam sent his men home and drove to Kabul to join his family. There he met Latif and Faizi, who had fought to the last round in Wardak. They sheltered together in Kabul. The U.S. government was making no effort to help soldiers like Salaam, Faizi, and Latif. Salaam pleaded with every American he ever fought alongside, and these pleas had led Salaam to Captain Zac.

Scott Mann's combat operations, including this one in Oruzgan province in Afghanistan in April 2004, helped him develop a deep bond with his Afghan partner forces.

Nezam's Afghan Special Forces patch identifies him as a member of the group that was trained and equipped almost as mirror images of their American comrades.

Scott and a young Nezam after completing a combat patrol during Village Stability Operations in Khakrez District in Kandahar province in June 2010.

Nezam (left), photographed with a fellow Afghan Commando during a combat operation in 2017; note the captured Taliban AK-47 slung over his shoulder.

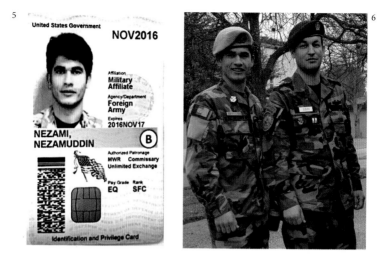

Left: Nezam achieved unprecedented trust within the U.S. military as an Afghan Special Forces partner. He even obtained his own U.S. military ID card while training at Special Forces schools in America.

Right: Nezam (left) and Major Abdul Jamil Malikzai were both part of the first group of Afghans to attend the Q Course at Fort Bragg. In 2018, Major Malikzai was assassinated by the Taliban in Kabul. TF Pineapple moved his widow and children out of Afghanistan after the U.S. withdrawal in 2021.

Left: Hafizullah—known as "Mustache"—was a member of the Afghan National Mine Reduction Group, the "guardian angels" of U.S. Special Forces in Afghanistan.

Right: Afghan Special Forces operator Salaam, like many others the author interviewed, fought to the last round until his government collapsed on August 15, 2021. He and his family were among the first group of passengers on the Pineapple Express.

9

Left: Green Berets forged partnerships that ran deep. Retired Colonel Matt Coburn (right) trained countless Afghan National Army units over his six deployments.

Right: Students in Zac Lois's eighth grade social studies class might not recognize the Green Beret "Captain Zac" here conducting village stability operations in the treacherous mountains of Sha Wali Khot in 2013.

Left: Master Sergeant Basira Baghrani (left) was the pride of the Afghan National Army, and one of the most prominent Afghan women to cast off cultural shackles and serve her country. General Austin "Scotty" Miller (second from right) was the NATO and U.S. Forces commander in Afghanistan until July 2021.

Right: Zac Lois (left) and his interpreter Mohammad Rahimi (center) forged bonds in combat that led to Zac's "Hail Mary" post on August 20.

The remote combat outpost securing the state-of-the-art Bayat power plant in Sheberghan, nestled in the far northern reaches of Afghanistan, should have been the last place Nezam would have to worry about the Taliban hunting him down.

"If you fight, you will win," Nezam (in ball cap) told Shebergan police officials during a last-ditch June 2021 meeting. He implored them to stand up to the encroaching Taliban.

Left: Fearing his camp would be overrun and he would be executed at any minute, Nezam made a video explaining his dire situation in Sheberghan. He feared this might be his last message to the world.

Right: A Covid mask covering his true emotions, an elated Nezam prepares to board an Afghan MI-17 out of Sheberghan.

Flanked by Commandos, Nezam (in *shalwar kameez*) poses with the friend who got him out of Sheberghan, Lieutenant-Colonel Zamarai Noorzai.

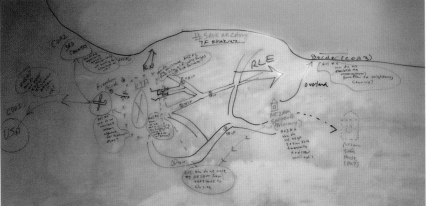

Scott used a whiteboard to sketch out a "scheme of maneuver" to get Nezam out of Kabul. On another next to it, he mapped out the small team that would rally to help Nezam find safe passage to America.

Arriving at HKIA on August 15, 2021, the paratroopers of Charlie Company, 2nd battalion, 504th Parachute Infantry Regiment ("White Devils") commandeered a fleet of abandoned vehicles to aid them in securing the airfield. The firetruck is driven by First Sergeant Jesse Kennedy.

On August 14, 2021, only hours before the Taliban engulfed Kabul, embassy personnel were being evacuated on a CH-46 "Frog" (visible in the background) while a literal dumpster fire burned in an effort to destroy massive amounts of sensitive and classified information.

From Nezam's view of East Gate on August 19, 2021, he watched as National Strike Unit 02 violently secured the airport perimeter. Their distinctive tiger stripes identified them as the CIA-paid paramilitary force that had previously been based in Jalalabad.

At 4:32 p.m., still outside HKIA, Nezam sent a selfie to the team to email to U.S. embassy officials and marines at East Gate so they could recognize him in the vast crowd.

23

Sergeant Jason Milstead of the 82nd Airborne was spotted by Finnish Special Envoy Jussi Tanner inside HKIA as he held a newborn Afghan. The action helped Jason cope with post-traumatic stress triggered by the last of many Afghanistan deployments.

24

25

Left: CIA paramilitary forces from the National Strike Units are shown being transported to HKIA during the August 2021 evacuation.

Right: Three hundred feet south of the Turkish Tower at Abbey Gate, British soldiers cut a hole in the chain-link fence for Jussi Tanner. This hole, marked with orange VS-17 signal cloth, became the key to the Pineapple Express.

On August 20, Jussi was trying to bring two Afghan women of special interest through the old Abbey Gate. Minutes later, he had the hole in the fence cut.

Jussi escorting three Afghan children away from Abbey Gate.

Afghan Minister of Women's Affairs Hasina Safi with First Sergeant Jesse Kennedy (left) and paratroopers from Charlie Company after he helped her and her family into HKIA on August 23, 2021.

Left: Captain John Folta (second from left), aka "Captain Red Sunglasses," and his paratroopers brought this group of Afghan special operations forces and family members into HKIA on the Pineapple Express in the early afternoon on August 26, 2021, just hours before the ISIS-K bomb detonated at Abbey Gate.

Right: Hafi sees a sniper rifle poking out of the open window of the "Turkish Tower" on August 23, 2021.

2:00 p.m. on August 24, 2021: U.S. Marines and NATO forces (left) stand on the wall of the sewage canal near Abbey Gate, which is clogged with Afghan civilians and former military members.

The man standing at the far left marks the spot where, only fifty-two hours after this photograph was taken, the ISIS-K bomb would explode, killing many of the people clogging the sewage canal in hopes of escaping Afghanistan.

This still from a U.S. drone video over Abbey Gate, taken minutes after the ISIS-K bombing at 5:36:52 p.m., shows Charlie Company providing trauma aide by the Turkish Tower, while a strike team aims rifles out from the retaining wall.

This slide from a two-thousand-page Centcom report on the Abbey Gate bombing shows the location of the ISIS-K blast and a view of what TF Pineapple shepherds called the "shit trench," as well as the bridge link-up site.

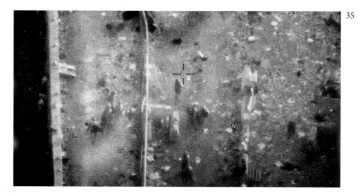

This still, taken right after the blast from drone video recorded directly over the Turkish Tower and chain-link fence, shows a U.S. service member carrying a wounded comrade on his back (far left) before ducking and passing through the hole in the fence.

Matt Coburn visits Afghan refugees in December 2021 in New Cumberland, Pennsylvania. Standing is Basira Baghrani. At the table is Command Sergeant Major Roheedullah Azizyar. Azizyar's son sits on Matt's lap.

Thanksgiving 2021: Zac Lois (right) and his wife Amanda (far left) host Mohammad Rahimi and his family for a celebratory dinner. The Rahimi's are resettled nearby in the Syracuse area.

Scott's Rooftop Leadership team made posters to welcome the Nezamis (Hassam, Hawa, and Elham with their mother, Uldoz, at back) to Tampa in February 2022.

Nezam and his friend and former commander, Scott Mann, are at Scott's home in Riverview, Florida. Today, they are neighbors, just as Scott promised.

Scott introduces Nezam's children to fishing on his pier on the Alafia River.

Elham, 11, supervises as Hassam, 6, and Hawa, 8, surprise Scott and his wife Monty with sketches of their family and American flags.

Now, as darkness fell, they were traveling from different points by taxi to a staging area designated by Captain Zac. Their phones were charged, and they had the bright yellow picture ready to show the soldiers near Abbey Gate. *After the sun sets,* Captain Zac texted, *and when the conductor is in place, you'll slip away from the crowd with your family to this location.* This was followed by another GPS pin, along with photos of the site.

> The conductor will signal you with a green light. When you see it, move closer and hold up the yellow screen on your phone. The conductor will then call out for your name and the number of people in your party. Once he checks it against the information I've sent him, he will summon you forward.

Zac had concluded the message with a threat update of a possible ISIS-K suicide bomber in the crowd, a map of Taliban checkpoints, and a warning to stay alert and be ready to move.

All Salaam and his people could do until then was wait.

Salaam stood beneath the wide branches of a tree in the darkness. Everyone in his large flock of sixteen people had converged on a residential side street near the HKIA terminal. They looked ordinary. The women wore hijabs and the men wore traditional shalwar kameez, scarves, and vests. Each family had used taxis to get close and then shuffled to the rendezvous one by one, staying away from the crowds on Airport Road, where the Taliban were firing their Kalashnikovs in the air.

Taxi horns beeped. A dog barked. The children in their group were restless and scared. Captain Zac had texted each man—Salaam, Latif, and Faizi—saying, *Wait for my signal to go.*

That time had come.

This is the plan, Zac texted. *I spoke to the American captain near Abbey Gate. People are getting through the gate slowly. They're going to try bringing you in.*

Salaam texted him a map, a GPS pin marking their location.

SALAAM
We are here. Moving forward.

ZAC
Send me a picture of everyone in your group and I will send it to the captain now.

Salaam and his friends used his iPhone to take pictures of each family member. In turn, Zac sent a pin drop of a spot near Abbey Gate.

ZAC
Get to this coordinate. This is the linkup point. The captain's men will meet you there.

SALAAM
Understood.

It sounded straightforward, but before they could get to the canal, they had to leave the staging area and cross the crowds—and the Taliban checkpoints.

They set off toward Abbey Gate. The Taliban had little control over the crowds. They'd placed Hiluxes and makeshift barricades made of large conex shipping containers in the road to try to slow the surge of people, but it wasn't working. Salaam's group pushed forward, and he felt his heart race; he squeezed his four-year-old son's hand. His wife cradled their infant, while his brother-in-law, Iqbal, carried Salaam's three-year-old daughter, who wore a purple jumper.

I cannot fail them, Salaam thought, silently rehearsing the story he would tell the Taliban if he were stopped. *I am an electrical engineer and a contractor at military bases, not a soldier.*

They were now within arm's reach of a Taliban checkpoint, but none of the Taliban asked any questions.

Instead, they began beating them.

A wire cable whipped Salaam's back with an awful sting. *Motherfucker!* he thought. Another Talib bastard struck his wife with an open palm. Latif was lost in a blur of wincing blows that landed on him, Faizi, and Iqbal. Half a dozen armed fighters had taken to beating them, using fists, the wire whips, and rubber batons. Salaam and the other men shielded the children, taking the brunt of each strike.

"Keep moving!" Salaam yelled. "Forward!"

"Traitors!" the Talibs screamed—but they weren't screaming it at Salaam and his group, they were screaming it at everyone trying to flee the country. The beating wasn't necessarily directed at them, it was more like they had to pass through it, as one might walk through a waterfall to get to a hidden tunnel.

Just as suddenly as the beating began, it ended. They were past their attackers, with other civilians on the far side of the Hiluxes, but not yet inside the HKIA wire.

For a moment, Salaam feared he'd lose his son in the melee, but he had held his trembling little hand tight, and now took a head count—everyone was there—and directed them toward another side street away from the crowded road. They rubbed their welts and spoke quietly. Over their shoulder, another large American C-17 lifted into the air, as if thumbing its nose at them. It was undoubtedly full of Afghans who were now free.

"Up until a week ago, *we* were the ones going after *them*," Faizi said in a rage-fueled whisper, his head shaking. He rubbed a tender red spot on his cheekbone from a Talib club.

Salaam felt a throbbing pain across his back.

"We hunted them, and they were scared of us," Salaam hissed. "Now they're beating us. This is the worst fucking day of my life."

86

Zac paced his kitchen, flipping back and forth from Fox to CNN to MSNBC, looking for any news from Kabul as his operation unfolded. But the crowds, the Taliban checkpoints, the unending panic—a gauntlet of obstacles were keeping his flocks out in the open. Mohammad Rahimi and his family had been camped out near North Gate for three days, trying unsuccessfully to convince the soldiers at the gate to let them enter, before giving up and going home. Zac worried that all the families he had in motion would get hurt—maybe fatally.

But what's the alternative? he asked himself. *Murdered in their homes?*

His phone buzzed. It was Salaam. He, Latif, Faizi, and their families had made it past two Taliban checkpoints. They were bruised and a little bloodied, but alive. They were also closer to the GPS pin indicating the friendly U.S. forces. Their IDs hadn't been examined by the Taliban and their bags had been left untouched, which surprised Zac. Salaam said the flock was trying to flank the crowd by walking a half mile around a fortified compound adjacent to the Baron Hotel, attempting to approach HKIA's perimeter from a side road.

ZAC
OK, when you get there, look for a green light across the sewage canal. A captain is coming to find you. He will be calling your name.

SALAAM
OK.

ZAC
Captain Folta is his name. Stay quiet and don't call out 'til you get close to his green light.

Zac calculated that Salaam's half-mile detour would take about ten minutes—maybe twenty with all the kids they had in their group.

After half an hour without word, Zac began to worry. He texted them again.

Move to the green light if you see it.

Nothing. It was now past midnight in Kabul. *I would kill to have drone video right now*, Zac thought. The only sound he heard was the tick-tock of the second hand on an antique clock in the foyer.

It felt like Harriet was heading for failure.

87

Salaam led his flock away from the crowds, staying in the shadows on a mostly empty road that passed the old Camp Sullivan compound next to the Baron Hotel. The hotel was still being secured by British troops and remained a gathering place for foreigners needing exfil. The families huddled there while Faizi went up the lane alone to scout out Captain Zac's linkup site.

Salaam waited with the families, his heart in his throat. After about twenty minutes, Faizi texted that he could see the green light, but that he had gotten caught inside the crowd and couldn't easily move out of it to cross the long concrete sewage canal that would get them close to Captain Zac's GPS pin.

Salaam texted Captain Zac.

> **SALAAM**
> We see the green light. We are near the bridge.

> **ZAC**
> Move towards it. Move quickly and quietly.

> **SALAAM**
> We can't move. There are a lot of people.

> **ZAC**
> Make sure you are at the pin-drop map location.

> **SALAAM**
> Yes, we are near Abbey Gate. Faizi is close and sees a Marine.

> **ZAC**
> That's probably our 82nd ABN guys. Are you able to talk to him?

SALAAM
No. Lot of people.

ZAC
Send me a picture of your location. I need to confirm.

Salaam took a picture, but when he went to send it, he had no signal. It had suddenly dropped. He tried to message Faizi, too, but nothing was transmitting. "Stay calm, everything is fine," he reassured his family. "I'm going forward to find Faizi. We'll try to contact the captain. Don't move until one of us comes for you or Latif says so." He wrapped his black-and-gray-checked scarf around his head to shroud his face and jogged up the road toward the airport.

Floodlights from behind the wire cast eerily long shadows of the crowd. He went near the GPS pin and found Faizi, who indicated a soldier waving a green glow stick like a sentinel at the footbridge crossing the canal—the meeting point. "I have not observed the enemy near here, only civilians," Faizi said.

Just then, their phones regained their signals.

Salaam texted Zac. *Network is slow. I see him now, CPT Zac.*

They're using cell phone jammers, I think that's why, Zac responded. *How close can you get to the American? He is at the little bridge standing on it next to the concertina wire. Move to him. Say Captain Zac sent you.*

Salaam, the highest-ranking officer in the group, instructed Faizi to return to their families and bring them here.

He turned around. As much as he wanted to, he couldn't cross the bridge. There were just too many people. *Fuck it,* he thought. He got to his knees and dropped down the canal's concrete wall and into the filth. The shin-deep muck was rank and thick. He wished he had worn something more substantial than his leather sandals. He pushed a handful of his scarf over his mouth and nose, the acrid odors stinging his nostrils.

Once he committed, he reached the soldier on the other side within only a few minutes. He held up his phone as high as he could, showing the bright yellow card Captain Zac had sent. The soldier with the green light above him on the embankment acknowledged him, then reached down for his hand. The soldier heaved and pulled Salaam out of the sewage and up onto the footpath on the other side.

"I am from Captain Zac, sir," Salaam said. "We have our families nearby. They are ready."

The soldier grinned. "Roger that. Let's get them over here and inside the airfield." Salaam could make out his captain's bars in the green glow of his chem light and a name tape that read FOLTA in black letters. "Yes, sir." He texted Faizi to bring everyone forward. Then his phone flashed a new text from Captain Zac.

Are you with the captain?

Captain Folta asked Salaam for his phone, and he handed it over.

88

Amanda narrowed her eyes as she watched Zac from the kitchen. He had been flitting around his sloppy workstation like a mad professor for twenty minutes and hadn't looked up once to acknowledge her presence. He fussed over Post-it notes, marked stuff on his dry erase board, and occasionally sat down long enough to speak to somebody on his cell phone. He was manic, scurrying around like he was on an episode of *Homeland*.

He hadn't showered in days. She could smell him from here. His beard was so unkempt his own children barely recognized him. It was happening again. The ghosts were back.

She knew he was saving people in Afghanistan, and she was beyond proud of him for what he was willing to do. But it wasn't what they had agreed on. Zac voluntarily chose to leave that world behind in 2014, ready to build a new life without the military puppeteer dictating his every move. Together they had started a family and repaired the damage war had done.

But not all wounds heal, and bringing the hell of Afghanistan into their quiet New York home was never part of the plan.

This was the government's problem. They weren't her promises to keep. Was anyone else fighting to protect the sanctity of their marriage, of their commitments to each other and their children? Was anyone else trying to keep the ghosts of Afghanistan from destroying their home? The Special Forces community was filled with forums discussing the despair and suicides of veterans. Damn if she was going to let that happen on her watch. If being a bitch was how she kept her husband alive and protected her children from the nightmares, then so be it. Nobody sends a casualty affairs officer to thank you for your husband's valiant service when you're no longer on their payroll.

She hurried out of the room. If she was going to cry, it was going to be in private.

The Army and the government hadn't been there when he came home broken inside. She was the one there when this peaceful, beautiful man stared out the window at distant bloody poppy fields that only he could see. She was the one who calmed him after the night terrors. She was the one who whispered softly to him when the war came violently out of nowhere in a public place. She had been the one who assured him through debilitating self-doubt during his first days as a social studies teacher that this was what he was born to do and that there was no one who could be better at it.

This was their life now; they had built it together. They had fought so hard for it. They'd moved beyond the ghosts, but now they were back in full force.

Just yesterday, Zac had suggested not returning to his teaching job to keep helping Afghans. Would these "Pineapple shepherds" be around when the demons came and took him back into the dark places?

She took a deep breath.

Zac had asked Amanda to watch their sons a bit longer, but she knew in doing that, she was helping him back onto the path of depression and isolation that had crushed him so badly after he left the Special Forces. That was the choice left to her. If she didn't take extra duties with the kids, the house, and hold space for him to do whatever crazy-ass schemes he was working, then innocent people would die.

She sighed again, wiped the tears with her palms, and straightened her back as she'd done countless times in the long war with the ghosts.

The boys would be waking up from their naps soon, and Zac would disappear into the guest bedroom to continue his endless uphill battle.

She pulled out her phone to check that she still had the number for the therapist, wondering if the practice had a two-for-one rate.

89

Zac was about to type another message when his phone pinged.

> **SALAAM**
> Zac, it's John Folta on Salaam's phone. Salaam is with me. We are working on a solution to get them all across.

> **ZAC**
> OUTSTANDING!!!!!

> **SALAAM**
> Thanks, sir. We are inside. God bless you.

Zac let out a whoop and typed the good news into the Pineapple Signal room.

90

Faizi hurried away from Salaam into the darkness. Even in the early-morning hours, people still clustered around the airport's perimeter, a slow churning movement, pushing like a current along the closed-off road alongside the trench. He shouldered his way through, moving as fast as he could without attracting attention.

The crowd thinned as he moved onto a side street leading away from the airport. He slipped quickly down the road, skirting the northern side of Camp Sullivan to his right and the back lot of the Baron Hotel to his left, where a helipad lay on the other side of the fence. He saw fewer people as he moved toward the airport's industrial outskirts of empty warehouses and still streets. He didn't know what the shadows might hide. The streets around him were quieter, but he could feel the city's unease, a crackling sense of chaos.

On missions, he always knew where he was going, what his task was, and how he would achieve it. This was different. The city was upside down, and he felt hunted, like prey. Cell phone coverage was spotty; if he disappeared, no one would ever know.

It took no more than ten minutes to reach the spot where the families were waiting. Latif was glad to greet his fellow operator and learn there was a plan.

The children were asleep, sprawled on the crowd of adults keeping vigil at the bags. At a signal from Latif, they quickly woke the children and set off. Retracing Faizi's steps took much longer with the sleepy children, but they soon were back among the airport crowds.

The families clung tightly to one another as they shouldered their way to the side of the canal. Salaam was there, standing beside a U.S. soldier with a green chemlight dangling from a cord around his neck. He beckoned them on. They were so close now.

Faizi and Latif went down into the ditch, splashing into the fetid water, then reaching up to grab the children and carry them across. One by one they brought them over. Then the last adults lowered themselves in, waded the fifteen feet or so to the other side, and grabbed the hands that reached down for them. Up and down the trench, people watched in disbelief as the soldiers brought them up.

"I'm Captain Folta," the soldier with the green light said to Faizi as he stepped up, the last of sixteen Afghans. The paratrooper looked over each member of the flock, checking them against a document on his phone. "Come on in," he said. Other soldiers near the fence searched them, one nametag read "Kennedy," and then they were guided toward the hole in the fence marked with the orange cloth.

PART IV

THE
LONG
NIGHT

91

Zac allowed himself to smile for about a minute and then got back to work. Operation Harriet had worked.

At around 7:00 p.m., he posted a photo John Folta had sent to him of the three Afghan Special Forces operators and their families that had just successfully ridden on the Pineapple Express. John, Jesse, and Doc Gundy stood side by side with Salaam, Faizi, and Latif in the dark, illuminated by the headlights of a truck. Sixteen Afghans had gotten to safety. Eight were children, and a few looked to be about the same age as Zac's boys. Four massive C-17 Globemaster airplanes and a single C-130 cargo plane filled the background.

Scott texted Zac: *That's some legit Green Beret shit right there, brother.*

With Salaam and his flock in HKIA, Zac turned to the other names on his board. One of them was Mohammad Rahimi. His former translator had camped near Abbey Gate starting on August 16. His family had spent three grueling days baking in the blistering heat, hemmed in by the crowds and random bursts of deadly force. More than one person had died right before his family's eyes. Mohammad had tried to be helpful to the U.S. Marines, hoping to gain enough of their trust that they would admit him, but they had largely ignored him. Finally, on August 19, he gave up, returning with his family to their rented apartment.

Zac felt certain that Mohammad's flock should be next. They *had* to be. They had a system, and while complications were inevitable—as John guaranteed—they now had proof. Operation Harriet was viable.

92

Hasina Safi felt sick: the Afghan Ministry of Women's Affairs was now the Ministry of Virtue and Vice. Before the United States toppled the Taliban in 2001, this had been the agency responsible for the beatings and executions of Afghan women deemed to have violated Sharia law. Like the Taliban, it was back, and it was occupying her building.

It won't be long before crowds are stoning women to death in the Kabul soccer stadium again, Hasina thought. She had been one of the most respected women in Afghanistan, and now she was one of the most wanted.

She hoped to remain in her country and help Afghan women, but that was impossible. Perhaps, outside her country, she could speak up again for the women she so believed in. But first she would have to lead her family through the obstacles between her and a flight to freedom. She remembered what her father had taught her: "There is no taste in life if there are no challenges." But what she faced now weren't just hurdles—the Taliban victory had put up an insurmountable wall before her.

She had a British visa that would get her on a flight to London, but no clear way to get into HKIA. A colleague and friend from the United States, Kelley Eckles Currie, ambassador-at-large for global women's issues during the Trump administration, had told her the day after Kabul fell, "Since you have a British visa, if we can get you through the gate, we can probably push you right through on a flight to the UK."

Hasina had grown up as a refugee in Pakistan after her family fled the Soviet invasion. So be it. She would be a refugee again.

Hasina made arrangements for her whole group of ten—including her husband, son, two daughters, mother, and mother-in-law—to get picked up and taken to the gate outside the Baron Hotel, a fortified compound adjacent to HKIA that was protected by British forces. But first they had to get there. A loyal bodyguard drove them as close as possible, and then they pushed into the crowds.

The women were shrouded in black, and the men wore humble, traditional clothing. But it didn't matter. They were stopped by the Taliban. They hadn't identified Hasina, thank God, but they still whipped her husband and young son with canes and rubber hoses. Her sixty-nine-year-old mother-in-law was slapped in the face.

Hasina's young daughter pleaded, "Mother, please, we cannot stay here. Take us home!"

They couldn't make it. They turned around and left.

93

Kelley Currie's hopes withered when she received news that Hasina had failed to get into HKIA. It was insane to Kelley that one of the highest-ranking women in Afghanistan, someone who faced certain punishment and even death at the hands of the Taliban, had been left to fight alone for her and her family's safety. Kelley had tried everything to get the White House and Department to notice Hasina's plight, but she'd had no success. Finally, a friend and Biden administration official told her, "You're wasting time with these lists that State keeps asking for. They're going into a black hole. The only thing that's working is the ad hoc groups."

Kelley reached out to everyone she could think of in D.C. She had been doing all she could to get at-risk women out, but she'd been told that a group of military veterans seemed to be having the most success at penetrating the complex security structure at HKIA. She called her friend Liv Gardner.

"Hey, Liv. I'm trying to help a lot of civil-society at-risk women like Hasina Safi get to safety. Can you help me connect to this 'bro network' I've been hearing so much about?"

"They might be able to get her out," Liv said. She explained that Task Force Pineapple—which Kelley had jokingly called "the bro network"—had just gotten three families to safety inside HKIA. Liv believed this would be the best—and quickest—way to get Hasina's flock out, too.

There was a complication, however. Unlike Nezam or any of the other Afghan Special Forces soldiers, she had no training and no experience operating in chaotic tactical situations. Worse than this, the former minister had a deep-seated fear of soldiers, a primal anxiety stemming from her childhood spent as a refugee, always running from the armed men who would do her and her loved ones harm.

Hasina would have to deal with soldiers if she wanted to escape.

Kelley weighed the risk. Given Hasina's high profile, it would have been suicide for her to attempt to run the gauntlet at the gates. She and her family couldn't spend a day or more pushing through the crowd and waving paperwork in the air, evading thieves and the crush of the crowd, all while trying to avoid the Taliban. They had been beaten on their previous attempt. If Hasina was recognized, she would be dragged away to prison.

Kelley made the decision for Hasina: the only way out was to trust this faceless group called Task Force Pineapple. She texted Liv and asked her to put it in motion.

Liv called Jesse at HKIA. As Zac had done before with John Folta, they went through all the details for how Hasina and her family would get into the airport. The approach routes. The obstacles. The sewage trench. The green light. The yellow card on the phone.

Kelley would be Hasina's shepherd. Liv would have to get this exactly right, precisely as Jesse described. She repeated the process one more time.

"That's it," Jesse said.

"Good. Her shepherd, Kelley Currie, will be in touch soon." Then Liv hung up and called Kelley to pass on the instructions.

94

Shortly after midnight, First Sergeant Jesse Kennedy signaled to Doc Gundy that it was time to go. He checked his equipment, making sure his weapon and kit were in order. Attention to detail had kept him alive in Iraq—it would keep him and his men alive here. He double-checked the information Liv had sent him about this incoming flock, Hasina Safi and her family, studying their photos and documents.

Jesse and Doc Gundy drove to Abbey Gate, where they parked their vehicles. They went the rest of the way on foot, passing through a concrete corridor. Jesse and John had decided they could pull more Afghans in if they worked independently when possible. John would take his radio operator with him on his runs, while Jesse would take Doc Gundy. When things got busy, the two would work together to pull more in.

As they got closer to the perimeter, the sound of the crowd outside grew louder. They approached a Marine on duty. "What's up, man? We're going to pull some more people tonight. How's the security posture looking?"

"Just trying to keep the zombies on the far side of the shit trench," he replied.

The two paratroopers walked down the length of the chain-link fence that jogged south from the Turkish Tower. When they reached the hole in the fence, they pushed the orange piece of cloth aside and ducked through. They then moved to the linkup site about four hundred feet down the canal. Behind him, Jesse heard the protests of an Afghan man being pushed back out the hole they had just come through; he wasn't on any of the exfil lists and the Marines weren't going to let him into HKIA. He briefly studied the man, noting his height and beard and clothing. He'd have to watch out for him later, to make sure he didn't jump into Hasina's group and try to sneak through again.

As Jesse moved to his spot on the airport side of the canal, the odor of the trench hit him like a sledgehammer. The crowd was packed tonight. The sense of desperation had grown along with the crowd size as the date of the retrograde approached, now less than a week away. Flashbangs went off nearby. He surveyed the roiling mass of people, cracked a green chem light, and hung it around his neck. He wondered if he'd even be able to see Hasina's yellow screen.

95

"Minister, we have another option for you."

Kelley told Hasina over the phone that if they returned to the airport and went to the Abbey Gate area, they could get into HKIA with the help of American soldiers, who would allow her to bypass the gates to enter the airport. They would have to approach the linkup point using the sewage trench that ran alongside that side of the airport. "I'll send you a GPS pin, but there's a fence on the other side. Some Americans will meet you there."

"From the State Department?"

"No, Hasina. From the military."

Hasina didn't like that—or any of it. But she knew of no alternative. "Let me discuss it with my family. What you are saying will be hard for all of us, but especially my mother and mother-in-law. Thank you, Kelley. I'll call you back shortly."

Hasina told the driver to stop, and in low tones so their nearby daughter wouldn't overhear, discussed this latest option with her husband.

As they spoke, her phone rang again. It was a friend—another of four female ministers who had served in the Afghan government. She told Hasina that she was in HKIA, thanks to some Norwegians who had gotten her out. She encouraged Hasina to try to get in however she could, too. If she could just find someone to help her inside the airport, her British visa would get her on a flight out.

"Time is running out, Hasina. You cannot lose this chance," her friend said. "You may not get another. You *must* go."

Hasina conferred once more with her husband, and together they decided that her friend was correct. They had to return to the airport, where they'd been beaten and turned back just minutes earlier.

The driver turned them around and returned in the direction of the airport, winding his way through back alleys and side streets to get them as close to Abbey Gate as possible.

They left the car and pressed toward the GPS pin. Finally, they reached it. The Taliban—who, only yards away, mercilessly beat the crowd—refused to follow them into the trench of excrement and filth.

She called Kelley. "We're here. We're at the trench." She peered into the darkness. She could make out soldiers along the wall, and on the footbridge over the trench. One of them had a green light hanging from his neck. She looked again at the contents of the canal. "It's going to be very bad," Hasina said.

"Hasina, you just have to cross over. A soldier is waiting for you," Kelley pleaded.

"Yes, I see him," Hasina managed to say over a sudden crescendo of noise: there was the din of the crowd, the roar of an airplane overhead, and horns honking everywhere. She looked back at her family, all huddled together, her husband practically wrapping all of them in his arms, her two bodyguards flanking the whole group like giant bookends. The bodyguards were loyal, there of their own accord. Though they knew there would be no protection from the Taliban beatings, they could at least prevent any harm coming to the family from the seething crowd.

"Kelley, I am scared for my family if we don't try it. But I am scared for my family if we do try it. Please tell me what to do, Kelley. Please."

Kelley took a deep breath. "I don't know what to tell you, Hasina. It's crazy, but whatever you do, you need to do it like a crazy person."

Like a crazy person, Hasina repeated in her head. Sanity had indeed left Afghanistan.

96

Like a crazy person, Hasina thought again.

All around her, people pushed and pulled, sometimes grabbing at her family's small bags and clothing. Her bodyguards flanked the group, even though she had asked them not to risk themselves. Now she stared down the edge of a sewage canal. Up and down its length, people used the viaduct as a watery passageway, a stinking approach to Abbey Gate that was so vile the Taliban wouldn't come near it.

"Are you ready?" she asked her husband.

He nodded.

Hasina texted Kelley. *OK. We are going in.*

Great, Kelly responded. *Remember to hold up the yellow card.*

Panic gripped Hasina as the reality of confronting these heavily armed soldiers settled clashed with the traumatic memories of her childhood.

Yellow card? What is she talking about? She began crying out of frustration.

I don't know what you mean, Hasina wrote.

Bring up the yellow card on your phone that I sent, Kelley texted, *and hold it up for the soldiers to see.*

Hasina suddenly remembered. Scrolling through the email she'd gotten from Kelley, she found the yellow digital card and held it up, thinking it was impossible that any of those hundreds of soldiers would see it, much less help her family, amid all of these thousands of people screaming for help.

But the soldier with the green light caught her eye. He looked like a giant as he stood on a bridge on the airport side of the canal in his battle gear, staring across the ditch at her. She felt as though her knees might buckle in fear.

"What is your name?" he called out loudly.

"Hasina Safi," the matriarch called back as bravely as she could, trying to push down her fear of men with guns.

"Okay," he said. "How many in your party?"

"Ten."

"Okay. Wait. Please stay right there." He stepped aside and studied something on his phone for a moment, then looked back up at her.

A cacophonous burst of gunfire from a nearby .50-caliber machine gun echoed over the streets. Hasina jumped at the noise. What was she doing here?

A few moments later, the soldier was back and indicating that she should come across the trench. "You first, ma'am," he instructed.

Hasina's stomach turned as she lowered herself down the stone trench wall into the mire. The fetid water came up over her ankles, but her loyal bodyguards were at her side. She moved through the warm, thick ooze. It was about ten feet to the far side. On one step, she felt a blinding pain on the bottom of her foot—it felt like she gashed it on something, razor wire or broken glass. She steadied herself on one of her bodyguard's arms and continued. It would need to be cleaned, but pain didn't matter now.

She looked up at the soldier, who was extending his hand. She swallowed the lump in her throat and extended her own hand. He grabbed her forearm and as she looked into his eyes, she saw he was smiling.

"I'm Jesse. You're safe now."

First Sergeant Jesse Kennedy pulled her up and turned to get the rest of her family from the other side.

"Do you know who I am, Jesse?" Hasina asked hopefully.

"I have no idea who you are. Liv said you were coming, though." He was polite but adamant about the task at hand—getting her family across. "Go stand with my medic, please, ma'am," he said, pointing toward the fence. Her foot bled badly from the cut she had received in the water, but she refused to leave the side of the canal.

"No, I am Hasina. That is my family. I'm going to help you."

She watched as her bodyguards waded back through the canal and up the other side to help the other family members across. One by one, Jesse pulled them out of the ditch. They lined up and he carefully counted them one last time. "Two are missing," he said out loud.

He turned to see Hasina's bodyguards retreating into the canal. He called to them.

"Guys, this is your chance. Let's go."

They waved and shook their heads. Stepping through the putrid trench water, they disappeared into the crowd on the other side.

He turned back to Hasina, who waited near the fence with her family. He escorted the family to the hole and then to the waiting trucks that would take them to the aircraft area, and to freedom.

97

Razaq and his family had tried twice to get into HKIA—and twice they had failed. The former interpreter had resigned himself to growing a beard and living a bleak life under the Taliban. He would do whatever it took to protect his wife and daughters.

But then an old friend called—a former Army captain named Steve Rulli. And Steve implored him: "Don't give up, Razaq."

Steve had first called about a week earlier, and it had taken Razaq a minute to remember him. But once he did, it all came flooding back.

The American had a boyish look with the wiry build of an endurance athlete, an infectious laugh and smile, and hard combat experience in the deserts of Iraq and Afghanistan. He had served as an assistant operations officer for Scott Mann in 2006 and had planned to become a Green Beret himself until his collapsing marriage forced him to drop out of the Q Course and the Army. It didn't help, and he ended up divorced.

Eager to serve anyway he could, he became a civilian consultant, a kind of troubleshooter for special ops. He would kit up, put on a uniform, carry a gun, and then deploy with Green Berets to determine how to improve operational organization and battlefield performance. It was in this capacity that he had met Razaq.

The new job had fewer deployments and less stress, but Steve still struggled when he returned stateside. A brain injury from an IED in Iraq, coupled with the post-traumatic stress, had taken him to dark places. His sense of despair deepened in the summer of 2021, as near-constant cable news in his den blared the latest Taliban advances, reporting in real time as Afghan provinces fell one after another. He'd remarried in 2016, and his new wife was an Army helicopter pilot. From her post within the 82nd Airborne Joint Operations Center, where she was assigned because she was pregnant, she confirmed every detail of the Afghan nightmare.

Feeling powerless, Steve had begun cold-calling former partners to offer help—and one of those calls had been to Razaq. It was Steve who had sent Razaq to the airport. Steve who had sent him to fail.

Since he'd last spoken with Razaq, though, Scott had folded Steve into Task Force Pineapple—and these guys were getting shit done. Steve still felt crushing guilt—he still felt as though he were failing the men who had bled with him—but, as Scott had told him, "At least we're doing something, brother."

Now Steve was urging Razaq to make another attempt. He promised that the situation had changed—they had a plan now, a strategy, and someone on the inside. But Razaq and his family still had to make it to Abbey Gate for the plan to work.

Reluctantly, Razaq gathered his family and they returned to the airport, this time in the dead of night. When he saw the crowd again, it took his breath away.

Razaq pressed into the crowd with everything he had, ensuring that he didn't lose the tight grip he had on his daughters and that his wife, who was seven months pregnant, never left his side. After a while, they could see the Taliban clearly. Several of them were on a truck with a .50-caliber machine gun firing tracer rounds wildly over the crowd, causing the mass of humanity to recoil and then surge back with a fury.

The Taliban manning the perimeter had loudspeakers and were announcing that *Daesh*—the term many Afghans used for ISIS-K—was in the crowd. Everyone had to be vigilant. Razaq noticed that the Taliban were visibly nervous about the possible presence of ISIS-K. Ironically, they could now be on the receiving end of a potential suicide bomber. It was, after all, the Taliban's Haqqani network—which now secured HKIA—that had introduced suicide bombings in 2005.

More gunfire. Screams broke out, and the crowd suddenly parted.

A man lay on the ground bleeding profusely from what had once been his head but was now a mass of gray matter and blood. The Taliban had turned the .50-cal on this man, dropping him instantly.

Razaq couldn't help himself. "Why did you shoot this guy?" he screamed at the triggerman.

He felt his wife go limp against his shoulder and then land on the ground with a thud. Terrified that she'd be trampled, he pushed the crowd back like a caged animal. Kneeling beside her, he gently tried to wake her. As she slowly started to regain consciousness, his phone rang.

Somehow, Razaq answered.

"Razaq, where are you?" It was Steve.

"A checkpoint near Abbey Gate," he said curtly. "They're shooting. They just shot some guy. My wife passed out."

"Razaq, you are fifty feet from freedom. I need you to press through."

Fuck you, Steve, Razaq thought, and hung up.

His two oldest daughters, ages four and eight, stood over their mother with worried looks as Razaq slowly lifted his wife to her feet and then shifted his youngest daughter onto his other hip. "Come on," he said just loudly enough for them to hear. "We're going home." He lent his wife an arm and his daughters grabbed onto his shirt as he led his family away.

When they got home, Razaq was terrified to see that his wife had started bleeding profusely. He called her doctor, who recommended they risk the city and bring her to the hospital immediately. Once there, they learned that although she was very weak and had lost a lot of blood, she would be all right—and so would the baby.

They returned home several hours later. Razaq's mother had somehow gotten their two daughters to fall asleep. Razaq texted Steve that they were home, and Steve called immediately. "You okay, brother? I'm so sorry."

"No, I'm sorry, brother," Razaq said slowly. "You are trying to help us. We'll go again tomorrow."

Razaq went to bed, utterly exhausted. He was asleep within seconds.

98

Scott sat on his back patio when a message from Will Lyles popped up on his phone. Scott hadn't heard from him in at least five years.

Can we talk on Signal? Will asked.

Scott was nearly certain he knew why Will was calling: someone in Afghanistan needed help. He texted back, *Of course.*

A few minutes later, Scott's phone rang. "Sir, it's Will. You're the only person I can think of who might be able to help. I need an assist—and it's going to be a pain in your ass."

He explained the situation of a lieutenant colonel in the Afghan National Directorate of Security named Kazem. "Dude's a fucking machine. He was my interpreter, sir. He helped save my life when I lost my legs in Oruzgan province. I owe this guy my life, sir." Scott felt a chill as he remembered that terrible day back in 2010 as he sat vigil outside the Kandahar field hospital, wondering if Will would survive. Will continued. "He had no intention of leaving. He was going to fight until no Taliban were left. But I think he's come around to the idea that it's better to live now and fight later. I'm only saying this because he was making no contingency plans—he's got no passport or visa. I know it sounds like a lost cause, but I owe this guy my life," Will repeated, his voice cracking. "He pulled me from that IED blast, sir. If I lose him, I don't . . . I don't . . ."

"I know, buddy," Scott said. "How's your wife dealing with all of this?"

"It's tough for her," Will said. "We weren't together when I was in the war. We've got little ones now, and it's a lot for her. I haven't slept in days. I'm not really here when I'm with the family. I mean, I'm here, but

I'm over there. You know what I mean? I'm on my damn phone dealing with shit I used to do in combat. Only now, I'm doing it at the breakfast table while my kids are trying to get my attention. I thought I left all that behind." A pause. "I thought this shit was over for me, you know, sir?"

"We all did, Will. Listen, I'm going to bring you into our Pineapple group. I can't promise we'll get Kazem out. It's pretty late to be trying to move someone like him, but this crew has been amazingly resourceful and truly collaborative. I promise you will be surrounded by people who will try their best, including me."

"That's all I could ask for, sir. Thank you."

"Tell Kazem to get near the airfield and lie low for now. Tell him to be ready to move. If the opportunity comes, he won't have much time."

"On it, sir."

99

"Okay, let's line up," the young American civilian told Bashir through a Dari interpreter, unaware that Bashir spoke perfect English. The former master sergeant stood in a group of Afghans at the edge of the runway. Commander James had submitted Bashir's paperwork and tried diligently to get his family into the airfield. It was too much for Bashir's fragile wife, but James had been true to his word. Although Bashir desired to wait for his family to join him, the U.S. security forces were eager to fly refugees out as fast as possible to make room for more. His heart pounded as he lifted the straps of his backpack onto his shoulders. He was about to take the longest walk of his life.

He'd been inside HKIA for four days, and every day he'd hoped to get his family inside, too, even his newborn baby girl, Zainab. He'd tried to act as a liaison between the Americans and his fellow Afghans—he especially wanted to help fellow Afghan Special Forces operators find their way into the airport like he had—but the Americans didn't want him. It was almost as if they'd been ordered *not* to help members of the Afghan special operations forces.

The only time they'd ever said anything meaningful to him had been just now, to tell him that it was time to go.

The line took shape. He could hear the screaming engines of a C-17 just a few hundred yards away. Like his walk from Camp Morehead to his house on the day that Kabul fell, he'd make this walk alone. His wife and six children would remain behind, at least for now.

He extended his arm and did one last 180-degree selfie pan of his beloved Afghanistan with his phone. *How could this have happened?* They had fought to the end. *They* hadn't given up. Their president had given up. The generals had given up. Even the Americans had given up. But Bashir and his brothers had kept their promise.

What kind of man leaves his family behind? he asked himself. He knew the answer. It didn't matter. It was too late now.

Commander James, who had convinced him to come here alone, had sworn it: "I'll take care of your family, Bashir. I'll get them to you. I promise." Bashir's own father had told him: "Get on the plane, my son. We will find our way to you."

A wave of nausea grew inside Bashir as he neared the plane's ramp. He fell to his knees on the tarmac. Everyone, even the U.S. Air Force crew, stared at him. But he didn't care. Tears rolled down his face as he bent down and kissed the Afghan ground one last time.

He then slowly rose, climbed the ramp, and found a place on the crowded floor of the cavernous metal bird.

100

Matt Coburn hammered the screen of his phone as he tapped out a long Signal text that he hoped would light a fire under the Army brass. The recipients were Major General Chris Donahue, the commander of the 82nd Airborne Division, who was on the ground at HKIA, and General Austin "Scotty" Miller, the last commander of the NATO mission in Afghanistan, who was now stateside but still influential in the Afghan recovery effort.

Both were former special operations commanders who had been Matt's bosses in Afghanistan in 2020. Both had firsthand experience of the Afghan interpreters and Special Operations Forces and the invaluable work they had done. To Matt's mind, these two high-ranking officers could head off the unfolding catastrophe that anyone with eyes could see coming: the wholesale abandonment of every Afghan special operator and their families once the Americans were completely gone.

He wrote:

Gentlemen,

We have highly loyal and dedicated Afghan Special Forces officers and NCOs at the SW Gate right now. They are with Sergeant Major Mirwais. They have their families with them. You know every one of these men. They have partnered with us loyally for years. Several of them went through their basic training with 1st Battalion, 3rd Special

Forces Group (Airborne) when I was a Captain and have been fighting "shoulder to shoulder" with us for 19+ years.

They have earned the right for refuge and sanctuary. I know that it is in your power to help them. I am sorry, but this is a moral imperative. Please, help us get them admitted to HKIA and flown out.

Our American military effort has been amazing given terrible circumstances.

The entire world has watched us fly out tens of thousands of Afghans who did not once pick up a rifle and fight in support of their country or our counterterrorism mission.

These men and their families have. There are 115 people plus 30 more members of Sergeant Major Mirwais's brothers and sisters and nieces and nephews. That is under 150. They are consolidated and organized.

I can give you the young Marine's name who is in contact with them.

Please Help Them.

Sincerely,
Matt

He pressed send. With luck, they would write back soon. In the meantime, he needed to look into other options—primarily Task Force Pineapple.

101

Captain John Folta followed First Sergeant Jesse Kennedy out of their makeshift company headquarters—which they had named the "shit shack"—and joined their radio operator and medic in two Hilux pickups for the short drive to the U.S. Marine command post at Abbey Gate for their daily threat brief.

"All clear, sir," the Marine sergeant said when they got there. "A few 'be on the lookout' reports about a vehicle-borne IED, but I don't see anything like that getting through this crowd. Go ahead and do your thing tonight, guys."

John thanked the Marine and headed toward the perimeter. He walked past the Turkish Tower alongside a dozen evenly-spaced concrete jersey barriers, then ducked through the open hole in the chain-link fence. Jesse followed. They moved along the footpath running between the perimeter fence and the sewage trench. About four hundred feet away, a short footbridge crossed the foul trench to the footpath on the other side; a coil of concertina wire blocked it to prevent people from crossing over. The roar from the crowd rolled over them. Neither man wore a helmet, just an armored vest with ammo magazines and headsets linked to their radios. They carried their M4 carbines, though.

Conductor is set, John texted Zac.

For the past two days, his and Jesse's phones had been ringing constantly with calls from all sorts of people in the United States who had somehow gotten their numbers. Every call mentioned a name, and every name had a story.

Some of the callers were too vague to be helped. They couldn't provide full names or lists of people, or even photos of the Afghans they wanted to get into HKIA. They were just trying anything they could. John sympathized with these folks, but he could not help them. The Pineapple plan had few ambiguities; it was tactical and could be executed with precision in a chaotic environment, and the group was experienced and reliable.

Zac had alerted John that on this night, the express would be even busier, moving dozens more Afghan special operators and their family members. The flocks would be stacked like trains at rush hour.

They were ready to receive these people—the only thing he might have changed was the code word. Zac had decided on "Seth Rogen," the name of an actor in the movie *Pineapple Express*. The conductor on the canal retaining wall would call out "Seth!" when he saw a yellow screen down in the trench. The reply from the Afghan would have to be "Rogen" for the conductor to pull the passengers up and out of the sewage canal. John wasn't sure it was the best choice, wondering if the Afghan flocks would even be able to pronounce it. "John Rambo" would have been simpler.

The sun was already setting on the western horizon. Rambo or Rogen, Pineapple Express was about to get underway for another night.

102

"Papa, where are we going?" Mohammad Rahimi's five-year-old son asked.

On their previous attempts to get into HKIA, the family had pressed against the fences outside Abbey Gate for forty-eight hours, just a few feet from U.S. Marines. They'd been caught in crossfire between American forces and the Taliban. His wife, Gulnar, had narrowly missed being struck by a Taliban bullet that instead killed an innocent man standing just behind her. They stood by as the NSU paramilitary guards in their tiger-striped fatigues fired indiscriminately into the crowd, shooting one man's arm completely off as he tried to enter the gate. His children had witnessed killings and cruelty and brutality—things children should never see.

These ordeals had left his five-year-old jumpy, terrified at any loud noise. Mohammad had tried to reassure him. "I am here, your mother is here. We are going to another place, a good place, where we will have a good life." He gently stroked the boy's dark hair to accentuate his words.

Mohammad zipped up a sports bag full of clothes. Mister Zac, one of his former American bosses when he was an interpreter, had urged him to return to the airfield once again. Previously, they'd begun at the Panjshir pumping station on the north side of HKIA, and ended at North Gate. This time, they would try a different approach, at Abbey Gate on the airport's southeastern side. Zac told his old friend that he had U.S. soldiers inside HKIA who would pull the family in. The night before, they'd managed to bring in twenty-five Afghans, including children.

"It's safe," Zac had promised. "It will work."

But when Mohammad told Gulnar they had to return to the gates outside HKIA, she protested. "We cannot go. They didn't let us in! I won't do this again."

"But Mister Zac says we can go inside this time. He even sent me a password and a yellow card to show on my phone." He showed her the yellow graphic. Even as a special operator, he felt foolish doing it. How could something so innocuous guarantee their safety?

Gulnar tearfully shook her head. He hugged her tightly and then gazed down at her face. He hated asking all of them to try again.

"My flower, if we can get to America, we will not be killed by Talibs. We can trust Mister Zac. We *must* trust Mister Zac."

Finally, she relented.

They piled into a taxi and made their way to Abbey Gate, taking side roads through the industrial park outside the airport. Mohammad led the older children while Gulnar carried their three-month-old infant. They were accompanied by Mohammad's two brothers, each carrying one of Mohammad and Gulnar's two-year-old twins.

They pressed into the crowd, heading directly for the sewage canal, while the rest of the crowd surged toward Abbey Gate. He spotted the soldier on the far bank with the green glow stick dangling from a cord around his neck.

Thirty more feet, Mohammad thought, *and my children won't grow up under the Taliban.*

Mohammad held his arm as high as it reached and waved his phone displaying the bright yellow card. The soldier yelled, "Seth!"

"Rogen!" Mohammad answered. The soldier waved them across.

They dropped into the muck, just as the other Pineapple flocks had done before them. They waded through the filth, carrying the children just above it, and crossed. On the other side, the Americans checked their names against a list. Then they were lifted out of the filth and onto the concrete embankment. Mohammad held out his phone to show the Army captain, whose name tape read FOLTA, texts from Mister Zac.

"This is my supervisor," Mohammad explained. "He's in Special Forces."

"You're good to go," John said. "On the other side of that fence is the United States of America."

Mohammad looked where the man pointed. It was a simple chain-link fence with a person-size hole snipped in the wire.

This attempt had taken under an hour. Soldiers ushered Mohammad and his family through the wire, and then searched them on the other side. More soldiers were there, guiding them to nearby trucks. Mohammad put his palm over his heart.

"Thank you. I am a lucky man right now," Mohammad told the Americans.

103

SF Peyton needed the man he called "Mustache" to survive. Hafi wasn't just his best friend in Afghanistan, but he also knew a ton of sensitive information about hundreds of American operators he'd served with over the course of a decade of war.

And now it wasn't just Hafi who had to get out. In Kabul, he had linked up with six other comrades from the National Mine Removal Group. These men had all brought their families. Hafi served as their group leader on the ground, bringing all of his organizational skills to bear, and SF Peyton served as their shepherd in the United States, working them into the Pineapple extraction queue.

Hafi and his flock were operating with military-level precision, and their group of forty-two people were able to get to the GPS points TF Pineapple issued them, but SF Peyton's main concern was that Hafi's flock was now too big. He texted Zac to make sure.

PEYTON
Is that too many?

ZAC
Don't know. Might be able to get all at once. I will talk with Folta. Give them my number and have them connect with me on Signal or WhatsApp and I can coordinate with them directly. Are they Afghan SF? Have they been submitted for SIV or humanitarian parole?

PEYTON
They are NMRG. They all have SIVs submitted 8 months ago with Liv and Congressman Waltz's help. They speak OK English but not great.

> **ZAC**
> OK. Send them to the staging area.

> **PEYTON**
> Roger that.

SF Peyton texted Hafi to move his group toward the airport immediately:

> I need you to get to Abbey Gate. Bring food and water. I will give you more instructions once you get there. We're going to sneak in your group in the middle of the night.

Then he waited.

Seven thousand miles away, Hafi gathered his men. They were now in two groups—one led by him, the other by another Afghan NMRG operator named Sayed.

A few hours later, Hafi sent a series of voice memos and a pair of photos to Peyton from the airport perimeter.

SF Peyton looked at the first image. It showed an enormous crowd of Afghans, many with scarves over their heads, pushing and jostling outside the gate. In the background, beyond the sewer trench, loomed the two-story, brown concrete guard tower with bullet-proof windows known as Turkish Tower. The middle window was open. Poking out of it SF Peyton could make out the barrel of a U.S. Marine's M110 sniper rifle, pointing in the direction of the Baron Hotel. The sniper was undoubtedly looking for threats like ISIS-K suicide bombers.

In one of the accompanying voice memos, Hafi said, "Sir, uh, the other NMRG Sayed, uh, he is already there." His voice was halting and staccato, as if he was being crushed in a crowd and unable to draw a full breath. "I, uh, I have a little bit of distance between them and us. So, yes, right now I'm watching because here is so many people. When I get close to the soldiers, uh, I'll let you know. But there might be no internet and just cell phone. The internet is not working there. So, uh, repeat: Sayed and his people are already there. By the Abbey Gate."

SF Peyton knew that the Marines were occasionally using cell phone jammers because of the IED threat. Hafi knew it, too. Communications would be tricky going forward.

As SF Peyton listened to this memo, another photo arrived. What it depicted was shocking.

It showed Hafi and his group exactly where they needed to be, directly across from the 82nd Airborne conductors' hole in the chain-link fence. But it also showed the massive crowd in which he was caught—easily four thousand people stretching a good half mile or farther down the narrow twenty-foot-wide path between the arching blast walls and the opposite wall bordering the shit trench. People had hooked shawls along the blast walls to create makeshift shelters from the sun, but now, since it was night, most everyone stood in the crowd.

You couldn't slip a sheet of paper between any of them, Peyton thought. It looked like the biggest mosh pit he'd ever seen.

SF Peyton wolfed down his lunch, watching Zac's updates on the group chat.

ZAC: *Mustache is on deck, Sayed is behind him.*
PEYTON: *You are awesome. I owe you a beer.*

There was nothing SF Peyton could do but continue to wait. As he sat in his quiet office, voice memos from Hafi rolled in sporadically. Over two hours, he received five. After what felt like hours of silence (but was only about fifteen minutes), SF Peyton sent a memo. "How's it going, brother? Have you made linkup yet?"

A garbled voice memo arrived a few minutes later. "Sir, right now, uh, we just, we just, uh, we are past the wadi by the wall of the, uh, airport." *Wadi* meant the sewage canal. "So there is a U.S. soldier. I ask them about Captain Zac. So we are with them right now. So hopefully we will go inside."

"Send me a message when you get there, brother," Peyton said in reply.

After another excruciating thirty minutes, Hafi sent a new memo. "Sir, we are inside right now, like, ten minutes ago. My internet was weak. So I just hear your message right now. I am inside, sir!"

"Awesome, brother! Can you give me an update on the rest of the NMRG? How many made it?"

"Forty-two people, sir," Hafi answered.

SF Peyton could hardly believe it. Zac told the main Pineapple chat room the good news. *Confirmed: 40+ from the NMRG team has conducted linkup!*

God loves the Airborne, Peyton mused to himself, *and so do I.*

104

SIGNAL CHAT ROOM–AUGUST 24, 2021

The Pineapple chat room was on fire. Shepherds from across the United States worked double time to move their flocks to safety. Many shepherds also celebrated as their people were inside HKIA and getting manifested onto American C-17s, and then just as quickly turned to other flocks. The successes just put more pressure on the shepherds whose people were still on the ground. Managing the chaotic flow of endless real-time updates was like looking through a digital soda straw into HKIA. Perspective was painfully limited as the messages cascaded so swiftly now that new postings buried old ones within seconds, and basic information had to be constantly reposted or repeated. Following the threads was like watching the scenery fly past while on a moving train. If a shepherd turned away from the screen for even a few seconds, new updates piled on top of old ones.

> STEVE RULLI: *I have two families to move to the airfield . . . father of a SIV that is already stateside. Some of them don't have passports . . . young children. What do you advise? Have them move to the airfield or wait? I can pass all of their info.*
>
> ZAC: *I can try to make it work later in the night. They've got seven families in front of them.*
>
> DAN: *7 pax wheels up thanks to TF Pineapple!*
>
> STEVE RULLI: *Zac, this is the group leader of the family I messaged about. . . . Name's Razaq. They are moving to the gate now and I'll send the number of pax as soon as I get it . . . along with passport/ID*

photo and phone number. I'm attaching a letter of recommendation
written for him by General Don Bolduc.

LIV: *If we have anyone inside HKIA who needs to be manifested I have a*
plane and someone trying to put butts in seats. Just need bodies to go
to ramp 8. They're manifesting in flight. The flight is to Uganda.

105

Somehow, Scott Mann had to help his youngest son, Brayden, move into his new college apartment. Boxes full of baseball trophies, lamps, and books, as well as furniture, were piled high in the pickup. Scott's wife, Monty, was helping, too. Their older sons, Cody and Cooper, had already left home, making this moment even more meaningful. When they returned home that evening, their baby boy would be gone. They would be empty nesters.

Monty had admonished Scott not to get embroiled in Pineapple today. "Babe," she'd said as they prepared to leave, "this is a big deal for Bray and me. Please keep the Afghan phone calls to a minimum, okay? It's his big day, and you'll regret it if you miss it."

Naturally, as Scott pulled a box of lamps out of the pickup, his phone rang. It was Matt Coburn.

Shit, Scott thought. He looked around. Monty and Brayden were upstairs. Maybe he could sneak a call. He answered on his wireless earbuds.

"What's up, Matt?"

"I believe General Miller and General Donahue are blocking the Afghan commandos from coming in. I don't think they want them in HKIA," Matt said in his usual no-bullshit tone.

"Why would they do that? It doesn't make any sense," Scott said, moving toward the apartment building.

"I know, but Miller told me we'll have to triage the Afghan special operations guys we bring in," Matt said.

"He told me the same fucking thing." Scott had texted his old boss

General Miller that morning about the situation at HKIA, and as he had told Matt, the general told Scott that "there has to be some level of triage with this." The response infuriated Scott, who couldn't believe that a bunch of retired officers, including himself, were triaging any of these Afghan Special Operations Forces, when the CIA managed to exfiltrate their entire thirty-five-thousand-man partner force and families. Scott's anger bubbled up as he walked into the building and up the stairs. He tried to gather himself. "I just can't accept that, man. I'm sure he has his reasons. I just don't understand what they are." Scott had reached the top of the stairs and didn't know which door was Bray's. He just stood there, awkwardly waiting for one of Brayden's friends to come out, hoping it wouldn't be Brayden himself. "I mean, how can these guys get left behind while those fucking NSU paramilitaries are getting every last person out?"

Matt sighed. "It's sick. I've talked to dozens of Afghan senior operators. The Taliban got a shit ton of data off the computers they've seized. They're going door-to-door looking for our SOF brothers right now. Command Sergeant Major Mirwais almost got rolled up at his house, but luckily he was out getting food." CSM Mirwais, who had been head of the Commando School of Excellence at Camp Morehead until a few days earlier, was a top target of the Taliban.

"Matt, you've got to keep going. Pineapple's getting some of them into HKIA in small groups, but you have the best chance at a full and proper evac. That's the key." Matt had been the last commander of the Combined Joint Special Operations Task Force–Afghanistan. In so many ways, Matt was the last direct representative of the Afghan special operations forces. He'd worked directly under Donahue and Miller. "If anyone can change their minds, it's you."

"Maybe, but the silence of these guys is deafening. I don't think they're listening. Bashir was evacuated with no effort by the U.S. forces to use him as a liaison to pull our guys in. I'm telling you, these generals do not intend to get our Afghan SOF guys inside the wire."

Just then, Brayden emerged from his apartment, catching Scott red-handed. Brayden shook his head and pointed to where his dad needed to be. Scott smiled meekly and shuffled off. He continued talking. It was impossible to miss his son's disappointment, but he had to finish this call with Matt.

"They sure as fuck aren't going to listen to me," Scott said. "I don't get many Christmas cards from SOF flag officers, bro."

Matt let out a laugh. "I'd take that as a badge of honor, man. This is wrong on *every* level, moral, force protection, you name it."

"Leaving these guys in the wind is also a massive national security threat," Scott reminded Matt, not that he needed it. "How many countries will want to work with us when we treat our partners like this?"

"I just want these generals to be held accountable when it's all said and done," Matt admitted.

Scott felt the same way—but now was not the time for that. "Later, man. For now, keep rattling cages."

"Rattling cages is still something I know how to do. In the meantime, can you bring me into Pineapple? Maybe I can get some of my guys out that way."

"I'm on it."

Scott looked up from his phone. He didn't realize it, but Monty stood just a few feet away, her fists balled on her hips, glaring at him.

Scott set down the box. "Shit, babe. I gotta get on a Zoom call." He stepped into Brayden's bedroom and slid his laptop out of his backpack. As he closed the door, he yelled, "Sorry!"

Monty didn't believe him, but he meant it.

106

TAMPA, FLORIDA—AUGUST 24, 2021

Dan O'Shea was retired, but he was still the same fast-talking SEAL. He was fueled by rage over the U.S. government's abandonment of its Afghan partners. The urgency spilled out of the Pineapple chat room as the days ticked down toward the retrograde and the shutdown that would precede it, which one shepherd reported was probably seventy-two hours away. After the U.S. planes went wheels up, it was all over for anyone still in Kabul. *Everyone remaining gets cut away*, the shepherd posted. *Plan accordingly.*

Dan's current concern was the Afghan-American Qais and his family. It was somewhat complicated because some didn't have green cards or citizenship, but that wouldn't stop Dan. Hell, saving Americans was why he volunteered in the first place.

Qais had made repeated attempts to get into HKIA following the instructions of U.S. officials—attempts that ended with him beaten and nearly killed. Dan was completely frustrated with the way Qais was being treated by the U.S. government. Embarrassed even.

The State Department had told Qais that he couldn't take his parents or siblings to the U.S. since they weren't citizens and had no SIVs. But the Afghan refused to leave without them, meaning they were all stuck.

Dan messaged Qais.

> **DAN**
> We will continue to work on getting you all out, but you may need to consider taking your immediate family who have US passports and green cards.

QAIS

My father, my mother, everyone needs to be helped—they're all on a hit list.

DAN

The window is rapidly closing to save anyone in Kabul. That includes American citizens.

QAIS

I know, but I am not leaving my family alone to face their death.

DAN

I would do the same, my friend.

107

Steve Rulli picked up the phone to the sound of Razaq's kids screaming in the background. They were clearly outside—he could hear the wind, horns honking, and occasional gunfire in the distance.

Following Steve's instructions, Razaq and his family had returned to Abbey Gate. This was their fourth attempt.

"You okay, Razaq?" Steve asked, moving out of earshot of his own wife and daughter, who were playing peacefully together in their living room.

"No, we're not. The Taliban are yelling at me to get my kids to shut up. My kids shouldn't have to see this. The Taliban have us sitting on a wall. They tell us if we move any more forward, they'll beat us."

Steve heard Razaq's fear. But based on the GPS pins he was dropping into the Pineapple chat room, Steve could also see just how close Razaq was to the linkup site and to the 82nd Airborne.

"I'm sorry, Razaq. Stay on the line." Steve put the call on speaker and furiously texted Zac. *Is the conductor still there?*

ZAC
Yes, the conductor is there, but not for much longer tonight. And we've switched from the yellow card to pineapples on the phones. Sending to you now.

Seconds later, Steve received a graphic of a bunch of tiny yellow pineapples arrayed against a garish pink backdrop. He immediately sent it to Razaq, who was still on speakerphone.

"Razaq," Steve said, "you have to do whatever you can to move, man.

We don't have much time. I'm sending you the new image to show to the conductor. You gotta go."

"Okay, Steve. Stay on the phone." Razaq started speaking to someone in Pashto. Then Steve heard someone shouting in Pashto, then screaming, and then Razaq again. "Oh, my God! No! Stop! Steve, they are beating my wife. Someone help me! They are beating my wife. Please make them stop!"

Then Steve heard the sharp snap of a bolt being drawn back, probably an AK-47. There was nothing Steve could do. He fell to his knees.

Did I just do this to him? Steve wondered. *Am I about to hear an execution?*

Then the line went dead.

108

Kazem read Will Lyles's words—*Hide up for the night*—from the driver's seat of a stolen car he'd hot-wired the day before.

Once the car was running, he picked up his baby brother, Ahmed, who had done contract work for the U.S. government. Together, they headed to HKIA. When they arrived at one of the gates, the U.S. soldiers hadn't exactly welcomed Kazem with open arms. After they ordered him away at gunpoint, Kazem signaled to his brother to back off. They pushed their way through the crowd, in the opposite direction of HKIA.

Kazem still didn't want to leave Afghanistan. But he wasn't suicidal, either. He loved his country, but if he stayed, he knew he would be killed in short order, erasing his chance at one day seeing the Taliban defeated. He trusted Will to get him out, so that, in time, he could return. And when he did, there would be hell to pay.

Motherfuckers, he thought.

Motherfuckers.

Kazem and his brother made their way back to the stolen car parked on the perimeter of the airfield. They would spend the night there and start again when Will told them it was time to move.

That night, hunkered next to the car, Kazem shaved his beard and changed his look. He snapped a selfie and sent it to Will, with a caption that he hoped would make Will laugh: *I look like a fucking crackhead.*

As he sat in the dark with his brother in the quiet car, he knew in his heart that this wouldn't be the end.

109

Scott was in his office again, where he spent a lot of his time unfortunately, far away from the simple life he had built with Monty when he had left the military.

As the U.S. evacuation operation neared its end, urgent requests for help flooded in from other veterans and friends. It wasn't just Afghan SOF and interpreters in duress. They wanted help with young girls on the run and women who were all alone with no chance of advocacy in the male-dominated society. And it wasn't just to Scott or the other shepherds. Thousands of frantic, graphic pleas for help were pouring in over social media to Scott's business staff, his non-profit staff, even his wife and kids. They wanted help with SIVs or getting people manifested onto flights or inside the wire. All the things Pineapple had been dealing with for the better part of a week.

Word of Pineapple Express's successes had spread like wildfire through Signal and WhatsApp chat rooms. Similar groups like Dunkirk, Sacred Promise, and Team America also hummed with volunteer efforts.

Some people asked straight-up to be brought into Task Force Pineapple's Signal group. Scott was selective though, he knew it could get out of hand fast, and he also felt that they might be walking the seams on legality. He did let in Johnny Utah, one of Nezam's old friends, who was shepherding a new group of NMRG operators. Utah had called, excited, when Pineapple got one of his guys into HKIA.

"Hey, bro, I just heard my dude Mustafa is inside the wire boarding a fuckin' plane! I checked with one of my teammates from Helmand and he told me the dude was safe at HKIA. He saved me and the whole team by tipping us off to an insider attack."

Scott immediately posted Utah's news, saying that a Pineapple shepherd—he wasn't sure which one—had helped evacuate an NMRG operative who had saved a team of Green Berets years earlier.

In addition to newcomers like Johnny Utah, J.P. had finally resurfaced after no contact for the past few days. He had been deeply immersed in getting out the embassy's local staff and their families—some three thousand in all—who had rolled up to Liberty Gate in dozens of buses before being ushered in through the CIA's back door. He was now involved with helping SF Peyton's flock. The seemingly sleepless diplomat was also actively aiding Qais.

Scott watched the Signal message stream flow by like an old teletype wire, dutifully ticking out news.

> ZAC: *OK everyone, I'm back up on the net. I had to read bedtime stories to my own little terrorists here. I'm rehashing the mechanism for the Pineapple Express for our next go under the cover of darkness.*
>
> MATT COBURN: *@Zac Is there a better gate to move my Afghan Special Operations forces to? Or another location to get them in the vicinity of the start point?*
>
> ZAC: *I would try to have them loiter in the general vicinity of Abbey Gate or if there's a house or safe house nearby they can stage in.*
>
> DAN: *I have an American Citizen with his extended family of 14 pax ready to move. Only 1 km away from HKIA.*
>
> ZAC: *Waiting to confirm if it is a go for tonight.*

Scott leaned back in his chair. Half a world away in Kabul, the sun was rising. Task Force Pineapple was preparing for what Scott feared might be their final run. "The airport isn't going to be viable much longer," he typed into the chat. "We've got one last shot in all likelihood."

110

James with the Hat didn't share the euphoria that some of the other shepherds were expressing on the chat board. In fact, he was at a low point.

He'd only gotten three guys into HKIA. Bashir plus two other NMRG guys, one of whom he barely knew—some guy named Mustafa.

"I'm barely making a dent," he told his wife, Sarah.

So he sat at his computer, nursing his Four Roses bourbon mixed with lukewarm coffee. Once again, he'd failed. He'd failed over a dozen other NMRG guys and their families—over 120 people in all—he was trying to get out. Some of the people in this flock were reluctant to go near the airport for fear of being recognized; others simply didn't trust that the Pineapple Express would work.

James with the Hat decided to shift his focus to overland routes and away from Task Force Pineapple.

111

Red GPS pin drops marking Taliban checkpoints and foot patrols spread like an infection over an evolving black map of Kabul.

Scott recorded a voice mail for the chatroom, setting the objective and quoting one of Task Force Dunkirk's lead volunteers, Worth Parker, "Save one more . . . and then just one more."

Zac Lois left a voice message for the group.

"Hey, everyone. I just wanted to send a quick message before the Pineapple Express gets rolling and we're trying to put out fires left and right. You guys are phenomenal. Let's try to keep the linkup site clear until a flock is called in. We don't want to attract the attention of the Taliban. We move slow, and we move steady. As we all know, this is probably our last night at this. So, let's go ahead and get our friends home and out of there. This is Zac. Good luck, guys."

THE
PIPELINE

112

As the sun rose, Scott ran his fingers over the totems that he displayed outside his home office, items that his sons had given him when he deployed so many years earlier. A *Star Wars* action figure from his eldest, Cody, now an Army infantryman. A cross from Cooper, who was studying to be a federal law enforcement officer. A green wristband from his youngest, Brayden.

He always followed the same ritual before going into combat, lightly touching them as a reminder of the precious people he needed to return to. He hadn't done this in a decade. Now, he wasn't going into combat, but the NATO warriors on the HKIA perimeter and the at-risk Afghans who had already risked so much were. Scott dropped to both knees and prayed, asking the Lord for the wisdom to make decisions worthy of the courage of those Afghans and volunteers he was about to lead.

Every day the task grew harder. The Pineapple group had no backup plan, and no official support. Everything was on the fly. Tempers were high. Sleep was non-existent.

All their successes had been due to human connections, force of will, and good luck.

He went inside and filled the Yeti mug he took everywhere with black coffee. The lack of sleep was getting to him also. Hell, it was getting to everyone in Pineapple. They couldn't sleep during the day because it was night in Kabul. And they couldn't sleep during the night, because they had to line up the next group of flocks. Scott could only imagine how exhausted the Afghans were.

He knew that tired people make mistakes. He hoped these would be minimal on this day.

Though the sun was coming up in Florida, it was getting ready to set in Kabul. Scott's main concern for this third night of their underground railroad was that so many Afghan Special Operations Forces and interpreters remained. Matt Coburn was shepherding a group of Afghan special operators and their families, a flock that counted over 150 people. Dan was shepherding Qais and his family. So many more were involved, Scott wasn't even sure he knew about everyone. All told, there were probably more than six hundred people in the pipeline. The retrograde was no more than six days off, but the shutdown of the airport would begin much sooner. At 6:36 a.m., one of the shepherds posted in the Pineapple chat that the window would close that day at 5:00 p.m. Kabul time.

But Scott's biggest worry was ISIS-K. The number of threats associated with the terrorist group was uncomfortably high. Their prime target was any U.S. or NATO forces that remained in Kabul, but the Afghans who worked for them might offer the easiest pickings. The biggest opportunity to sow terror was in the tumultuous chaos at Abbey Gate.

Pineapple knew all this even without relying on rumor or having access to classified intelligence. They could tell by the posture of the coalition forces and their jagged use of cell phone jammers. They could tell by the sniper rifle visible in the window of Turkish Tower, its shooter surveying the massive crowd across the sewage canal. And then there were the U.S. Marines and NATO forces with binoculars, which flocks had constantly seen looking out at the crowds around Abbey and North Gates. These men were on high alert. There was also the nervous demeanor of the Taliban checkpoints and the reporting coming from the flocks themselves who had their ears to the ground on threat streams.

ISIS-K couldn't get any vehicles near the area along the sewage canal, but they could get a man on foot in there. The Taliban were barely checking anyone at their "checkpoints"—instead they just randomly struck civilians with wire cables or batons. A determined ISIS-K bomber could easily sneak past in the crowd, a suicide vest under a shalwar kameez or burqa, and no one would catch him or her.

For this reason, John told Zac that the U.S. and NATO security forces had collapsed back to the jersey barriers behind the fence line due to the threat. The footbridge was no longer controlled, and there were no guarantees the Express could even open on this night. It might be too risky to post a conductor along the canal. If it did open, the window for extraction could be very short.

The group decided to stage the flocks at "offset" positions away from the gate, but still near enough so they could move quickly to the canal when the time came. Zac, the engineer, queued them up like planes waiting for their turn to taxi to the runway. When one flock got in, then the next in line got the signal from their shepherd to approach the conductor at the gate. The smaller the flock, the better, meaning guys like Matt had to break his Afghan SOF into more than a dozen groups.

Relaying this information to the flocks was not easy. Their lives hung on messages from their shepherds. To a man, these operators said the same thing. "We will take our families and get in position. And then we will wait."

113

Zac looked at the whiteboard to see the day's order of movement. Over its first two days, Pineapple Express had pulled in 130 Afghans. Now they were going for 600 in one night.

Zac hadn't showered or shaved in days, and he was barely sleeping. He'd all but abandoned his wife, Amanda, and their two small boys. He practically vanished from the lives of his young children.

As he prepared for the long night ahead, he heard their car pull up in the driveway. He removed his earbuds and went out to greet Amanda and the boys.

"Hey," he said as she got out of the car.

As he tried to explain, he could tell she was still upset. He had stepped out of their lives for days, living among them like a phantom, slipping back into being that other guy he'd been in Afghanistan: Captain America, the Operator.

"I know I've been crazy the past couple of days," he conceded, looking into her eyes. "And you're not happy with me. But if we can pull this off tonight, it will be monumental. I know you're mad, but please let me work on this. I'm working with a bunch of people. We have a chance to save a lot of lives."

"And then are you really going to be done?" she asked. "I mean really done? Because I need you not to tell me things that you think I want to hear, Zac."

He didn't answer. He couldn't lie to her.

"You smell," she went on. "Your physical presence is confusing the children and me. Mentally you're not here. It's like you're the star of *The Zac Lois Show*, and we're just watching it. "

They went into the house in silence.

Just a little longer and it'll be over, he thought. *I'll make it up to her. Just a little longer.*

114

The latest summons from the State Department was urgent. The U.S. government was instructing Qais to come to the airport again.

"Please go to the New Ministry of the Interior (MOI) compound today at 00:00 hrs (midnight) with your husband or wife and children under 21 only. Please bring small bags only (no large suitcases). You will be transported to the Hamid Karzai International Airport."

The summons repeated their one caveat: "Do not arrive with your extended Afghan family. U.S. citizens only."

Qais read that one awful phrase over and over—"with your husband or wife and children under 21 only." The federal agency he worked for had finally given its clearance for his Afghan relatives to come, too, but that permission was null and void on the ground in this goatfuck of an operation.

Qais refused. He wouldn't do it.

He told his family that escaping Kabul was their "do-or-die mission." They would have to act as a combat team. His brother. His two sisters. His mother. And his father. All would-be warriors in this operation. The Taliban might not let George W. Bush into HKIA, but damned if Qais wasn't going to find a way.

Task Force Pineapple ensured Qais was in touch with a diplomat at HKIA, J.P. Feldmayer, who told Qais if they could get to a gate, they could march right in and get on a flight.

At around 2:30 p.m. Kabul time, Qais suggested to Dan that rather than going to the Ministry of the Interior linkup, he would go to Ramp 7, the area of HKIA where the CIA had been based. The NSU Tiger Stripes now worked the gate there.

Qais wrote, "Americans can come out and escort us easily from this gate. All I want is someone to escort us in. There is no threat for any Americans coming out through here. It's 500 meters from the airport's main entrance door."

In theory this was a good idea, but Dan explained that at this late stage the only locations admitting people were Abbey Gate due to the fact that the entire NEO was on the verge of collapse. Dan told Qais that some gates had already been welded shut, and that the same would soon be true for Abbey Gate. The ISIS-K threat was that high. His best bet was to go to the Ministry of the Interior linkup, as instructed. They told him to bring everyone, and they'd find a way.

115

Ismail "Ish" Khan, a former interpreter for the American Green Berets, settled onto the pillows and cushions arranged across the floor of his traditional Afghan parlor in Seattle. Looking at his phone, he read a message Scott had just left in the Signal chat.

"Hey, everybody. I want you to welcome Ish to Pineapple. He's done tons of work with Jim Gant in Afghanistan. He's media savvy, is fluent in English, Dari, and Pashto, and he knows Kabul like the back of his hand. He'll be a huge addition to our efforts. Welcome, Ish."

Ish was grateful to see the message at this low point in his life. For years, he'd worked alongside the legendary Green Beret Jim Gant as his interpreter, bodyguard, and adviser. This was during some of the worst combat in the Kunar River Valley and had lasted for over two years. After the Army dismissed Jim and forced him into retirement, Jim helped Ish immigrate to Seattle in November 2014.

Now that Afghanistan was falling, Ish was grateful to be in the United States. The only problem was that his family had all stayed behind. His mother, six brothers, four sisters, and eight nieces and nephews had all remained. And like the families of all Afghans affiliated with the Special Forces, they were now threatened by the Taliban.

Ish had already begun a separate exfiltration operation, building up a small tactical operations center of his own. Dozens of Afghans filled his modest Seattle home, working around the clock on their laptops to get friends and family out. He brought Pineapple a new perspective and real-time picture of facts on the ground in Kabul.

116

Scott sat on his back deck.

The sun would soon set in Kabul. Scott scrolled through the message board, scanning hundreds of "baseball cards," single files for every flock they were trying to get out. The baseball cards included names, ages, affiliations, and "day of" photos of every member of each flock. This was the vital info that would let John and Jesse identify who they were pulling in. Scott couldn't stop looking at these images—some hopeful, some frozen in fear, often selfies taken at arm's length with the chaotic crowds framing them in the background.

The Pineapple Express would soon open, and messages flew back and forth. Mullah Mike was back and helping a Special Forces major and his family; Johnny Utah had his own group of NMRG guys; and Jim Gant was trying his best to keep everyone level headed.

It was getting to be too much, and Scott sighed, then typed a message. "We are going to push our start to twenty-two hundred local time. We have saturated the Pineapple Express and our capacity to move people through. Please do not bring anyone else into this room for the movement of people. This is a terrible call to make and I'm making it."

117

John couldn't believe the size of the crowd around Abbey Gate. *This is three times the number of people at the other gates*, he thought. Zac had agreed to push the linkup time to later in the evening, and he was glad. The Marines were using flash-bangs and warning shots to scare people back, and for the most part, these worked. Still, what John was looking at was complete chaos.

He turned to the sewage canal. It had been mostly clear the night before—with the exception of the flocks they'd pulled in, people were reluctant to get into the foul water. But that had changed. Tonight, the canal was clogged with people, not just the footpaths above it. Maybe they'd seen flocks come in and thought they could get in that way, too. Maybe they were just reaching a new level of desperation. Whatever their reasons, John knew it wouldn't be as easy for the Pineapple flocks to use the canal, and it would be harder to identify those who did manage to make it to the linkup point at the bridge, a few hundred feet away from the hole in the fence.

He got out his phone and texted Zac. *Flocks will have to make sure other people aren't jumping onto the train with them. Advise them that we'll probably have to use force to keep others back as they wade through water.*

John exhaled. *These people know exactly what's happening*, he thought. Time was running out.

118

Night had fallen. Qais brought his family together in their home and asked them to sit. This might be the last time they gathered together like this. It was time to go, he told them. *All* of them.

"I've been listening to you my entire life," he gently told his parents. "But this time, you must listen to me." They had come face-to-face with the Taliban twice and had been threatened or beaten both times. This time, if they ran into a Taliban foot patrol while making their trek to the MOI, they might have to fight.

"If it comes to that, I will reach for his weapon, and use his weapon against him," Qais said, pantomiming how he would grab an AK-47 out of the hands of an opponent, charge the bolt, shoulder the weapon, and fire at his enemy.

"We will all have to do things like this. I mean you, too, Maadar," he said, addressing his mother. She nodded. He turned to his two sisters, one of whom stood with her husband and his brother. "And you all as well. You may have to fight for all of our lives. So long as we fight, we have a chance."

He told his dad, a retired Army colonel, that his job was to help him wrest the gun away from the hypothetical Taliban if he proved strong. And he told his brother and brother-in-law that they would do the same if there were other Taliban.

"I don't want you to cry or be scared. All of you need to be a part of the fight," he instructed. "If you see that the Talib is going to yank his rifle back, then you have to grab him. Bite. Scratch. Kick. We are going to leave together, or we are going to die together."

They agreed, and everyone went to their rooms to make final preparations.

For a moment, it was just Qais and his wife, Rania. She looked determined but displeased. "Qais, you're not worried about me. You're not worried about the kids. I understand that you're standing on your own word. You just want to save them. I get it. But what's going to happen to us?"

Qais was dumbfounded. "If you were in my situation, what would you do, Rania? Would you let your parents die? What would *you* do? That's what I'm doing."

She turned and walked away. He'd never felt so alone.

And then, what felt like only seconds later, his father pulled him aside. He was weeping. He urged Qais to leave with Rania and their children. "I will forgive you," his father said.

"Don't forgive me—we're leaving together," Qais told him.

Qais thought, *O Allah, protect us from the fire.*

119

Razaq and his friend Akmal—the same friend who had asked him for a ride to the U.S. embassy on the day Kabul fell—climbed out of a taxi and made their way toward HKIA. Despite the fact the crowd was even bigger tonight, Razaq felt oddly upbeat. He had shed the sense of dread he'd carried since escorting his pregnant wife and little girls through this nightmare. Leaving his family was the toughest thing he had ever done. But he and his wife both knew she would not have survived another run through the crowd.

"You go, Razaq," she had said in a whisper at their kitchen table as the girls slept. "We will wait for you to bring us in." Once they were inside, Razaq planned to work with the Americans to pull his family in through one of the other, quieter gates he'd heard about.

Razaq and Akmal made it to the first Taliban checkpoint. On this day, the Talibs were in rare form as they thrashed Afghans trying to get past. Razaq swallowed hard as they pressed into what was certainly going to be a gauntlet of pain to get through the checkpoint. His hands shaking, he said loud enough for Akmal to hear, "Normal people don't hit other people like this."

Soon the blows started to rain down on Razaq's head. A moment later, the blunt instruments started to pummel Akmal as well. Dazed, Razaq pulled himself up, trying to catch his breath. Blood oozed from his head into his eyes. He knew he needed to stop the bleeding. Taking a page from how he'd stopped Akmal's bleeding several days earlier, he took dirt and rubbed it on his bleeding head.

He blinked through blood-smeared eyelashes to see Akmal in the fetal position absorbing endless blows to the torso and legs. Razek grimaced and rose with a gasp, helped Akmal stand as the blows transferred back to him. With one final burst, he pushed Akmal through the flurry of cable whips and blunt instruments and through the checkpoint opening, out of the reach of the violently swinging Talibs.

120

SYRACUSE, NEW YORK–AUGUST 25, 2021

Zac paced his kitchen, worried. The conductors had first postponed the start of the express from 8:00 p.m. to 10:00 p.m., and now they were pushing it back again, to midnight. If they didn't start soon, they would lose the nighttime hours at HKIA. Every second counted. He did the only thing he could, ensuring his shepherds were ready to go and had all the information they needed. With nothing to do but wait, he sent an update into the Signal chat.

> ZAC: *The conductor is not visible yet, but he is monitoring the situation. He's still leery. He's pushing till midnight.*
>
> JAY REDMAN: *Is that the call? Have all wait until midnight?*
>
> ZAC: *Unfortunately, yes. We are at the mercy of the conductor.*

121

Was it over? Scott wondered.

Their midnight start had never come to fruition. Not a single one of the six-hundred-odd Afghans waiting nearby had crossed into HKIA.

The 82nd had been away from the linkup point for over seven hours. No conductor, no Pineapple Express. Dawn in Kabul was only two hours away. John told them this would only work at night, and Scott wasn't sure if they could pull people out in the daytime. One commenter on the thread expressed Scott's sense of dread when he posted, *I got it from a well-informed source on the ground that the Taliban have all roads blocked and people are bribing them to get through. $3k a person is what I heard. The gates are essentially getting walled up because it's about to be chaos as people overrun the roadblocks. Military withdrawal is beginning now. ISIS-K threat stream is increasing with possibility of attack on civilians at gates.*

The only thing that brought Scott any solace was Zac's reply to this message.

Please do not stress the timeline right now, Zac wrote. *We are going to extend the operational timeline to continue to try to get our people in and adjust to the fluid situation. Shepherds, please pass along to your passengers about the extension of the timeline. That might help them not be so stressed about the clock ticking away.*

Texts starting flowing into the chatroom.

Oh shit, thought Scott.

JAY REDMAN: *Lost comms with several of my teams. Is anyone else*
  facing this issue?
ISH: *I don't have comms with my guys now.*
PEYTON: *Same, no comms. Are there jammers?*

Some shepherds speculated the Taliban were dropping local cell towers. Others believed it was U.S. cell jammers trying to prevent remote-
controlled IEDs.

A few minutes later, a flurry of new messages appeared. "Back on-
line." "Comms with my guys—good to go." "I've got comms with my
folks. They can go wherever we need."

Just as suddenly as communications had gone down, they had come
back up.

Scott breathed again. It was the last run for freedom, and if they lost
communication with their Afghan partners, it was all over.

122

Norwegian ambassador Jussi Tanner walked briskly back to his makeshift headquarters near the field hospital. Operations at HKIA were coming off the rails. The remaining troops were utterly exhausted. The lack of sleep coupled with endless threat reports and near-constant exposure to the suffering masses had taken a physical and mental toll.

Things weren't going well inside the airfield, either. Conspicuous-looking armed groups, who had not been inside the perimeter before he arrived, skulked around in the darkness—Jussi had no idea who these men were. Plumes of smoke billowed from burn barrels outside the various temporary headquarters as NATO staff shoveled sensitive and classified papers into the flames, lighting up the night and casting shadows on the sides of buildings.

As he walked, Jussi slipped on something. He caught himself before falling and turned on his phone's flashlight.

In front of him, a vast field of thousands of tan body armor vests littered the ground. The arrangement was so dense he couldn't see the ground underneath for one hundred feet. In their haste to evacuate, NATO members had flung their vests on the ground like snakes shedding skin. They didn't want the planes to be overburdened with unnecessary weight.

Just then he heard a violent, crunching sound. Jussi squinted through the darkness. In the flickering shadow of a burn barrel, he could barely make out the silhouette of a squatting NATO soldier smashing combat helmets with a hammer to render them useless.

This can't last much longer, he thought.

123

Hour after hour had passed as Master Sergeant Basira dozed in her seat. Eventually, dawn came. The sun rose higher and higher. Still they waited. It was quiet inside the bus, and outside as well. Away from the gates, there were no crowds. No shoving. No yelling. Only waiting. Basira felt blessed to be with this group. Morning had turned to afternoon. She had an uneasy sense that something was wrong. Two full days had gone by since she first boarded the bus.

Azizyar and Pashtoon and other senior leaders spent a lot of time outside having conversations with other commandos. Then, without any fanfare, two of the Afghan command's top leaders, a general and a senior NCO, got off the bus and left with their families. The Americans had summoned them.

Why only those two? Basira wondered. She wasn't the only one. Azizyar spent the rest of that day and much of the evening outside speaking with other families. Another night came. Basira slept uneasily in her bus seat. No other people were taken into HKIA.

Some of the commandos had had enough of waiting. Throughout the night these men took their families and quietly left, disappearing into the city.

Basira stayed. She would not go back home—that would just put her family at risk. Pashtoon and Azizyar stayed as well. They would stay more than seventy-two hours.

124

Matt Coburn hadn't given up on enlisting his two former bosses, General Scotty Miller and Major General Chris Donahue, to help with Pineapple's efforts. He had sent his Afghan SOF Command Sergeant Majors Pashtoon and Azizyar (along with Master Sergeant Basira, who was posing as Azizyar's wife), to the Panjshir pumping station across from Liberty Gate and told his former commanders they were there, waiting. The Afghans might as well have had a red bow tied around them—it was that easy to pull them in. Yet only two senior leaders had been pulled through the gate—and one of those, a general, had for some reason abruptly left immediately after getting onto the airfield, disappearing back into the madness of Kabul.

Matt had sent a flurry of inquiries via Signal to Miller and Donahue, but all he got in return was silence. Or, something worse than silence. One of Donahue's subordinates, a colonel, phoned Matt to offer himself as a "liaison" between him and the major general.

Matt nearly hung up on him. Donahue was sending a clear message he had zero interest in working with Matt to save this group of Afghan partner forces.

Exhausted, Matt closed his eyes. He had failed.

Then his phone dinged. He opened one eye and glanced at the Signal message.

AZIZYAR
Sir, We're in.

They had been lucky, Azizyar had called every number on his cell and an old friend had answered who was inside HKIA working as an interpreter. He had let them in.

Matt felt relief, but only for a second.

The Afghan explained it was just the three of them: Azizyar, Pashtoon, and Basira. Everyone else had left.

125

The sun was about to rise in Kabul and the conductors *still* weren't in place or pulling anyone into HKIA. Everyone on the chat was understandably fed up with the waiting, but Zac was confident from his discussions with the 82nd Airborne that the Pineapple Express would be back up soon—they were going to go ahead and run it in the daytime.

"Hey! I just wanted everyone to know that you guys are doing a phenomenal job!" Zac said in a voice memo to the chat room. "Shepherds, you are moving your teams across the battlespace, you're getting everyone in position, our intel folks are giving us the best updates they can. We've got a nice pause of a couple of hours before we try this again. One step at a time. Let's play this like a chessboard. Move our pieces around and not do anything too hasty. Okay? One step at a time."

126

Over the lip of her coffee mug, Liv Gardner glanced at the sign hanging on her kitchen wall. It showed a smiling woman holding up a ceramic cup. COFFEE—YOU CAN SLEEP WHEN YOU'RE DEAD.

Not wrong, Liv thought.

Liv had been going back and forth with the Marines for hours, but none of her calls had resolved anything. The Marines, who monitored the threat level around Abbey Gate, gave the word when it was safe to bring people in either through the gate or through the hole in the fence. Even at night, when Abbey Gate was closed, if the Marines said it was too dangerous to bring anyone through the wire, Pineapple Express couldn't run.

She read yet another pep talk that Zac had dropped into the Pineapple room. *Shepherds, motivate your guys any way you can. Tell them to think about the future, their children, their children's future. We've just got to get over this last little hump.*

Liv understood that the ISIS-K suicide bomb threat was at its highest now that the NEO was wrapping up—but that threat had been a factor since August 16.

127

STEVE RULLI: *US embassy alert—leave certain gates immediately, avoid airport. U.S. citizens who are at Abbey Gate, East Gate, or North Gate should leave immediately.*

ISH: *I'm holding my folks.*

WILL: *No comms with mine.*

128

Scott was stunned. A shepherd just reported that a six-year-old girl in one of the flocks had been trampled to death.

Is this much risk worth it? Scott wondered. *Should we have expected children to behave like clandestine operatives? No, we shouldn't have.*

But still, the alternative was worse. The wives and daughters would be raped. The small boys would be torn from their families and put into reactionary madrassas, becoming indoctrinated as Taliban themselves. Other family members would be decapitated, their severed heads placed on their chests on the ground out in public for all to see—the common Taliban practice for dealing with "apostates." This whole "kindler, gentler Taliban" was bullshit and Scott knew it. The whole team knew it.

But the girl's death was a grim reminder of the stakes. Retired SEAL Jay Redman also reported that one of his families had given up after a two-year-old fell in the sewage canal and nearly drowned in the water.

The only way forward was to keep trying.

"Everybody, stay in the game," Scott said in a voice memo. "Zac and Liv are working it. If there's a way to come through today, they'll do it. You guys are doing great. I can't imagine what your flocks are going through. It's absolutely critical to keep them postured for when we break it loose."

129

JAY REDMAN: *One of my families has two kids—one two years old and the other four months. They have been on the move for over 48 hours. They are carrying around little weight bags. Might be beneficial to link them up with another team. . . . If possible and close by.*
SCOTT: *Any other Shepherds that can help Jay out?*
ISH: *My guys are close by and can help.*

Scott thought about how most of these families had been out in that madness for hours. The children of these Afghan special operators had been roughed up and even trampled. Ish's own family had been out in the crowd for twenty hours. No more food. No more water. Ish was in Seattle doing his best to guide them, moving them to a prime piece of refugee real estate near the shit trench. And now they were dropping everything to go help Jay's flock. It was beyond admirable.

This is why we are here, Scott reminded himself.

Scott's fatigue dissipated some as he considered what these Afghans had been through. Tired? He didn't have the right to be tired.

JOHNNY UTAH: *Trying to keep my groups calm and their morale up by reassuring them. My groups are still intact and on site but are restless.*
ISH: *I don't know how long I can hold these guys.*

Scott looked at his watch in the darkness as he lay propped up in bed, with Monty beside him. The sun was already up in Kabul, but his house was still. *Not exactly the empty-nesting I imagined,* he thought.

He couldn't stop thinking about the trampled six-year-old.

He was haunted by the death of another young girl, back in 2005. *She was six, too,* Scott thought. He had cleared the use of a five-hundred-pound burst bomb to terminate a Taliban commander Scott had been fighting against in the mountains of Oruzgan province. The little girl was never supposed to be there. But there she was when the bomb detonated, sending metal fragments screaming into the commander's house.

She was six, but it was impossible to tell from the pictures after the bombing.

Scott had grown accustomed to many things through multiple combat tours, but not the death of little ones. Those things never left.

He looked at his watch again. The odds that the Pineapple Express would ever open again were slim. He checked the chat. Nothing from Zac in over an hour.

Scott felt they were at a critical decision point. Should he tell the shepherds to keep holding the Afghans near the gate, or level with them that it all might be over and that they had to make their own call? If he kept pressing them to stay, many of them would, but at what cost? He knew that the crowds clustered around Abbey Gate were a suicide bomber's dream.

Scott took a breath and looked up at the ceiling. He felt like he was at a breaking point. The flocks were experiencing unbearable suffering outside the airport walls, and it seemed that the threat of an attack increased every second. He desperately wished he didn't have to make these calls anymore. But this responsibility was his and his alone. He looked at his watch one more time. He started typing.

Hey, guys. Sorry to tell you this but we have hit a log jam on the Abbey Gate issue. It's a General Officer food fight going all the way back to DC. It may swing our way—it may not. Liv and Zac worked it hard but so far, no joy. Liv is still engaged with them. I think at this point you have to do what is best for your guys. You have to make the call on whether to stay or leave and try something else. We will keep working Abbey and advise if that or any other opportunities pop. Godspeed.

It was unfortunate, but the suffering was out of control. He had just let in another shepherd too, Rob, who was helping his flock from his posting as a contractor in Iraq. There was still some hope, but not much.

Scott hit send and lay his phone on his chest. He closed his eyes. A few minutes passed. Then his phone buzzed loudly, accompanied by the *whoosh* of a new message. It sounded eerily loud in the dark, quiet room.

Scott picked up his phone.

LIV
Scott, call me. Our conductors just pinged me they're back up.

"Damn!" Scott exclaimed, rolling out of the bed and getting dressed. He called her immediately. "What's up, Liv?"

"They are back up," she said. "Jesse just texted me. I don't know for how long, though."

"Shit, I just told the shepherds to have their passengers bail if they thought their people couldn't hold any longer."

"Try and get them back, Scott. Probably our last chance."

"On it."

SCOTT: *Just spoke with Liv—looks like the conductor is back—stand by.*
ISH: *Standing by.*
ZAC: *Shepherds: if your passengers are up to it, the conductor is back at the original linkup site near the bridge. He is accepting passengers.*
ISH: *Go to Abbey Gate?*
JOHNNY UTAH: *Do they just go up and show the pineapple? I got guys at Abbey who are really close. I don't want to move them to the original linkup unless we know that's 100%.*

ZAC: *I haven't heard back from the conductor for details. I just lost a group of passengers.*

SCOTT: *What happened?*

ZAC: *They hadn't made it to Abbey Gate yet and they were getting the crap kicked out of them by Taliban at a checkpoint. They couldn't find a way around.*

SCOTT: *Shit.*

CAPTAIN RED SUNGLASSES

130

Captain John Folta rifled through his rucksack at Charlie Company's makeshift field headquarters. The Pineapple Express would be a daylight operation now. This was the only option, due to the delays caused by potential ISIS-K suicide bombers during the previous night.

During the night, the operation hinged on the ability of the Afghan flocks to pick out the conductor's green glow stick, the one thing that differentiated him from the multitudes of Marines, 82nd Airborne, and NATO troops lining the airport side of the shit trench.

The threat reporting throughout the night had been too dangerous to risk exposing his paratroopers to a potential suicide bomber and threatened the overall security of the entire NEO. It was two bad choices: either expose his troops and save more Afghans, or hold the troops back and miss the last period of darkness to pull Afghans to safety. Folta's upbringing had always encouraged him to look for ways to serve something larger than himself. Pulling at risk Afghans inside the wire was a way for him to fulfill on a legacy of service that was instilled in him long ago by his parents. After some conversations with Jesse, he had decided to assume some risk and try and pull Afghans in during the daylight.

The glow stick would be useless in bright sunlight, so John would need some other way for the traumatized Afghans to recognize him easily.

Finally, his hand found what he was looking for. He pulled out a pair of chunky Oakley sunglasses with bright red frames. When he wore them, he looked like an Elvis impersonator, or a Mafia don trying, and failing, to go incognito. There was no way he could be missed. He typed a quick text to Zac, along with a selfie: *I'm wearing red shades. You can't miss them. That's my far-recognition signal.*

John and his radioman drove their Hilux to Turkish Tower. From there, they moved quickly along the chain-link fence toward the hole with the orange cloth. Daylight ops added a new level of risk, but he knew that time was running out for these folks.

They walked toward the hole in the fence. John could see people already in the canal and he wondered how many of these were pineapples. After about 125 feet, he passed Turkish Tower again, this time on his left. It was surrounded by Marines, all stationed on the other side of the fence and jersey barriers. He stepped through the slit in the wire. The Marines had reduced their presence outside the fence and, glancing at the footbridge where he and Jesse had pulled up passengers the previous night, he saw that it was now swarming with Afghans.

Using the putrid waste corridor for rapid movement wasn't going to work for these Afghans today. He scanned the area, looking up and down the canal, and sure enough, almost as soon as he arrived he saw a man down in the canal holding up his phone showing the yellow pineapples on a pink background.

John asked for his name, which he then checked against his list of "baseball cards." He found the one he was looking for—it came from a stateside shepherd named Donny—and pulled it up. He asked how many the man had in his flock. "Seven," the man called out. Correct again.

Just as John was about to pull them up, a British paratrooper approached.

"What the fuck, mate, you sure these're yours?" the paratrooper asked.

John gave the paratrooper a quizzical look. "Yep, just checked them through. They're on the Pineapple Express."

"Fuck me. I'm looking for pineapples, too," the Brit muttered as he walked a few yards down the line to another group of pineapples waiting in the shit trench.

I guess you guys have gone international, John thought, laughing to himself. He looked down at the trench filled with men and women trying to get his attention. He'd been wrong on his walk out to the linkup point. The people in the trench *were* pineapples. By the looks of it, nearly all of them were.

131

Scott read messages at a breakneck pace, chiming in with his own. John and Jesse were pulling people out of the canal at a furious rate, with help from other Charlie Company paratroopers and—surprisingly—Brits who were lending a hand, thanks to an active duty Pineapple Shepherd with deep connections to the British military who was passing information of the exodus in real time. The pace of the extractions was dizzying, and some of the protocols were falling away in the chaos.

> DONNY: *The conductor got two other groups in. That's 25 pax.*
>
> LIV: *They just got 3 groups of Donny's out plus 5 others.*
>
> ZAC: *If anyone sees a British soldier around them, the pax can show them the pineapple, and they will get picked up. The conductor confirmed he got 29 of Donny's.*

Scott was elated. But then another series of messages started popping up.

> ROB: *Fuck. Both my groups left and went home . . . shit!!*
>
> JAY REDMAN: *Scott, my guy is at the hospital. His 2-year-old, the one that fell in the water, wasn't breathing. She's apparently ok but I have no idea how long before he can be ready.*
>
> ISH: *One of my group left and one other is divided into two.*
>
> ROB: *WTF?!? Will there even be another chance after today?*
>
> ISH: *This is so hard.*

"Fuck!" Scott slammed his fist onto his oak desk. He'd moved to his office now that things had picked up. Had he jumped the gun on his instruction for the shepherds to make their own calls about whether to carry on or go home?

He shook his head and rubbed his face. He had to get with it and keep people moving. He put in a quick call to Zac. They would pull out all the stops and reach out to any uniformed contacts they had along the HKIA perimeter. They needed all the help they could get.

132

Dan O'Shea woke up on his living room sofa. He'd passed out from sheer exhaustion, his iPhone buzzing on his chest. It was still dark outside. His thoughts immediately turned to Qais and his family. They had been instructed to queue at the Ministry of the Interior and wait for a bus to take him and his family inside. At one point Qais spoke to the driver, who repeated that he would only transport Qais and his immediate family—no non-U.S. citizens, no extended family.

Furious, Dan had spoken to this man himself. He'd bluffed, bloviating to the Afghan bus driver as he knew an active-duty officer would. "This is U.S. Navy Captain Bob MacKenzie from Special Operations Command," Dan had barked, lying through his teeth. "This man's entire family must be transported to HKIA, do you understand? They are all expected by the State Department inside. I need you to promise they will all be boarded on the bus, got it?"

"Yes, sir," the driver had said, totally cowed. "I'll get them on."

It was after this exchange that Dan took a chance at some sleep, his first in nearly thirty hours. Qais would be on a bus around 10:30 a.m. Kabul time, and since he and his whole family were now backstopped by J.P., all was in the clear.

Dan stretched and rubbed his bloodshot eyes. He focused on his iPhone: 4:15 a.m. *Fuck it's early*, he thought. Then he noticed text alerts stacked up from Qais.

QAIS
It's after 10:30. We're still waiting. Any updates?

QAIS
Should we go back home? We've all been here since 3:00 a.m.

Dan snapped awake. He did the math. It was now 12:45 p.m. in Kabul—more than two hours after Qais should have been picked up at the MOI—but apparently he was still there.

He kept scrolling through his chat room messages and came across something he'd missed. It was a reply to one of his earlier SOS posts about Qais's trouble with the bus driver. A pin drop had been shared for a spot off Russian Road near the Panjshir pumping station, which J.P. confirmed was the location of the same secret gate he had brought Nezam's wife and kids through on August 22. Since Qais was an American citizen and a federal law enforcement employee, perhaps he would qualify as one of the "special interest" cases that occasionally entered HKIA through Liberty Gate. He had to try.

DAN
Qais, do you know where Liberty Gate is?

QAIS
Yes.

DAN
Can you make it there?

QAIS
We will try. Walking there now.

133

Zac was ecstatic. He just wished it hadn't taken so long to get off the ground. How many more could they have rescued if they could only have gotten the leaders inside HKIA to play ball? With a little more coordination, they could have brought in their flocks en masse.

As he pondered this, Zac caught up on the texts streaming in. Information was flowing faster than ever, almost impossible to follow.

JOHNNY UTAH
My groups are heading to the conductor. Having some issues navigating the checkpoints but they're on their way.

ADAM E
Is the conductor still at canal? Will he move to Abbey Gate? I have 3 groups at the gate.

DONNY
People need to physically get into the canal for this guy. He's got red shades on and is actively looking for people, looking for pineapples.

ROB
Zac, any possibility for tonight?

ZAC
No. It's today only.

JOHNNY UTAH
Yo we got people moving to the canal.

ISH
I don't have comms with my folks but they are at Abbey Gate. Please help.

ROB
This is the last push?

JAY REDMAN

Guys, I'm going offline. Our guy's daughter was hurt and they can't leave the hospital. They'll have to try some other way. Thanks for all that you're doing. Good to know there are still amazing Americans despite the craziness in our world.

ROB

Zac, how long do you think the express will be running?

ZAC

It's pretty fluid right now just walk up to the American with the red sunglasses and show them the pineapple.

JOHNNY UTAH

2 groups in the water, 4 pax and 2 pax.

DONNY

lol yeah it's turned into a free for all.

ISH

My guys turned back, one of them is really hurt.

ZAC

Just got this from the conductor: "We're on stand down due to high-risk threat at Abbey."

SCOTT

Rob, at this point, don't know if it's worth it? With the stand down. Thoughts?

ZAC

Seems like using the canal is helping. Anyone else having luck in the canal?

JOHNNY UTAH

Yes. Both my groups took the canal. No complaints. Earlier when they went to Abbey Gate they got their asses kicked.

ROB

I think the canal is key. The Talibs don't want to get in that nasty, shitty water. But it can be the key to freedom. They can get a tetanus shot later.

JOHNNY UTAH

They couldn't move so we told them to jump in.

ZAC

I'm pushing all my remaining people to the canal. Abbey is a mess. I told the conductor to spread the word to his guys that we are pushing into the canal.

DONNY

Sounds like the conductor is pulling people out of the water like the *Titanic* just went down. He may be very busy going back and forth. Recommend they walk the canal north, then turn south. Keep checking until they see him. He's out there.

ZAC

Conductors will be coming back up soon. I told him if he can tell all of his guys to look for pineapples that would help. So if you have passengers in the canal have them find a soldier and show the pineapple.

DONNY

Is this going to be a free for all or are we going to have direct contact with the conductor?

134

Dan nervously tracked Qais's progress to Liberty Gate. An Army Ranger had been sent to meet him by the State Department.

Dan had sent Qais a selfie of the Ranger, who had a dark beard and wore a gray T-shirt and a tan armor vest. On the vest was a full-color American flag patch; the Ranger's distinctive crest, showing a lightning bolt, sun, and star, was stitched over the flag.

> **DAN**
> Qais, keep moving to North Gate. The Ranger is waiting for you there. You need to find him. Get to the pin drop as soon as possible.

Finally, at 7:42 a.m., two full hours after Dan had told Qais to try Liberty Gate, Qais texted.

He and his whole family had passed through the passport checkpoint, had done a biometric scan, and were now safely "on the truck" inside Liberty. He thanked Task Force Pineapple profusely, strangers he had never met halfway around the world.

Dan added, *Qais, you had some of my Irish luck today. May it stay with you on your journey home to America. Everyone on this thread played a critical role getting you and your ENTIRE family onto HKIA.*

135

LIV: *Everyone, one of the 82nd conductors says that operations may end indefinitely at 1700. They start moving out tomorrow.*

STEVE RULLI: *USMIL has apparently begun retrograde ops.*

DONNY: *Just to clarify, 1700 Kabul time?*

LIV: *Yes, so 2 hours.*

DONNY: *ALL IN PINEAPPLE: 1SG Jesse is near the bridge now. He is looking for pineapples. I don't have a description other than he's the only 82nd guy up there, has a flash-bang on his chest, and is carrying a rifle. If you are near Abbey, get your dudes in the canal. Into the water, near the bridge that runs over the canal near Abbey Gate. This may be your last chance. Have pineapple photo out so he can see, make eye contact, yell. dude's name is "Jesse."*

JOHNNY UTAH: *We just got one group in!!!*

136

Razaq and his friend Akmal couldn't take it any longer. For three hours they'd stood in shit and sewage holding their cell phones up with the pineapples, but none of the soldiers they saw seemed to be looking for them. No one had offered them help.

"Bro, my leg is really messed up," Akmal said at one point. "I think I need to go to the hospital."

Razaq inspected Akmal's leg, which the Talibs had lacerated as they jostled with desperate Afghans in the canal.

As Razaq poked around the red and swollen wound, Akmal winced. He pulled out his cell phone. One more thing to do before departing.

He texted his shepherds: *Fuck you, Zac, you mess with my emotions. Fuck you, Steve. This is bullshit. Good joke. You guys win. You got me. Fuck this.*

They walked down the service road of HKIA in silence. People were everywhere, but it was nothing like the nightmare they'd left behind. Or maybe it was. Akmal wept under his Ray-Bans.

"Why are you crying, man?" Razaq asked him.

Akmal gestured maniacally, using both arms. "Look around you!"

Razaq's stomach dropped as his eyes landed on a pregnant woman, her burqa hiked up past her waist as several other women knelt around her. She groaned and cried as she writhed in the dirt, giving birth for all to see—in the dirt.

"This is our future," said Akmal. "This is what the Taliban are bringing to us. Our lives are fucked for working with those assholes for the past twenty years."

137

Kazem got angrier with every step he took down the disgusting trench. He'd gone from being a highly respected fighter against the Taliban, to making a last stand against the enemy just days earlier, to wading through human shit and rubbish begging for rescue. At least he had his baby brother with him. He'd wanted to bring his whole family, but his brother was the only one who would stand a chance in the crowds.

Kazem's shoulder ached from holding it up for so long, just like Will Lyles had told him to do, showing the pineapple graphic. Throughout, he screamed, "Pineapple!" over and over.

All around them, hundreds of other people also yelled, "Pineapple!" Some were doing it because it had worked for others, not because they'd been vetted by some group of random American veterans on the other side of the globe. But many of them—maybe even most—had the very same graphic as Kazem. It was a shitstorm, and it happened to be in an actual shit trench.

Suddenly, a soldier with big red sunglasses made eye contact with him.

"It's Captain Red Sunglasses," Kazem said to his brother.

The captain pointed at Kazem and asked his name. He checked it against a list on his phone, and then reached down, pulling the brothers out of the canal and to safety.

138

Will Lyles was getting ready to go to work. His little ones ate breakfast and packed their bags for the school day. They were oblivious to the violent virtual world their dad had been navigating from his wheelchair for the past week.

As he went into the kitchen, he felt that familiar buzz alerting him to a new text. He pulled his phone to his face.

KAZEM
Boss, I'm inside.

Will pounded his kitchen counter with joy when he saw the text. His kids nearly jumped out of their chairs.

"Daddy, are you all right?" his older child asked.

Will smiled so much it hurt. "Yes! Yes, I'm sorry. I'm really, really all right."

He was overcome with joy, but more than that what he felt was relief. Kazem was going to get out. He and TF Pineapple had given it all they had, and the guy who had helped save his life so many years ago was coming to America.

Promise kept.

Will texted Kazem to congratulate him and then switched to the group.

My guy is in, he just sent me a message. Thank all of you.

139

For the first time in days, June reappeared in the Pineapple chat room. The USAID official and former Marine intelligence officer had been busy finding safe passage for at-risk girls and women through the CIA's Eagle Base four miles away. She'd leveraged a Delta Force contact there to ferry the women out—that is, until the CIA torched the base to prevent it from falling into the hands of the Taliban.

When she returned, she found a chat room that was far different than the small group of volunteers who'd helped Nezam. The half dozen or so original members had grown to about sixty. These shepherds were leading hundreds of Afghans into HKIA. The contrasting emotions of relief and chaos were palpable as flock after flock made its way through the wire.

She had a large flock herself, and now that Eagle Base was up in flames, she needed help. She had two groups of young girls that needed exfiltration—one from a soccer team and another from a music school— and now the Pineapple Express was their best option.

She took a chance and posted onto the chat:

> Guys can you also send the canal coordinates or description? I have a large group of young girls moving to base.

> **ZAC**
> Have your pax get in the canal and walk in the water all the way down to the bridge. There are guys from the 82nd picking up anyone who shows a pineapple.

140

TAMPA, FLORIDA–AUGUST 26, 2021–4:39 P.M. KABUL

Scott's head swam as he rushed to dress and shave. He was about to be late to meet Monty at a car dealership to shop for her new car. Based on his lack of presence over the last month, this was a little thing that was a big thing. Even though he was running behind, he kept one eye on Pineapple. He glimpsed at June's post about her flock of girls and paused.

These girls. Maybe there's one last chance to . . . He shook his head. It wasn't his flock and he needed to pay attention to his family. *Focus, man.*

He splashed water on his face and looked in the mirror for several long moments. He barely recognized the man staring back at him. An old face. It had been young when Afghanistan first called to him. But war had taken care of all that. *Snap out of it*, he told himself. There were only a few hours of Pineapple Express left. He'd have to work the final run on the move.

He snatched his keys and jogged outside to his truck. Traffic to the dealership was terrible. As he drove, Signal messages poured in like machine-gun fire. He found himself trying to read the texts while hurtling down the highway at sixty-five miles per hour. He was going to get someone killed. He pulled over.

> SCOTT: *June . . . Do you have the pineapple phone graphic for those girls to show? They have to have it on their phone. Can one of our guys guide June on that?*
>
> JUNE: *Yes to pineapples. But wondering how to walk them into this location. Or walk them into canal?*

SCOTT: *Need one of the old-hand shepherds to talk to June. She's got to move girls through this it won't be easy.*

ZAC: *I'm trying to communicate with the guys to start grabbing the girls.*

JOHNNY UTAH: *We have NMRG guys outside, June. We can probably kill two birds with one stone if you wanna link your girls up with our NMRG guys. They can escort them in. They'll protect. They are outside trying to get in as well.*

Scott pulled back into traffic. He couldn't text and drive, so he brought Zac up on a Signal voice call. Zac picked up on the first ring. "Hey, man," Scott said, "which way are we going with this? We need to get these girls in. Is the conductor coming back onto the bridge?"

"He just messaged that they're going to make one more run at it," Zac responded. "Looks like they're moving that way now. We have been having them show the pineapple to anyone who is standing on the airport side of the trench. Lots of other people outside of Captain Folta's group are pulling them in."

"Great. I really hope they can get there in time," Scott said. He ended the call.

He drove for several minutes, once again scanning texts. No mention of the girls. He pulled over again, cursing his inability to be someplace stationary. The girls suddenly felt urgent. The world pressed down on him. It felt all too familiar. Once more, everything was slipping through his fingers. He was losing control.

All his years of training. All his experience. And there wasn't a fucking thing he could do. Time was the real enemy. He hadn't been able to beat time in over twenty years of war, and now it was about to win again. Like it always would in the end.

Scott typed into his phone.

SCOTT: *Do the 82nd guys know that these girls are coming? Has someone personally talked to the conductor? I don't want them to pull off the link up site for something else and I don't think they will if they know these girls are coming.*

ZAC: *Yes I have texted the first sergeant and captain. They haven't replied. They're swamped.*

Scott cursed again as he pulled back into traffic and drove toward the dealership.

He was so fucking late.

141

Something didn't feel right to Ish. He had a gut instinct for situations that felt wrong, and this felt wrong. Something was spiraling out of control. He didn't know what, but he'd learned to trust his gut through years of fighting the Taliban. It had kept him alive more than once.

Ish's family, plus the two families they were helping for Zac, had gone back to Abbey Gate to recover from the horrific experience of standing in the sewage canal.

His makeshift tactical operations center in his Seattle home was a roar of activity as his Afghan friends frantically talked on their cell phones and laptops. But for Ish, everything got quiet.

He quickly dialed his brother. The *number not in service* tone pierced his ears. Fucking jammers. He kept dialing, feverishly, trying everyone in his party. On the twenty-sixth attempt, his brother-in-law picked up.

"Listen to me. All of you need to leave the area immediately. Stop calling or texting anyone. Leave now and call me when you are away from the airport. Go!"

142

ZAC
30 mins left!!!

143

The deafening sound of the C-17s taking off every few minutes had become commonplace. John glanced around the "shit shack." Troopers were propped up on their rucksacks eating blueberry Pop-Tarts, the only remaining food they'd found in the abandoned HKIA shops. Pop-Tarts were still better than MREs. Several of his guys were crashed out, trying to find some respite from the heat, under the wings of abandoned airplanes. Everyone was exhausted.

Abbey Gate, where he'd recently left to check on his men at the shit shack, was crazy. They'd pulled about 330 people out just today. It was all coming to an end, though. The Marines had kept Abbey Gate open past 1700, but not for much longer—they were about to shut it down. John and Jesse were making one more pull at the trench before it all ended.

As they gathered their kit, Jesse pulled out a pack of Italian Milano cigarettes and croaked, "Going to burn one more real quick, Captain."

John smiled. Jesse had been the glue keeping his company together since landing at this fragile airfield. His big heart had also been a key driver in pulling so many people from the clutches of despair.

"Take your time, Top," he said. He pulled his phone out and sent one more message to Zac.

> FOLTA: Back up, though almost dead again. Boys have kept at it. Final run if we can squeeze any. If you have people near Abbey Gate, get them there, use the pineapple bona fides.

144

Jesse and Doc Gundy parked their truck facing the airstrip as John parked his alongside. They were just outside Abbey Gate. Doc did a final check on his aid bag. John and his radio operator finalized their checks. As they conducted their pre-combat inspections, more Charlie Company vehicles pulled up.

Drivers stayed with the vehicles while the band of paratroopers moved in unison for one last big pull on the Pineapple Express.

Jesse took the lead. John was behind his left shoulder. Doc trailed a few steps behind, his aid bag slung over his right shoulder. The roar from a sea of Afghans simultaneously clamoring for freedom grew louder.

Without being prompted, the troops merged into a loosely organized single-file line so they could move through a concrete alleyway that led to a gap in the blast wall.

As the paratroopers got within thirty yards of the blast walls, a deafening concussion split the dry air like a thunderclap and almost knocked Jesse to the ground. His ears rang amid the eerie silence that follows massive explosions. He dropped into a prone position, his M4 carbine pointed in the direction of the explosion, scanning for threats. Gunshots popped.

His gaze lifted up to the sky over the Turkish Tower, eyes locking on debris rocketing overhead, almost stalling in slow motion, then landing beside him in all directions with a *whump. Whump. Whump.* An arm bent at the elbow. A leg. A face. Flying through the air from the mushrooming cloud of smoke. He steeled himself for what lay beyond that wall.

145

DAN: *ALERT ALERT! Report of IED at Abbey Gate! Waiting for confirmation.*

JOHNNY UTAH: *No comms from NMRG, outside of linkup point.*

DAN: *Detonated. Confirmed by HKIA JOC.*

SCOTT: *June—where are your girls? Any updates?*

MULLAH MIKE: *I'm hearing reports of an explosion.*

DAN: *Confirmed by HKIA JOC only 300m away. Unconfirmed – possible U.S. casualties.*

ZAC: *My guy says he sees multiple fatalities.*

JOHNNY UTAH: *Damn.*

ZAC: *Keep pushing until I get confirmation everything is done. I am hearing of an explosion at canal area.*

SCOTT: *What about the girls?*

IN MEMORIAM

U.S. SERVICE MEMBERS KILLED IN ACTION AT ABBEY GATE ON AUGUST 26, 2021

Marine Corps Lance Cpl. David L. Espinoza, 20, of Rio Bravo, TX

Marine Corps Sgt. Nicole L. Gee, 23, of Sacramento, CA

Marine Corps Staff Sgt. Darin T. Hoover, 31, of Salt Lake City, UT

U.S. Army Staff Sgt. Ryan C. Knauss, 23, of Corryton, TN

Marine Corps Cpl. Hunter Lopez, 22, of Indio, CA

Marine Corps Lance Cpl. Rylee J. McCollum, 20, of Jackson, WY

Marine Corps Lance Cpl. Dylan R. Merola, 20, of Rancho Cucamonga, CA

Marine Corps Lance Cpl. Kareem M. Nikoui, 20, of Norco, CA

Marine Corps Cpl. Daegan W. Page, 23, of Omaha, NE

Marine Corps Sgt. Johanny Rosario Pichardo, 25, of Lawrence, MA

Marine Corps Cpl. Humberto A. Sanchez, 22, of Logansport, IN

Marine Corps Lance Cpl. Jared M. Schmitz, 20, of St. Charles, MO

Navy Hospital Corpsman Max W. Soviak, 22, of Berlin Heights, OH

PART V

THE DUST CLEARS

146

Hovering high above Abbey Gate was a U.S. Air Force MQ-9 Reaper drone, its lens panning over the carnage below. Dozens of figures, appearing as light gray silhouettes, ran single-file past Turkish Tower along the trash-strewn path toward Abbey Gate.

Clustered near the shit trench were about a dozen other figures, moving around and over each other like a group of busy worker bees. Many figures in the frame moved away from the blast site, but not this group.

First Sergeant Jesse Kennedy and Doc Gundy were at the center of this cluster of troops. Captain John Folta stood nearby. After the blast had delivered the gruesome rain of flesh and body parts over the wall, everything became kinetic. Screams and wails rose from the street beyond the fence. Shouting. Boots pounding on the ground. John had summoned a quick reaction force, which took positions along the canal wall, rifles aimed out, looking for follow-on attacks and protecting the men who helped the wounded.

The ISIS-K suicide bomber had set off his IED on the street across the shit trench, just behind a low wall. It exploded outward at 5:48 p.m., sending a fusillade of ball bearings in every direction and a high plume of dark smoke into the sky. The tiny projectiles shredded anyone they hit, including the security forces who had been posted on the far side of the canal. Most of the injuries suffered by these warriors were above the waist. The detonation killed two hundred people crowded around Abbey Gate, including thirteen U.S. service members.

Bodies lay jumbled everywhere in the canal below. Afghans who had been spared staggered in shock along the opposite wall, staring at the human remains in the stagnant sewage.

"Doc!" John yelled to his medic. "Trucks are ready for medevac!" Everywhere he looked, U.S. servicemen applied pressure to wounds and tightened tourniquets to ruptured arteries. One casualty had already been slung over the shoulders of able-bodied men and carried behind the wire.

"Get 'em to the Norwegian field hospital!" Doc Gundy hollered back as he worked on a soldier who had lost a limb.

John sprinted back to the vehicles with several other paratroopers. He jumped behind the wheel of a Hilux whose bed was full of casualties. He paused for only a split second to look left and right for inbound aircraft before gunning the truck across the runway. His eyes settled in on the Norwegian field hospital on Apron 8, making a beeline for it.

Some among the badly wounded would live.

147

Scott was nearly forty-five minutes late as he pulled into the Toyota dealership. Monty was waiting in the parking lot, her hands on her hips. He pulled in and parked, taking up two spaces.

She opened his door. She said nothing. She knew.

"There was an explosion," he said finally. "There were these little girls that were in the canal. We almost had them. I don't . . . I don't really know . . ."

Scott turned to her and buried his face into her chest, sobbing. He wept so hard it was as if the pain of twenty years poured out. All the friends killed, countless more wounded, innocents killed along the way, the lost time with Monty and the boys, and now all those people who had stood with them—abandoned to die in a river of shit.

"Hey, why don't you take a walk and get your thoughts together?" Monty offered. "I'll be right here to drive us home when you're ready."

Scott nodded, wiping away the tears. He walked away from the car lot into a patch of grass and watched the traffic stream by. Reflexively, he checked Signal. Dozens of frantic messages filled the Pineapple chat trying to determine the status of flocks and loved ones. His stomach did somersaults. He felt as though he might throw up.

What just happened? How many are dead?

Scott thought about the U.S. servicemen and women on that wall. About their families. He knew the mother of a young Marine who was serving at HKIA. Would she now fly a Gold Star? What about John and his company? He thought about the families who'd soon hear a knock at the door.

He suddenly realized there was one thing he needed to do. He pulled himself together. He could break down again later.

He recorded a voice memo and dropped it into the chat room.

"Hey, everybody, please listen to this carefully. We need to make sure that we do not pass any information about U.S. KIAs because there's a notification process that must take place. As helpful as this platform has been, we need to ensure that we do not get in front of the military process for notification. That usually takes twenty-four to forty-eight hours. This could be ridiculously heartbreaking to a family if they get word through one of these chat rooms or the media that their loved one was killed. Please remind everybody you're talking to not to discuss any military KIAs because frankly there's nothing we can do about it on this network."

148

Jussi Tanner was working in the makeshift Finnish consulate adjacent to the field hospital when he heard the sickening explosion in the distance. He knew exactly what it was.

He walked outside and looked in the direction of the blast. A column of smoke billowed from the edge of the airport near Abbey Gate. Within minutes, vehicles screamed across the runway toward his location. They reached him in under a minute.

Dead and wounded Marines lay in the back of one pickup's bed. Their buddies sat on the edge, holding hands and comforting them.

Jussi's eyes fixed on an Afghan girl in another truck. She couldn't have been more than ten years old. As he watched, a paratrooper carried her from the truck to the field hospital. She wore a light red dress, as if she were coming from a party. The folds of the dress, from the waist down, were a different shade of red, darker than the top.

Later, he asked one of the medics about the girl, the one in the red dress. The medic just shook his head.

149

James with the Hat walked into his kitchen and poured a splash of bourbon into his West Point mug. Through the window, he could hear the drone of a lawn mower ripping away at a neighbor's grass.

He felt like he had failed. Utterly. Of the 180 people he'd told TF Pineapple about, only a few had gotten out. Scott had told him that one had been a man named Mustafa, who had saved the lives of Johnny Utah's team from an IED years ago. So maybe it wasn't all for nothing. Still, the bombing just steeled his resolution to keep going. He called Scott. "It's been real, but I've got to move on to working overland exfils."

One of the stranded flocks he was determined to save was Bashir's wife, Laila, and their children.

James with the Hat texted an operative still in Afghanistan: *Execute. Let me know when they are out.*

The operative would soon knock on Laila's door. Bashir had told her to expect a slight, unassuming man in a COVID mask. He would say, "James sends his greetings. Are you ready to go?"

She would have just one bag for herself, the children, and baby Zainab. They would be loaded up in a four-door Corolla and would head for the Pakistan border.

James with the Hat stared blankly out the window at his tranquil neighborhood. He didn't even notice his wife sitting at the kitchen table behind him, staring at her distant husband, unsure of what to do.

"There are so many," he said through a hoarse whisper. "This is never going to end."

150

All Ish could think about was that he had condemned his family to death. He had called his brothers dozens of times. No answer.

His downward spiral continued for hours.

Then his phone rang. It was Najibullah, his seventeen-year-old brother. He was alive. They were *all* alive. They had followed Ish's premonitory warning to leave Abbey Gate without hesitation. It had taken them this long to get to safety and into working cell service.

"What about the other families?" Ish asked, concerned for two of Zac's flocks who had joined them for safety.

"They are with us, brother. They are okay."

Ish couldn't answer. All he could do was cry.

151

HAMID KARZAI INTERNATIONAL AIRPORT, KABUL—AUGUST 26, 2021

In the final few days on HKIA, the mission atmosphere changed dramatically. After the explosion, gates were welded shut and internal force protection measures made unannounced entry requests by Afghans all but impossible. It was more profound than just changes in security. Palpable anguish descended on the remaining forces following the loss of thirteen American lives. It infected the entire HKIA task force.

The remaining State Department officials were all exhausted. It was time to go. They had done what they could.

A small group watched the flag folding ceremony between Ambassador Ross Wilson and Major General Chris Donahue in numb silence. As the ceremony ended, some shouldered their bags and filed up the ramp of the C17 Starlifter without a backward glance.

152

First Sergeant Jesse Kennedy shook himself awake, stretched, and jumped from the pickup truck where he was napping. He was almost ready to go. Charlie Company had been pulled off the security mission after the explosion and redirected to the retrograde. They would be part of the rear guard for the entire operation, securing the airfield while the planes departed, and then board the last planes out. It had to be carefully choreographed. Captain John Folta prepared the company with numerous rehearsal exercises before executing it for real.

As Jesse emerged from the shit shack, he noticed a company of Marines baking in the sun. There was no shelter from Kabul's oppressive heat. These Marines had suffered grievous losses the day before and had been pulled off the airfield perimeter. This was their chance to decompress and process their friends' deaths before making the long trek home.

Charlie Company still had one large box of blueberry Pop-Tarts from the HKIA gift shop. It was a coveted box.

Jesse approached the company's executive officer. He didn't want to intrude on the Marines, knowing their nerves and emotions were still raw.

"Would it be okay if we dropped off some food and medical supplies for your guys?" he asked. The XO nodded.

First Sergeant Kennedy grabbed the Pop-Tarts off his Hilux and walked it over. Weary smiles crossed dirt-streaked faces as the Marines eyed it. They stood and exchanged solemn handshakes and hugs with the paratrooper.

Charlie Company got into its vehicles and moved out to their rehearsal area for the retrograde. Jesse rode in silence, thinking of his dad and hoping he'd made him proud.

Tactics and experience save lives during combat, but sometimes luck is more effective. He had paused to smoke one last Milano cigarette at the shit shack before the final run of the Pineapple Express. That brief smoke had saved his life and his captain's.

153

June, where are your girls?

Scott texted this question minutes after the Abbey Gate attack. But June didn't know the answer right away. Some of the girls—school-age orphans—had been trying to link up with Johnny Utah's NMRG operatives in the canal less than an hour before everything went dark.

"I still don't know who lived or died," June had told him. "I don't even really know who was there. But I got a video sent to me in my WhatsApp of the carnage from one of the women who was with this group of girls." She was choking back tears. "I don't think they made it. All I know, Scott, is that Task Force Pineapple gave them something they didn't have."

Scott could hardly imagine what that was, since they and other flocks were now dead. "What was that?"

"Hope, Scott. We gave them hope."

154

Major Ian Wookey was in a hurry. He and the other remaining pilots had a final, critical mission: deny the Taliban an air force. Seventy fixed-wing and rotary aircraft littered Aprons 8 and 9. The group of aviators were making buckets of slimy crud consisting of chemicals and sand to pour into the fuel tanks of all the planes and helicopters they could not fly out of Afghanistan.

The U.S. embassy's CH-46 helicopter, the very one that had evacuated acting ambassador Ross Wilson from the Green Zone. Expensive Connecticut-manufactured Black Hawks. A-29 Super Tucanos. The light scout choppers known as "Little Birds." C-130s. A-206 Cessnas. PC-12 spy planes. All were soon rendered unflyable by the pilots pouring the grimy cocktail into the fuel system and yanking out electrical cords in a discreet manner so little outside damage would be noticed or make headlines in propaganda pictures.

The 82nd Airborne had its own four CH-47 Chinooks at HKIA. Whether the U.S. troops would be taking them with them was far from certain. Wookey had prepared three contingency plans: 1) load the Chinooks onto Air Force C-17s, if any arrived; 2) fly the helicopters into neighboring Pakistan; 3) toss thermite grenades in each chopper and go.

Late in the day, more giant C-17s arrived, and Wookey and the aircrews folded the rotors of the Chinooks and watched the loadmasters push them inside the bellies of each bird. The major and his men loaded up. And then they were gone.

155

All of the airport's gates had been welded shut. All the equipment that wouldn't be taken had been destroyed or decommissioned. All the remaining vehicles rendered inoperative, all the papers burned, all the hard drives smashed. All that remained was for Charlie Company and the rest of the 82nd to get out alive.

During evacuation operations in rough places, the most terrifying moment comes when the last flights leave, when there's no one behind to provide cover or watch your tail. HKIA was no exception. Charlie Company had arrived amid chaos, and they were leaving in chaos.

"Prepare to execute," Captain John Folta heard over the radio.

The brigade headquarters began to call the companies one by one. Each company loaded up their commandeered vehicles and consolidated on their assigned planes. Charlie Company was the last one off the airport perimeter.

As he watched First Sergeant Jesse Kennedy count his men onto the plane, John glanced at the last plane that would take General Donahue after they lifted off.

John went through the contingency plans in his head. What if the plane broke down? What if they started receiving fire? What if . . . What if . . . And he prayed the plane would take off, and fly away, and maybe he could finally get some sleep.

The paratroopers broke from their formation and began hastily filing into the C-17. Jesse counted them one by one as their boots pounded up the tail ramp into the plane's vast cargo bay—the most important head count of his career. Then he boarded.

The massive cargo plane lumbered down the long runway and lifted into the night sky over Kabul. Jesse could feel the tension among his guys as the plane climbed, holding their breath for incoming rockets that could kill them all. He went around to each of his men. Their work had been "epic," he told them. They had gone above and beyond the call of duty and had saved hundreds of lives.

"You made the history books," he told them. "Everything will be fine. We're almost home."

Jesse took his seat. There would be time for reflection and processing when they landed in Kuwait. For now, Jesse closed his eyes and leaned his head against the red cargo netting, quietly hoping he was right.

156

About a week after the Abbey Gate bombing, Scott received a text while eating dinner at home.

> Mark Milley here . . . if you get a chance give me a call.

He'd blinked and read the text again. *General* Mark Milley? The chairman of the Joint Chiefs of Staff? The president's most senior military adviser? In disbelief, Scott held the text for Monty.

"Maybe they're actually going to do something, baby," she said. She was the optimist in the Mann family.

"Fuck it, let's see if he picks up." He tapped call.

"This is Mark Milley," came the gruff, Massachusetts-accented answer.

The call was surreal. As Milley spoke, all Scott could think about was how mad he was about how the NEO had been handled.

"Scott, I want you to come to D.C. I want to work together to get more out," Milley said.

"Yes, sir. When do you want me there?"

"Immediately."

"Yes, sir."

Scott hung up, his heart racing. He looked at Monty like a kid who'd just been offered a free pass to Disney World. She rolled her eyes. "I'll cancel your workshop tomorrow, contact your clients, and start working flights."

For the first time since the bombing, Scott felt something like hope.

Six days later, Scott found himself following a Pentagon escort down a long, wide hallway to the chairman's conference room, their footsteps echoing off the polished floors. Now that it was happening, he didn't want to be in this sterile, squeaky-clean palace of dread. Twenty years of pain and loss and disillusionment had begun here, almost to the day. It had been the 9/11 battleground where his Ranger buddy Cliff had died after American Airlines Flight 77 pierced the west side of the building. Losing Cliff had fueled Scott's rage and thirst for revenge in his first blistering years of combat in Afghanistan. Over those years, Scott had lost twenty-two more brothers in arms.

Click, click, click, the footsteps continued down the nearly empty hallways. *The chairman's conference room*, Scott thought. How could this be? He had never been summoned by the chairman even when he was in uniform. Now he was in a blue suit, brown leather dress shoes, and a yellow tie about to meet the top man.

When they reached Chairman Milley's conference room, Scott took out his cell phone and placed it in a lockbox. An Air Force major led him inside. Scott wasn't alone. Other former officers were seated around the table. Major General Ed Reeder, Nezam's former boss, was one of them. They barely spoke. There wasn't much to say. At the far end, digital clocks displayed time zones from around the world. Scott imagined the topics of conversation that high-level officers must have had in this very room: Panama. Afghanistan. The bin Laden raid.

How many high-level plans have been hatched here? Scott wondered. Would recovery of the Afghan Special Operations Forces be solved here today? That was the only reason he was in this room.

General Milley entered with his entire staff. He made a joke that fell flat about "having pineapples and other kinds of fruit in the room." Then he said, "Let's see who all are here." One by one, everyone introduced themselves.

After the intros, General Milley launched into a thundering diatribe. "This was the greatest airlift in American history," he said. Wearing his khaki windbreaker with four stars on each shoulder, he continued, "Over a hundred twenty-five thousand American citizens and Afghans were lifted out. It's unprecedented!"

In an instant, Scott realized this was nothing more than political theater. Legacy damage control. Every ounce of hope he had felt coming in drained away.

All he could think about at that moment were the hundreds of Afghan commandos and their families that Matt Coburn had organized onto buses outside Liberty Gate—people who had been denied entry by American commanders. The greatest airlift in history was also one of the greatest American betrayals of its allies. People had been left on rental buses with engines running. If that wasn't an apt metaphor for what had happened, Scott didn't know what was.

"There is still more work to do," Milley continued. "We can do better. But we need your help. I'm going to recommend to the National Security Council that we establish a public-private task force to work on getting more at-risk Afghans out of the country. DoD won't lead, but we'll be in support. State will have the lead. We'll work with your private groups to get more people out."

Scott raised his hand. The general nodded. "What does that look like, sir?" Scott asked. "I mean, will there be DoD assets for this? Do we hand our manifests off to you?"

"No, like I said, State will continue to be in the lead. DoD will not commit assets, but we will be in support."

There it was. The real truth of the NEO. The buck had been passed—and saluted. This whole thing was bullshit.

After a few more comments, General Milley turned to his operations officer and directed him to get everyone connected on this private-public collaboration. Then the chairman rose and left the room, his entourage streaming behind him.

Scott left the Pentagon without saying a word to his escort. On the flight home, all he thought about was whether Task Force Pineapple should participate at all. Or should they fold their tents and go home, as other groups had done? If they closed up, all of those Afghans who were still there—over six thousand people were now on Pineapple's manifest—would have no lifeline to the outside world. Many would be hunted, captured, and killed.

By the time Scott arrived in Tampa, he'd made his decision. He was skeptical, but he decided that they were going to do it. Task Force Pineapple was about to play the long game.

Zac had shown interest in signing up to do this full time, possibly quitting his teaching job. It was a start.

Six months later, Scott's skepticism was justified. The entire private-public cooperation had been a complete illusion. They received little help from the State Department, the Pentagon, or any other U.S. government agency, despite Milley's promises.

Their only choice was to do what they'd been doing. Press on with other volunteer groups, and fight the fight alone.

157

It was fall in the nation's capital. Scott and J.P. Feldmayer met in the lobby of the Crystal City Marriott in Arlington. Scott had been trying to continue the long-term effort of Afghan relief by turning Pineapple into the public-private effort General Milley had suggested. J.P. was in town for post-mission briefings. Even though they'd both been Green Berets serving in Afghanistan in 2004 and 2005, it was the first time they had met in person.

Smiling and easy-going, J.P. looked less like a former Green Beret Engineer Sergeant than a cool, bearded, and bespectacled lit professor.

Scott spoke first, unsure how to show his gratitude. "I know we burned your phone up, man. I'll never forget what you did. None of us will."

"You know, there were some days over there that I would look out at that crowd and my eyes would settle on one face. Real panic. Fear. Desperation. It crushed me."

"That had to be tough."

"Yeah. It was. When I finally got to see my wife and kids a few days later, it hit me even harder." J.P. paused and took a sip of his coffee. "The point is that every time you guys called, somebody's life was hanging by a thread outside the wire. I always knew that."

"There are thousands that didn't make it out who should have," Scott said. "A lot of the Shepherds want to keep going. I feel like I'm too old for this shit, but I'm in it now."

"Okay, I'm heading over to Qatar. If I can help from that side, you shoot me a note on Signal and I'll try my best."

Scott thanked J.P. again and the two fell silent with their thoughts.

J.P. stared across the lobby. "You know," he said quietly. "You know this thing isn't going to end the way either of us want it to? You do know that, right?"

Scott looked down for a moment as if consuming the whole Afghan forever war into one last inhale. "Yeah. It never does."

158

Bashir was glad Scott had come to see him. He hadn't had many visitors since moving into his new apartment in Dallas. The two men had dinner, mostly eating in silence, at the "Back Yard Chicken Shack." Bashir would have liked to have prepared his friend an Afghan meal, but he only had a short break from work.

It had been months since he had flown from Qatar to Texas, where he lived with four other Afghan men. Bashir was back in uniform. He was a security guard for a grocery and liquor store. It was a bizarre posting, after so much time spent at war.

"How's the job, Bashir?" Scott asked.

"It's fine, sir. I am able to save money. I work seven days a week, and I am putting money away for when my family gets here." His eyes dropped and his voice trailed off at that thought.

"How's your little girl?"

"She's amazing." Bashir's face lit up. "She's growing so fast." Bashir pulled out his phone and the two men looked at pictures as proud dads do.

"Listen, man," Scott said. "Commander James and I are doing everything we can to get your family back to you. I just talked to the chairman of the Joint Chiefs. They have this on their radar. We won't stop until they're here. I promise."

Bashir looked at his watch. "I have to get back to work." The two men hugged. Before parting ways, Bashir said, "Sir?"

"Yeah?"

"When I landed in Germany, I had only my backpack and my

sandals. I called Green Berets I knew from 10th Group. They were there at the camp in forty-five minutes with food and clothes for me. When I landed in Wisconsin at that refugee camp, same thing. Green Berets were there before I even called. And here you are now," he said through tears. "Everything I have in my life now came from Green Berets."

"Green Berets will get your family here, too." Scott turned to go back to his rental car. Bashir watched his friend walk away, head down, into the busy parking lot.

159

Hasina Safi was living in a London hotel, no longer a minister. She was a refugee again, although one with a powerful voice for her homeland.

She'd taken some trouble to find the mysterious soldier named Jesse who'd pulled her and her family from the canal. After they got onto the airfield, he had waited with them and ensured her family was loaded onto an RAF plane. Just before they boarded, First Sergeant Kennedy ripped the small black and tan American flag Velcroed to his sleeve and gave it to her.

"Something to remember," the sergeant said with an awkward smile. Then he disappeared.

First Sergeant Jesse Kennedy had permanently changed Hasina's view of soldiers. Once she was settled in the UK, she took it upon herself to learn everything she could about the 82nd Airborne, the "all-American" division. And she treasured the tiny flag he had given her.

She wanted to understand the character of this man—this stranger—who had helped her in an impossible situation. She wanted to know why he had come from so far away to afford protection and human decency to Hasina and her precious family amid the failures of so many powerful institutions, including the American government and her own. He would always be a *brother of quality* to her, the highest praise from an Afghan.

Eventually, she was able to contact Sergeant Kennedy. And when she did, she told him, "Jesse, you are my brother. Whenever I think about my brothers, I don't have five, now I have six. You are my sixth brother.

I pray for your long life with dignity. I pray that even the wind does not touch you."

When the Taliban was pushed out of power in 2001, American officials told women to stand tall. And they did. Hasina Safi knows they will stand tall again. This remains her life's work.

160

In a ramshackle row house, former Command Sergeant Major Azizullah Azizyar spooned out Afghan lamb and long rice onto plates on a donated dining table. Sitting next to Azizullah's wife, Matt Coburn gratefully accepted a plate. Azizullah's five-year-old son, wearing a Spider-Man costume, sat in Matt's lap. When he arrived at the house, Matt had surprised all three kids with new superhero-themed bicycles.

The family's new home was a rental provided by Catholic Charities. Azizullah wore a teal Adopt-a-Pet T-shirt—also donated—while his housemate, former Command Sergeant Major Pashtoon Peer Mohammad, sat across the table in a gray tracksuit, a beanie pulled low over his ears, translating for Matt.

The conversation turned to the fall of Kabul and President Ghani's flight. Azizullah burst into tears. As did Pashtoon. They had lost everything except their lives. Azizullah's six-year-old daughter glanced back and forth at the broken soldiers with her sad brown eyes, revealing her own trauma.

Matt excused himself. The moon-faced and bespectacled young woman who lived with them, Master Sergeant Basira, needed a ride to a job interview at an auto parts warehouse business that was owned by another veteran. Matt would never have guessed it, but the retired Green Beret's own survival felt like it hinged on the fate of this young Afghan woman who, in her country, had achieved so much.

Basira got the job, and for two months Matt drove her to work at 4:30 a.m. every day. Not long after, all three Afghan veterans were hired at the warehouse, and Matt helped them buy a used car.

Basira had a name for the retired Green Beret colonel. Burly Matt Coburn was simply "Big Brother."

161

Mohammad Rahimi settled into his chair in his tiny Syracuse apartment. His oldest son snuggled in his lap. Sometimes Mohammad couldn't believe he and his family were in the United States. Living near Mister Zac made it even better. He saw him regularly—and the other Afghan families that Zac was sponsoring in the area.

But this dislocation was a strange new experience. Profound sadness often overtook him and his family for reasons he couldn't understand. It was paralyzing. He looked down at his son, and pressed the remote for the TV. Watching a movie with him seemed like the best way to end a day of unsuccessfully looking for work.

The movie started, as many American movies do, with a shoot-out. Within seconds, Mohammad felt his son shaking. Sobbing hysterically, he buried his face in Mohammad's chest, tears soaking his father's shirt. He had that same look on his face when he'd seen the man shot in the head near HKIA.

Mohammad quickly turned off the show and tried to calm his son, but it was too late. He would sleep with his mother and father that night. Carrying his whimpering son into their bedroom, tears fell down Mohammad's face as he tried to shake the bloody HKIA images from his mind as well. Tomorrow would be a better day.

162

Razaq had watched the buildings burn near HKIA from a friend's house. He'd wept as a massive C-17 lumbered into the air, the very last American plane to leave Kabul. Its taillights grew smaller as it gained altitude, and finally vanished into the distance. HKIA's lights then winked out, as if the Taliban had snuffed out all electrical power in Afghanistan.

His mom called soon afterward. "Come home, Razaq," she had said. "Your wife has lost the baby." For him, this loss had been the last victim of the nightmarish evacuation, a personal sequel to America's longest war.

Months later, Razaq found himself still moving from one Kabul safe house to another. He prayed that his SIV would finally get approved after years of waiting. He had no job and was afraid to apply for a new one lest a biometric scan reveal his name and the fact that he had worked as a contractor for the Americans. Under the Taliban's resurrected rules, his wife couldn't teach. They had practically no money on which to survive. They sold her jewelry, their car, their furniture. The only other income they had came from donations through Pineapple.

But Razaq was defiant. He sometimes wore a jacket adorned with an American flag in the streets. He attended evening prayers—mandatory for men under Taliban law—and sent his American friends videos that he surreptitiously recorded in the mosque. These showed the imam, flanked by Talibs in camouflage jackets and cradling AK-47s, as he sermonized from the Qu'ran.

As with most things under the Taliban, even religion was to be received from the end of a gun.

163

Kazem landed well, relative to other Afghan refugees, accepting the sponsorship of a Duke University professor who lived in a renovated Victorian house in a leafy corner of North Carolina's Research Triangle. She was a kind and generous woman, but she did not like Kazem smoking in the house. He would step onto the back deck to feed his habit. He had switched to Marlboro Reds.

Kazem and his brother had barely made it into HKIA before the bomb went off. They were hustled off to processing, where they stood in line with other Afghan refugees for hours. After their initial paperwork had been reviewed, an American soldier approached them.

"Your brother can't fly with you, sir," the American said bluntly.

Anger boiled inside Kazem. "What the fuck are you talking about?"

"He has no visa. He didn't work for the U.S. government."

"Yes, he did. He did contracting for you guys," Kazem said. He explained that Task Force Pineapple people had submitted paperwork for his brother.

But the soldier wouldn't budge from his position.

"So, you're telling me this seventy-year-old motherfucker here," he said, pointing to a fragile old man staring off into space in the corner of the terminal, "that *he* risked his life for the U.S.?" He gestured toward another Afghan avoiding eye contact. "And how about this douchebag who I know is a fucking taxi driver that jumped the fence. Did he work for the U.S. government?"

The soldier insisted that his brother had to go. The decision was final. The brothers hugged. Kazem promised him he would get him out, somehow, and his brother went into hiding in Kabul.

Kazem eventually arrived in the United States and was taken to a refugee camp at Fort Dix, New Jersey. Then he was flown to Raleigh-Durham and taken to his new home. Winter had been in full swing when he stepped out on the deck for a smoke and dialed Will Lyles in Texas.

"Hey, boss, I don't think I'm gonna be staying here too long," he told him.

"Whaddya mean? You just got there. What's going on?"

"I mean, I'm like what, thirty-seven? I'm too fucking old to be learning something new. No offense, but this country is all about having nice stuff. This life here isn't for me. I don't care about nice clothes. Nice car. Nice house. I don't even care how food fucking tastes, boss. Do you understand what I'm saying?"

Will was bewildered. "What do you want to do, then?"

"I just wanna go back and start killing the motherfuckers again. And again and again and again."

As crocuses in Durham heralded spring, Kazem vanished. He had not answered texts on Signal. Will knew in his heart what it meant. Kazem had changed his nickname on Signal from "Life Fucking Sucks" to "Live to Fight Another Day."

Kazem had returned home.

164

Scott was nervous with anticipation as he prepared his barbecue grill for their very special guests. Nezam was coming over with his family this afternoon. As he cleaned the cast iron grill, he thought about what J.P. had said. He thought about the others they had helped get to freedom.

Qais's family members were still living with six thousand other Afghan refugees at the U.S. Marine Corps base at Quantico, Virginia. After arriving back home in northern Virginia, Qais surprised even himself by immediately volunteering as a linguist with the Department of Homeland Security, which was processing refugees for resettlement.

Peyton had managed to get eighteen of his twenty-one NMRG out and was now working on the Ukraine problem with his active duty unit. John and Jesse were preparing for similar deployments there.

Liv had been initially traumatized by the explosion and extreme loss of life, but she did manage a quiet smile when she learned that Jesse and John were able to navigate directly to the Level II Hospital because of the connection she had made with them and Khalid's pregnant wife. Leveraging the lessons she'd learned during the Afghan collapse, she had jumped in to help out displaced Ukrainians as well. Pineapple 2.0.

As time wore on, and the voices of those left behind grew quiet, Scott wondered how many were actually saved. Hundreds. More than a thousand? Not enough. That much was certain. The truth was, he was still discovering who had made it out and who didn't. Every day he received new information on heartbreaks and victories.

But he had to ask himself, what was the cost? To him, his family, his friends, the shepherds.

And was it worth it? Of that, he had no doubt.

Was it necessary? Now, that was the question.

Or better yet, why had it been left to them, Task Force Pineapple and all the other volunteer groups?

About an hour later, Nezam and his wife, Uldoz, walked through the front door. Scott felt a wave of emotion wash over him. They were here. Finally. They were safe. Nezam's three little ones rushed right up to him and Monty with neck-squeezing hugs that they'd been waiting six months to give. As Nezam and his wife brought their customary housewarming gifts into the kitchen, Scott motioned for the kids to follow him down to the dock by the river. Elham, eleven, just beamed with excitement in her new dress. The boys—Hawa, eight, and Hassam, six—squealed with delight as Scott pulled out rods and reels from a locker.

"Fishing!" Hassam shouted, using one of his new English words.

Scott sat on the edge of the dock with all three as they took turns learning to cast a line under his watchful eye.

Nezam sat back in the Adirondack chair on the dock and smiled at the contented scene. The kids didn't catch any fish, but nobody cared.

Later, Nezam deftly wielded an axe under a stand of live oak, quartering a log with a set of on-target blows. He and Scott picked up the wood from the ground and tossed it into the firepit.

The two men stood quietly over the fire watching the kids play tag in the yard, as the golden light of sunset faded. The light reflected on the river, rippling in the wake of a passing fishing skiff.

Monty called them up hill to dinner.

Scott marveled at the turn of events as they ate and told stories. Seven months prior, Nezam had been a dead man walking. Now he had a Florida driver's license, was already working on his GED, and lived with his family on a pleasant suburban block a short drive from the bay. Scott was training him to be a story coach to other veterans while he also followed his passion for working with horses at a local equine clinic. The Tampa community had rallied for them, furnishing their new rental house and providing clothes for his wife and their three kids, now happily enrolled in public school, learning English, and making friends.

After the adults were finishing up dinner, Elham and Hawa emerged from the kitchen with papers in their hands and presented them with carefully drawn renditions of the American flag with the family beneath it. Scott was speechless and hugged each of the little ones tightly.

In the twilight, Nezam and Scott went back down to the fire. After years of moving from battle to battle and never settling down with his family, Nezamuddin Nezami, the "backpack man," didn't have to run anymore. Surrounded by his new family, and sitting next to the brother who had refused to give up on him, honoring a promise that their respective governments had not, Nezam finally had a home.

"What do you think you want to do?" Scott asked after a long silence, his gaze straight ahead.

Nezam thought for a moment, furrowing his eyebrows and staring into the fire's dancing orange blades.

"I don't know yet."

"Do you want to still be a soldier?" Scott asked.

Nezam remained silent. A crack of sparks flew skyward and he watched it dance into the starry night. "I want to move on," he finally said. "I think I have been through a lot."

Scott nodded. They all had.

EPILOGUE

Since the end of the NEO on August 31, 2021, General Mark Milley had countered requests from Capitol Hill calling for his resignation by declaring the evacuation the greatest airlift in American history. Privately he groused that his critics just didn't know what they were talking about. According to him, the Pentagon had not failed but instead snatched *victory from the jaws of defeat.*

The fall of Kabul and the two weeks that followed at HKIA, America's last outpost in Afghanistan, were hardly high points in our humanitarian history—far from it. Over the course of its history, America had liberated Nazi concentration camps, pulled off the Berlin Airlift, and delivered aid to disaster-struck countries across the globe. To claim victory in the events that occurred in Afghanistan belies the purpose of the airlift in the first place, which was to save American citizens and at-risk Afghans from the violence of the Taliban. The thousands left behind who continue to face that violence every day simply do not support any claims of success.

WHY DID WE FAIL?

Beyond these myths of victory, how and why had America failed in this final mission in Afghanistan? Was it a lack of intelligence? Willingness? Capabilities? Planning? Humanity? All of these?

In the spring of 2021, in a House hearing, Texas Congressman Michael T. McCaul grilled U.S. Special Envoy Zalmay Khalilzad. He specifically discussed the threat Nezam was facing from vengeful Taliban while the State Department dawdled on his SIV application. There were, he noted, 18,000 similar applicants whose cases had not been resolved. "I'm concerned that his prediction, and many predictions, will come true, that these people will be slaughtered by the Taliban," the congressman said.

Khalilzad was dismissive, even saying, "I personally believe that the predictions that the Afghan forces will collapse right away, they are not right."

In June, Secretary of State Antony Blinken said at another hearing that a collapse wouldn't "be something that happens from a Friday to a Monday." And before a Senate committee, General Milley himself said, "My professional opinion, I do not see that unfolding. I may be wrong. Who knows? You can't predict the future. But I don't see Saigon 1975 in Afghanistan. The Taliban just isn't the North Vietnamese Army." Other senior leaders made similar comments.

Senior leaders in the administration, from the president down, were briefed as early as March 2021 that Afghanistan would fall after America withdrew, that it was simply a matter of time. And yet, when President Biden was asked on July 8, 2021, if his own intelligence community had assessed that the Afghan government would likely collapse, he replied, "That's not true," and that "there is going to be no circumstance where you see people being lifted off the roof of an embassy of the United States in Afghanistan."

In one sense, the president was right—American officials at the U.S. embassy in Kabul were lifted off the soccer field adjacent to the embassy, not the roof.

And the slaughter came after the U.S. exit. Overhead imagery and inside source reporting revealed bodies littering the Kabul streets once NATO forces were gone, media assets moved on to other stories, and the Taliban's campaign of vengeance gained momentum over the brutal Afghan winter.

THE RISK TO OUR NATIONAL SECURITY

America's broken promises are a risk to national security. In this era of near-peer threats, it's unlikely the United States will take on China or Russia in direct combat. Blunting totalitarianism as well as violent extremism will be done through the partnership with indigenous forces around the globe. The wholesale abandonment of Afghanistan casts serious doubt on the U.S.'s willingness to honor its promises to its allies.

Partners will have every right to question the word of Green Berets and other U.S. forces by simply recalling Afghanistan.

How will these broken promises play out when the Taliban or their Russian and Chinese allies interrogate captured Afghan special operations soldiers and extract personal information about our own warriors and their families for further exploitation in strategic conflicts in Eastern Europe, like Ukraine, or even at the hands of the Chinese in Taiwan?

What if Americans are sent back to Afghanistan following another catastrophic terrorist attack at home or if they confront a global terror threat emanating from this now-unfettered sanctuary where al Qaeda has reconstituted and where ISIS-K's strategic capability was kicked up a notch? Will our sons and daughters face pissed-off, well equipped, U.S.-trained commandos carrying the grudge of betrayal?

Many in Washington speak of "over-the-horizon" strike capabilities with the same gleeful confidence they conveyed when trying to target Osama Bin Laden in Afghanistan before the attacks of September 11, 2001. As we saw with the failed retribution strike against ISIS-K, on August 29, 2021, where ten innocent Afghans (including seven children) were killed, this capability falls far short.

Vowing "never again," after the 9/11 attacks, our nation built a robust intelligence and partner network in Afghanistan, which our brothers and sisters fought for, bled for, and died for, for two decades. As things fell apart in mid-August 2021, these high-value individuals reached out to the U.S. men and women they had served with as a lifeline. Throughout the weeks of chaos in Afghanistan, SOF veterans were encouraging strategically vital, yet fragile, human networks to hang on until the cavalry came—in this case, United States Special Operations Command. Numerous attempts were made to hand off these networks to USSOF. The message was urgently passed from Veteran volunteer SOF groups to general officers in USSOCOM, U.S. Army Special Operations Command, and U.S. Special Forces Command, but no one came. The United States surrendered twenty years of strategic social capital in the blink of an eye, a strategic blunder that will haunt our society for years to come. And that is to say nothing of the moral injury.

As we learned all too painfully in Afghanistan, Iraq, and elsewhere, except in the case of total war, we cannot kill our way to security. In most modern near-peer conflicts today, a strong military alone isn't enough to triumph over the enemies of democracy. The secret to countering major threats to our national security lies as much in relationships as it does in unilateral strength. Relationships with partner forces. Relationships with NATO. Relationships we have squandered.

RELATIONSHIPS MATTER

Incredibly, there was not one single U.S. Green Beret team inside Afghanistan in the final weeks leading up to the collapse, or inside HKIA during the NEO. How could this happen? As the nation's premier elite force for mobilizing indigenous forces, Green Beret "horse soldiers" were among the first SOF inserted into the Afghanistan twenty-year war, specifically because of their deep relationships with indigenous people. Just one twelve-person SF team could have worked with Afghan SF like Nezam or Bashir from inside HKIA to facilitate and speed up the process of bringing in vetted Afghan Commandos and Special Forces partners. At the very least, they could have helped those left behind to prepare to survive and resist, thus preserving the vast intelligence and indigenous networks we built, and possibly preventing another attack like the ones in September 2001.

Recognizing these military shortcomings in the fall of Afghanistan is not the domain of high-level military strategists. They were pointed out by the very volunteers who stepped in during the collapse. During more than seventy interviews, over and over, special operations veterans, particularly former Green Berets, kept asking the same questions about the failures of our policymakers and military leaders in preserving what the 9/11 Commission had demanded of them.

They also grappled with helping the abandoned Afghans who had served shoulder-to-shoulder with them. Colonel Matt Coburn was still stunned that 150 of his Commandos were locked out of HKIA by American commanders on the airfield who refused to answer his direct pleas for assistance, even as the CIA's thuggish partner forces were evacuated wholesale out of Kabul after brutalizing Afghan civilians and soldiers alike at the airport's edges.

The paramilitary force paid by U.S. taxpayers physically denied access to many Afghan SOF partners even as they were witnessed bringing in their own families, including 8,500 NSU members who were airlifted or driven from the CIA's Eagle Base to HKIA by August 26, contributing to the logjam of thousands of unprocessed passengers that prevented entry to more of our valued partner forces on those final days.

Today many of those U.S.-funded paramilitaries—who had to rebrand after years of credible reports that some of their units had committed war crimes—are roaming American streets. Axios obtained minutes of a National Security Council meeting on August 14, 2021, where officials prioritized evacuees such as "Central Intelligence Agency priority partners" and local U.S. embassy staff like the several thousand J. P. brought in, but Afghan SOF and aviators didn't make the list.

One counterpoint, however, came from Pineapple's chief conductor, Captain John Folta of the 82nd Airborne. He said that the NSU taking over security at North and East gates enabled his company to adjust their security mission, which allowed them to facilitate the Pineapple Express.

But should it have come down to such a deal with the Devil?

"The agency honors its commitments," former CIA Director George Tenet told Washington Post columnist David Ignatius about the CIA's paramilitary evacuees.

Why didn't the U.S. military honor its own commitments?

WHERE WERE THE LEADERS?

There is little doubt that the Afghan evacuation failed, in part, to decisions made at the highest level of our government: President Trump's wrong-headed peace deal with the Taliban where he excluded the Afghan government and our allies, President Biden's inept withdrawal plan, and the State Department's inexcusable and hopelessly bureaucratic SIV process and chaotic NEO. It's deeper than that, however. The silence from senior military leaders in response to these numerous strategic failings is bewildering.

Major General Donahue stated in an interview that from his point of view, many of the Afghan SOF were not well organized for safe passage through HKIA and that some of them had even turned to the Taliban. Still, with this in mind, it's hard to fathom how large manifests of highly vetted Afghan SOF, particularly those presented by Matt Coburn, a former CJSOTF-A Commander who worked for Donahue, were not processed through the NEO Task Force.

Yet, leveling accountability singularly on MG Donahue is not fair either. In post-mission interviews with him, it was clear that he was task-saturated and managing an unimaginable strategic load. The same can be said for Rear Admiral Vasely and Major General Sullivan. Their bandwidth was stretched to the max. Major General Donahue further stated that the calls and emails from Matt Coburn were "wildly unhelpful," hence his decision to push him off to one of his colonels. Yet, what could have been expected of a retired Green Beret officer, plagued with years of survivor's guilt and post-traumatic stress, receiving endless phone calls from dozens of his partners he'd advised for two decades? The burden of recovering the high-risk Afghan SOF partners and salvaging the vital Afghan human network shouldn't have fallen to either.

But what about the senior military officers, particularly from the SOF community who served in Afghanistan and in the U.S. in the final months leading up to the collapse? What responsibility do they have in this abandonment? What needs to be set right? And what can we learn from it?

With the exception of one or two colonels from the Army SOF Command HQ, most senior SOF officers, including the last NATO commander in Afghanistan, General Miller, and the USSOCOM commander, General Clarke, did not personally speak out about the situation. Senior SOF leaders did not resign in protest. They did not assume responsibility for the abandonment of their own loyal partner forces. And most did not overtly assist their Afghan partners who were calling them with pleas for help. Instead, the majority of these active-duty senior officers passed off the risk and the moral injury to more junior active-duty members of their organizations as well as the combat-fatigued SOF veteran population.

These senior leaders are good people with far more contributions to the nation than most. These leaders understood the importance of good partnership. They knew that an Afghan partnership was not transactional. They knew the right thing to do, yet they chose not to do it. Instead, they sat silent while many of their own sergeants, captains, majors, and veterans who had served them faithfully for years, stood up to help their partners—to honor the promise.

Why?

What did these senior leaders have to lose at that point in their thirty-plus-year careers when the largest moral injury in modern military history was playing out in real-time? Why did they not at least reach out to these vulnerable veteran populations who had served them so faithfully to assist them with the emotional burden they carried from this abandonment? We requested interviews to gain these answers, but only Major General Donahue agreed. Yet, these are questions that must be answered, not to the author, but to our own military community, if we are going to restore trust between the leaders and the led, as we turn the page on the failed twenty-year Afghan campaign.

MORAL INJURY

Some promises are written in blood.

Embedded deeply in special operations culture is an operational truth: when you build teams in foreign lands which blend American and foreign partner forces to stand against oppression, there is an understood and eternal promise: "I have your back." Without it, the team will not function. It's what every special operator knows at a fundamental level. That implicit promise is the glue that holds a team together.

It matters less where it comes from than that it is kept.

At the heart of this Afghan atrocity is the "moral injury" suffered by our comrades who answered the call to besieged Afghans when the U.S. government didn't. The men and women who became shepherds in August 2021 and who are largely continuing to assist our Afghan partners and friends since the last U.S. plane took off on August 31, 2021. What choice do they have? Service members, especially SOF, are trained to stand by their partners through thick and thin until properly relieved of their post. The U.S. government, despite General Milley's outreach to TF Pineapple and others, has done very little to relieve these beleaguered veterans.

These veterans remained at their posts and are in fact still there, answering the calls from Afghanistan.

Senior Pentagon generals and admirals are also known to have said privately that while there was a "moral obligation" to save Afghan partners, the United States had no "legal obligation" to do so.

Legal obligation or not, what does an American promise mean in the world right now?

President Biden told reporters on July 7, 2021, "We will ensure they have the capacity to maintain their air force." And yet by that date, the U.S. government had already taken away the U.S. contractor support for Afghanistan's aviation assets, surveillance, medevac capability, and all U.S. combat advisors. The very capabilities that were instrumental to their effectiveness when we built their military from the ground up.

What is the promise of any U.S. president worth these days?

President Ghani's National Security Adviser Hamdullah Mohib said in an interview that while he has been blamed by Afghans and Americans alike for ill-conceived military decisions, contractor support was all that kept the helicopters, drones, and A-29 attack aircraft flying, and the major airports operating. "Nobody was expecting contractors to be pulled out. When they were pulled out, that was a clear signal of abandonment," he said.

In another interview, a former Afghan Commando battalion commander asked, "Would American special operators conduct a combat mission if there was no air medevac?" Well, that's exactly what Afghan SOF were doing all the way up until August 15 when the government evaporated.

While it's easy to blame the Trump and Biden administrations for botching the withdrawal, accountability should go deeper. No military officer at the rank of colonel or above threw their rank on the table in protest. Nor did anyone in the State Department. Quite the contrary. They kept to the party line that they had achieved a victory with the airlift, thus preserving their careers and quietly shifting responsibility for the evacuation of at-risk partners to others, mostly veterans. This added insult to an already painful moral injury.

But what is moral injury, and who are the injured?

Moral injury can be defined as the "psychological consequence of a betrayal of what's right by someone who holds legitimate authority in a high-stakes situation."

Honoring a promise isn't just for Afghans. What about the promise to honor the service of our soldiers and their families? The infliction of a moral injury after the Taliban regained power following a twenty-year war, which cost the United States 2,465 lives and NATO allies another 1,144 lives, was as predictable as the collapse itself. The institutional intent to save political face and turn the page on this long war is palpable. But it's not that simple. Countless veterans, Gold Star families, and loved ones of the fallen were thrown into severe mental anguish over what it all had been for. Bonnie Carroll, the president and founder of the Tragedy Assistance Program for Survivors, an organization that provides care, welfare, and support to people who have lost loved ones in military service, confirmed there was a palpable spike in veteran mental health incidents following the Afghan collapse which still coninues today. Take retired Major James Gant, who was in pieces from emotional turmoil when Kabul fell. Jim stated that he felt all the blood, sweat, and tears shed in Afghanistan were "for nothing." It would be a phrase repeated by shattered vets. More than 800,000 Americans served in Afghanistan. Another iconic Beret NCO who was a Pineapple shepherd said through tears and a clenched jaw, "If I knew on September 12, 2001, what I know today about how our government would treat Afghanistan, I never would have walked into the recruiter's office and joined Special Forces in the first place."

Do our politicians, diplomats, and senior military leaders grasp the magnitude of the burden born by these veterans? The dozens of Afghan War Veterans we interviewed don't think so. In fact, a special advisor from Vice President Kamala Harris's office contacted Task Force Pineapple directly during the evacuation, asking for help getting one of the West Wing's favored Afghans out of the country. This kind of private career-preserving shift of responsibility for saving our Afghan partners to veterans and other volunteers, coupled with the deafening public silence from politicians, diplomats, and senior military officers has not altered the tenacity of volunteers who still maintain strained, yet vigilant ties to Afghan interpreters, special operators, at-risk girls and women, government officials, and others they worked with during those deployments over two decades. Hundreds of veterans and civilian volunteers watched President Biden's State of the Union in March 2022, hoping for some word that someone would relieve them of their humanitarian duties with Afghanistan. At the bare minimum, they expected some acknowledgment for the work and sacrifice they had dedicated to helping the Afghan people when the government did not. All they heard was silence on the part of their commander-in-chief.

Imagine a 911 emergency call that lasts over 250 days and counting, with no relief shift. Or imagine a friend or family member contacting you, begging you to help them as predators are actively hunting them down. As the keeper of this lifeline, deep down you recognize there is nothing you can do to stop it from happening today, tomorrow, next month, or next year. Yet, outwardly, your moral responsibility is to keep them hopeful and—to the best of your ability—alive.

This is the nightmare some of our active-duty warriors and many vets—many of them already traumatized by the pain and guilt of numerous deployments—have been living.

And then there are special operations veterans who deployed to Afghanistan year after year, in three trips, or maybe ten, or a dozen or even fifteen times since 9/11. Men and women who forged bonds with Afghans they fought and worked shoulder-to-shoulder with, who they made promises to stand by—because it was the job they volunteered for and were trained to do, in the national interest—only to watch as they were left behind by an America that had lost its political will to carry on the fight, according to generals and admirals in the sanctum of their Pentagon offices.

The motto of the Special Forces is *De Oppresso Liber* means "free the oppressed." But one of Task Force Pineapple's most active Green Beret shepherds Master Sergeant Geoff Dardia told me, "Rather than liberate the oppressed, I feel like we oppressed the liberated."

Army intelligence NCO Johnny Utah, with four trips to Afghanistan, is retiring with a high level of contempt for how the USG handled the Afghan Campaign. He said the promises he and other Americans made to Afghan partners were sacred—and then they were canceled by Washington. "The promise was broken, and our government was like, 'Sorry, it didn't work out. I think we're going to go play the field. We're done with you.' They ghosted Afghanistan like a bad Tinder date. Well, that's good and all, except for the fact that regardless of whether we were under the banner of the United States, we were the people who spoke those fucking words and we gave the promise."

As of April 2022, many of the unsung heroes of this book are still facing the mental and physical hardships of the Afghan fallout. One of Nezam's SF comrades was ambushed by the Taliban outside his home in

Kabul. He escaped, but with two gunshot wounds. Over 25,000 Afghan SOF and aviators are trapped and hunted along with thousands of legitimate SIV applicants who were completely abandoned. And Bashir, now in Texas, is still trying to reunite with his family and meet the baby girl whose birth he missed.

The cost of this moral injury to our warrior community has yet to be fully realized. Some former members of the U.S. Special Operations Forces have left the military or retired in disgust. Others are still on active duty, though now are disillusioned and determined to leave uniformed service. We also are losing scores of veterans to suicide every week and this abandonment only makes things worse.

The dissonance between senior leaders and the men and women who actually carried this emotional load is staggering. One general officer, who was deeply involved in the NEO and responsible for leading one of the nation's premier combat units, said in an interview in early 2022 that he was surprised to hear of so many broken, elite warriors. "I thought they would have gotten over this by now," he said.

IN THE END, AMERICANS SHOWED UP

Pineapple's sublime "engineer" Zac Lois, who has since returned to his life as a Syracuse school teacher, said to me, "When institutions failed in 2021, the best of America showed up." Like most of the citizen liaison networks, the members of Task Force Pineapple, who eventually numbered more than one hundred volunteers, were a mix of retired and active-duty U.S. special operations forces, foreign service officers, congressional staff from both parties, former intelligence officers, a Biden political appointee, and more. As just one group among groups, they looked at the massive collapse, saw that no one else was coming, and stepped forward and showed America what leadership looks like in the darkest of times.

The members of the Pineapple Express are still learning about the Afghans that were saved during those dark times, such as Afghan Minister for Women's Affairs Hasina Safi. The total number tops one thousand, plus at least six thousand more still in Afghanistan, sustained by Operation Recovery who are providing food, rent, and fuel for them through the winter. In many cases, these numbers pale in comparison to the Herculean efforts of other volunteer groups like Afghan Free, Afghan Evac, Save Our Allies, Project Dynamo, Project Exodus Relief, Moral Compass, Team America Relief, and many others who are still sustaining and safely moving Afghans out of harm's way.

The bravery of our Afghan partners supported by these volunteer organizations brought hope even in a divided nation. It was apparent from the beginning that HKIA could not stay in allied hands for long, and ISIS-K had a vote, too. The clock was running out and the shepherds, enablers, and active-duty warriors on the HKIA perimeter got after it. The numerous volunteer groups simply got to work, even though they had every reason to get angry. Hopefully, this unified action foretells a brighter future for America; even now, it is echoed as shepherds become involved in Ukraine.

Pineapple made its share of mistakes. As its leader, I accept the responsibility. There were redundancies where we were helping the same Afghans as other groups and missed opportunities to get people to safety during chaotic moments. We were working with limited information, limited resources, and limited access. We were volunteers with experience and relationships using cell phones to address an "Uncle Sam–sized problem." Yet, Mick Mulroy, a retired CIA paramilitary officer and former senior Pentagon policy appointee working in Task Force Dunkirk, said 125,000 wouldn't have been evacuated were it not for the volunteers who carried out the effort to get people to that airport. "We became absolutely essential for it to be successful at all," he argues.

George Packer, writing in the Atlantic, summarized the administration's boasting another way: "The achievement belonged mainly to the troops and civilians who worked tirelessly at the airport, and to the ordinary people who worked tirelessly overseas on WhatsApp and Signal, and above all to the courage, born of mortal panic and tenacious hope, of the Afghans who lost everything. Without the unofficial evacuation efforts, many of them funded by private citizens, the number would have been far lower."

Yet, when the top U.S. ground commanders inside HKIA were interviewed by DoD investigators, they made no mention of volunteer groups facilitating movements through Kabul of vetted Afghans. It was as if they learned nothing about the value of public-private partnerships, and the critical role these volunteer networks played in presenting American citizens and highly vetted Afghans to U.S. forces struggling to bring in the right people. A good step in the right direction to overcoming this moral injury would be for the Presidential Administration, Congress, State, and the Pentagon to formally recognize the contributions of not only veterans' groups but all of these volunteer groups.

When it was all over, there were no high-fives or Pineapple memes. Many shepherds bore guilt that they didn't get more Afghans inside the wire. There isn't a day that goes by that we don't think about those young girls and the other Afghans that were killed in the explosion, and what we might have done differently to pull them in. Even Matt Coburn, who rescued 127, told me he thought more about those left behind than those now in America.

"I don't think that anybody who didn't have the heart for these people would have ever been involved through this God-awful mess," Liv Gardner said to me.

THE U.S. GOVERNMENT NEEDS TO STEP UP

Most social scientists believe that for liberal democracies to succeed, there must be collective trust in the institutions that govern them. Much of the trust in our political administrations, diplomacy, and security has been damaged by this "forever war" in Afghanistan, and in the botched withdrawal that ended it.

None of us expect the entire country to be evacuated, that would be absurd. However, there are select members of the Afghan population to whom a promise was made. It's time for our government to step up.

While the volunteers detailed in this book, and thousands of others, will never stop working on the behalf of their Afghan partners, this problem requires more than they are capable of giving. It requires the strength of U.S. instruments of power.

How many American citizens and legal permanent residents remain behind in Afghanistan? The American people deserve to know. How will the Department of State honor the explicit promises of the nearly 75,000 pending SIV cases that have not been recovered? Will we stand by while women, girls, and LBGTQ community members are cast back into draconian Taliban measures of retribution and oppression? And what of the more than 20,000 Afghan special operators and aviators who fought to the last bullet?

The United States invested twenty years in Afghanistan and its people. Not only must the moral burden of the fall of Kabul be removed from our veterans, but we, as a nation, cannot allow the people of Afghanistan to suffer due to politics, indifference, or the mistakes of the past two decades. It is incumbent on the United States government to do more than offer statements and aid to those who remain trapped in Afghanistan.

Policy experts have analyzed the deteriorating conditions in Afghanistan, and there are immediate steps the international community can take today. Additionally, these recommendations must be considered separate from any ongoing discussions with the Taliban. The focus must remain on the people of Afghanistan and not what the Taliban can "get" at their expense, including recognition. Our recommendations include:

1. Working with the United Nations to establish a humanitarian corridor that would allow for much-needed aid to flow into Afghanistan, while also providing for safe passage to a neighboring country for at-risk Afghans.
2. Creating a special parole program, using the administration's discretionary authorities, which would not require additional legislation and would allow for the immediate evacuation of those most at-risk.

3. Utilizing the aid networks established by U.S. veterans. Many of us have spent the past nine months ensuring those who worked alongside the United States for over twenty years did not starve through the winter of 2021–22. Through the generosity of the American people, food, clothing, and heating supplies have been delivered to the tens of thousands in hiding. These men, women, and children cannot risk going to the village elders to register for international distribution without fear of retribution or fear of death. Aid organizations should review and support these networks, as well as look to model at-risk distribution for Afghanistan and future contexts.

It is important to reiterate that none of these recommendations should provide the Taliban with any recognition implicitly or otherwise. Their takeover of Afghanistan was a coup, and until free and fair elections are once again held in Afghanistan, the United States should not recognize the Taliban as the government of Afghanistan. In fact, based on the significant and justified support the U.S. has given the resistance in Ukraine, it's high time we support the Afghan resistance against the Taliban as well. These recommendations are centered around coordinating with America's allies and partners.

MORE IS REQUIRED

Volunteer groups have always been an integral part of any successful civil society. Citizen leadership played a big role in America coming out of dark times in the early 1900s, giving an upswing to better days in America for decades. Hopefully, our country will make it through this dark period and find its way back to the responsible institutional leadership we can count on as citizens.

It appears like another upswing is on the horizon. TF Pineapple and other volunteer movements could be just the first step forward.

When no one showed up from our government. Veterans and civilian volunteers honored a promise and demonstrated what leadership looked like. Operation Pineapple Express tells the story of a group of friends who honored a promise in Afghanistan when others did not.

For a fleeting moment, they defined what America could be once again.

What about you? When no one is coming, will you step forward?

What will your Pineapple Express be?

ACRONYMS

AMCIT	American Citizen
ANA	Afghan National Army
BAF	Bagram Airfield
CTPT	Counter-Terrorism Pursuit Teams, a CIA-funded and controlled Afghan paramilitary force
DoD	Department of Defense
GPS	Global Positioning System
GRU	Russian military intelligence
HKIA	Hamid Karzai International Airport, in Kabul, Afghanistan
IED	Improvised explosive device
ISI	Inter-Services Intelligence, Pakistan's main intelligence service
ISIS-K	Islamic State Khorasan Province, Afghan branch of the Islamic State
KAF	Kandahar Airfield
KKA	Ktah Khas Afghanistan, also known as the Afghan Partnering Unit (APU), an elite special operations unit created by U.S. Delta Force and Rangers
LNO	Liaison officer
MSG	Master Sergeant
NATO	North Atlantic Treaty Organization
NDS	National Directorate of Security, the Afghan intelligence service
NEO	Noncombatant Evacuation Operation
NMRG	National Mine Removal Group, experts at spotting and removing IEDs. Regularly worked with American SF.
NSU	National Strike Unit, the CIA-sponsored black ops groups known for their tiger-striped fatigues

Q Course Special Forces Qualification Course

SECDEF Defense Secretary

SIV Special Immigration Visa

SOF Special operations forces

TOC Tactical Operations Center

USAID United States Agency for International Development

VBIED Vehicle-Borne Improvised Explosive Device

VPN Virtual Private Network

VSO Village Stability Operations. U.S. forces would fan out across the country in teams to the most remote villages, working with elders and tribes as vanguards for the fledgling Afghan government.

A NOTE ON THIS BOOK

What is the meaning of a promise?
How far would you go to honor one?
How do you tell the stories of heroes who have no voice?
How do you write a book about chaos?
How do you tell that story that doesn't have an ending?
And who the hell am I to tell it?

These were the questions I faced when I sat down to write this book. Let's start with the last one.

This is not my story. But I had damn good seats to the events, played what part I could, and have tried to advocate for the ongoing fight to honor our promises in Afghanistan. And after hundreds of hours of interviews with people who don't usually get interviewed, I feel I can tell this story. Their story.

Let me explain.

I am an oral storyteller far more than I am a writer. That means I'm more comfortable telling the story of others than penning a memoir. Which is perfect for this book, because it is the story of Afghans who risked everything for freedom and the volunteers who stood at their shoulder when they did it. Due to the richness of these characters and the dramatic twists and turns as events unfolded, I have chosen to tell the story from many perspectives. As challenging as it was to step outside of my own experience, it means a great deal to me to be sharing with you the thoughts, experiences, and emotions of these amazing people. I hope that comes through. This story is about love, friendship, and hope as much as it is about accountability.

As much as I want this to be an authoritative work on Afghanistan,

I know it's not. It's too fresh. Too raw. Those works will come. I look forward to them. Task Force Pineapple is just one group of many such groups. I hope those other stories get told. Things fell apart quickly. There will be things I overlooked in preparing this book. Things I got wrong. The limited access to Afghanistan after the fall relegated a few of the events to single-source interviews that are normally not my way of working through tough stories. That said, these are highly vetted and highly trusted sources.

Lapses in memory are endemic to chaos and crisis. In most cases, the Afghans featured in this book endured horrific trauma as they saw their country seized and then ran the gauntlet of HKIA. Some of them are still stuck in Afghanistan. But for all, the pain endures. This is equally true of many of the veterans who joined Pineapple. Our non-profit is working with them to resolve the night terrors, but as with so many of our U.S. combat veterans, it will take time. There was a lot of due diligence in this book, but invariably it is a story forged in disaster. It's about rising from the ashes and dusting yourself off.

While this is a story mostly set in the panicked streets of Kabul and American living rooms, I made an effort to gain the perspective of U.S. senior leaders. I contacted all the prominent flag officers and civilian leaders involved in the Afghan collapse and requested interviews. With one exception, they all declined or only spoke on deep background. Major General Chris Donahue, though, agreed to go on the record with me. He was very forthcoming about not only the Herculean task he faced on HKIA, but also in allowing his paratroopers to talk with me on the record. I remain humbled by the trust they all placed in me by agreeing to talk.

Some of the characters in this book are at risk of retribution from the Taliban and other extremist forces. Others are still on active duty or in government service. Balancing the importance of telling this story to the world with their safety is no small task. I have used pseudonyms where it was requested or I deemed it prudent, but the stories and events are accurate and as we remember them.

It has been a dynamic journey to bring this story to you. I was constantly astounded by what folks could recall of the trauma and chaos they endured. Any errors with dates, specific details of the Afghan collapse, and anything else associated with telling of this difficult, but immensely important, story are mine and mine alone.

ACKNOWLEDGMENTS

To the American people and citizens of the world who heard our story and became supporters of Task Force Pineapple and held us up on your shoulders. Thank you for believing in us during those dark times. It sustained us.

To Howard Yoon, my literary agent. You believed in me when no one else would. Thank you for making the impossible possible.

To Robert Messenger and the Simon & Schuster crew. Thanks for seeing the story before it was written and believing it could help bring focus where it belongs: on the Afghan people.

To our creatives, Theo and Nils. Just stunning work. You are the best of the best. Thank you for fighting so hard for this book and putting in the sixteen-hour days. You all poured your hearts into this project, and we'll never forget you as teammates.

To SGM, Retired, Randy Surles whose work on this project cannot be overstated. You were at my shoulder every step of the way: writing, editing, troubleshooting. The Story Grid oughta be damn proud of what you brought to the party. Any warrior out there who ever contemplates writing a book should make their first call to Randy Surles.

To CJ, for keeping me straight. The work you did was top-notch and thank you for fact-checking this book.

To Congressman Mike Waltz, Green Beret and old friend, for standing with me always. You were there in the darkest hours for the Afghan people.

To the Special Operations Association of America (SOAA) and the volunteers of Moral Compass Federation. Thank you for taking a stand for our Afghan SOF partners and our U.S. SOF veterans in these trying times. Your work is legendary and you are our last best hope for providing our Afghan SOF partners with a pathway to safe passage and resettlement.

A massive salute to the Afghan special operations forces who fought to the last bullet. May history always illuminate the way you stood for your country when your leaders and the United States did not.

To the women and girls of Afghanistan. Thank you for showing us what real courage looks like. May your future be filled with happiness and empowerment overcoming these dark times you are in. I pray your true moment of reckoning and leading all of us is still in front of you.

To the Afghan New Resistance Front. We should have stood with you as a nation. You are the hope for Afghanistan. Don't ever quit. Keep fighting.

To our 800,000 (+) U.S. Afghan campaign combat veterans, along with our NATO partners. Thank you for your sacrifice in that tough place called Afghanistan. A special thanks to your families as well for their sacrifice.

To the civilian volunteers, active-duty members, and veterans who stepped up for the Afghan people during the collapse. Thank you for showing us what leadership actually looks like when nobody else is coming.

To Zeke and Mary with Operation Angel Wing. Thank you so much for the trauma intervention work you did getting dirt under your nails in the thorny situations that our Afghan partners and veterans were dealing with in this horrific collapse. Your work saved lives and still does.

To Ed, Geoff Dardia, and all the active-duty shepherds who can't be named because of the risk to their careers. You know who you are. Thank you for your moral courage when other leaders shifted responsibility from themselves to veterans.

To all of the volunteers and volunteer groups beyond TF Pineapple who continue to work so hard to provide safe passage and resettlement to the Afghan people. Your actions are epic.

To CPT John Folta and 1SG Jesse Kennedy and the "White Devils" of the 82nd Airborne, along with the USMC, and all the other US/NATO

Warriors who stood watch until the very end at HKIA. Thanks for being the vanguards of freedom and holding the line.

To our NATO partners over the last twenty years and at HKIA. America did you wrong at the end. I hope you'll forgive us and accept our gratitude for all that you did to pull in our people when hope was fading.

To the Rooftop Leadership Team for holding down the fort so that I could crash on this book: Eric, Caitlyn, Earnest, Stacey, Alliy, Emma, Amanda, Wes, and Mark.

To the Heroes Journey team for holding down the fort so that Scott could crash on this book: Kim, Kari, Chris, Jamie, Brianna, Alliy.

To Kevin Lang for capturing all the beautiful resettlement moments on video.

To Josh, Danny, Wes, John, Alliy, and the rest of Operation Recovery. You all did a phenomenal job of caring for our Afghan Partners long after the guns went silent. You are truly guardian angels. Thank you.

To Mark Nutsch, Jim Gant, Jay Redman, Mike Adams, Perry Blackburn, Fred Dumar, Worth Parker, Mike Edwards, Daniel Elkins, Amy Mitchell, Travis Pederson, Duke, Heather Nauert, Matt Coburn, and Ismael Khan for taking a stand publicly on behalf of the Afghan people and our veteran population while our retired senior leaders remained in the shadows.

To my parents, Rex and Anita. Thank you for teaching me what a promise is and what it means to honor it.

To Nezam for sharing your life with us and having the courage to try.

To Nezam's family and all of the Afghan families for your bravery. "Freedom is just another word for nothing left to lose."

To all the Pineapple shepherds and Pineapple support team. You know who you are. God bless you and thank you for stepping up when our politicians and generals stepped back.

To all the contributors of this book. Those whose stories were told explicitly and those that are hidden. Thank you for sharing your heart and soul with us.

To the people of Afghanistan. Thank you for opening your heart and country to us. May you find peace and the ability to stand against evil and find your own version of freedom and happiness that is right for you, not us.

To all of the men and women, civilians, military, and journalists who served in the forever war. It was not in vain. "Nothing is written."

To my incredible wife, Monty, the love of my life, and my boys, Cody, Cooper, and Brayden. Thank for all that you've endured over the last year (and last twenty years) to allow me to serve the nation. You are my heroes.

To Jane Horton, Holly, and the all the Gold Star Families of the Afghan War. I know your heart breaks but it was not in vain. The story is not yet fully told. The sacrifices of your loved one will come full circle and be known for the ages.

To the thirteen U.S. service members who fell at HKIA and the wounded from that horrific day, and your families. Thank you for holding the line and risking everything so that our American citizens and other Afghans who risked for us might see their children experience freedom.

To all of the U.S. Warriors who gave their lives in Afghanistan and their amazing families. We love you, and we will never stop telling your story.

IMAGE CREDITS

1. Courtesy of Scott Mann
2. Courtesy of Nezamuddin Nezami
3. Courtesy of Scott Mann
4. Courtesy of Nezamuddin Nezami
5. Courtesy of Nezamuddin Nezami
6. Courtesy of Nezamuddin Nezami
7. Courtesy of Hafizullah Abdulghani
8. Courtesy of Salaam
9. Courtesy of Matt Coburn
10. Courtesy of Zac Lois
11. Courtesy of Basira Mohammady
12. Courtesy of Mohammad Rahimi
13. Courtesy of Nezamuddin Nezami
14. Courtesy of Nezamuddin Nezami
15. Courtesy of Nezamuddin Nezami
16. Courtesy of Nezamuddin Nezami
17. Courtesy of Nezamuddin Nezami
18. Courtesy of Scott Mann
19. Courtesy of Ian Wookey
20. Courtesy of Tao Zeng, via U.S. Department of State website
21. Courtesy of Nezamuddin Nezami
22. Courtesy of Nezamuddin Nezami
23. Courtesy of Jussi Tanner, Finland Ministry of Foreign Affairs
24. Courtesy of Ian Wookey
25. Courtesy of Chris Bradley
26. Courtesy of Jussi Tanner, Finland Ministry of Foreign Affairs
27. Courtesy of Jussi Tanner, Finland Ministry of Foreign Affairs
28. Courtesy of Jesse Kennedy
29. Courtesy of John Folta
30. Courtesy of Hafizullah
31. Courtesy of Jussi Tanner, Finland Ministry of Foreign Affairs
32. Courtesy of Jussi Tanner, Finland Ministry of Foreign Affairs

ABOUT THE AUTHOR

LT. COL. SCOTT MANN (RET.) is a retired Green Beret with more than twenty years of Army and Special Operations experience. He has deployed to Ecuador, Colombia, Peru, Iraq, and Afghanistan. He is the CEO of Rooftop Leadership, a professional training and coaching company specializing in human connection skills, and the founder of The Heroes Journey, a 501c3 committed to helping U.S. and Afghan veterans tell their stories and transition to civilian life. Scott regularly speaks to corporate leaders, industry associations, law enforcement officers, and special operations forces on how to forge deeper connections with the people they serve and create more powerful outcomes in business and life. He is also an actor and playwright who has written and performed in a play about the war called *Last Out—Elegy of a Green Beret* which can be seen on Amazon Prime. A recent empty nester to three grown boys, Scott lives in Tampa, Florida, where he chases his wife Monty around the house on every possible occasion.

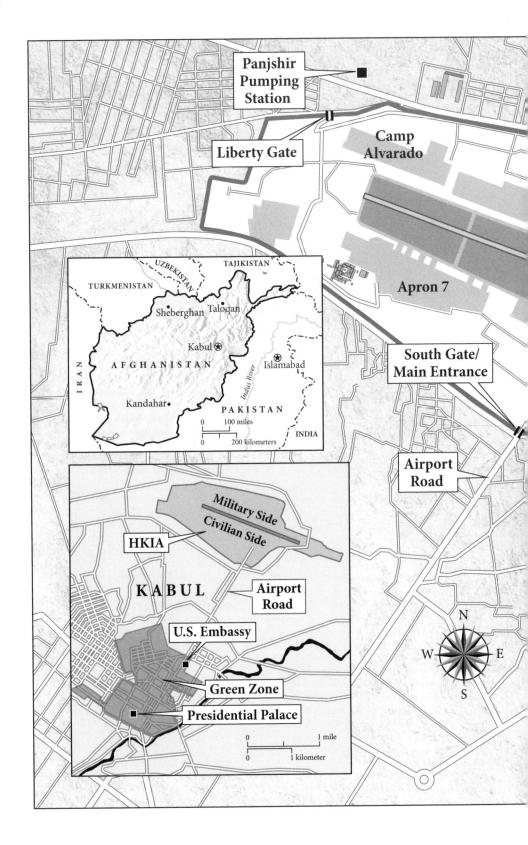

Panjshir Pumping Station

Camp Alvarado

Liberty Gate

Apron 7

South Gate/ Main Entrance

Airport Road

UZBEKISTAN **TAJIKISTAN**

TURKMENISTAN

Sheberghan Taloqan

Kabul ✪

AFGHANISTAN Islamabad ✪

Kandahar ● **PAKISTAN**

INDIA

0   100 miles

0   200 kilometers

IRAN Indus River

Military Side
Civilian Side

HKIA

KABUL

Airport Road

U.S. Embassy

Green Zone

Presidential Palace

0   1 mile

0   1 kilometer

N
W   E
S